Papers of the Forty-Ninth Algonquian Conference

Actes du quarante-neuvième Congrès des Algonquinistes

PAPERS OF THE ALGONQUIAN CONFERENCES
ACTES DU CONGRÈS DES ALGONQUINISTES

49

Papers of the Forty-Ninth Algonquian Conference

Actes du quarante-neuvième Congrès des Algonquinistes

EDITED BY Monica Macaulay and Margaret Noodin

MICHIGAN STATE UNIVERSITY PRESS | EAST LANSING

∞ The paper used in this publication meets the minimum requirements of ANSI/NISO Z39.48-1992 (R 1997) (Permanence of Paper).

Michigan State University Press
East Lansing, Michigan 48823-5245

Paper ISBN: 978-1-61186-344-4
PDF ISBN: 978-1-60917-620-4

Book design by Charlie Sharp, Sharp Des!gns, East Lansing, Michigan
Cover design by Erin Kirk New
Cover detail of a quill box is used courtesy of Julie L. Loehr

Michigan State University Press is a member of the Green Press Initiative and is committed to developing and encouraging ecologically responsible publishing practices. For more information about the Green Press Initiative and the use of recycled paper in book publishing, please visit *www.greenpressinitiative.org*.

Visit Michigan State University Press at *www.msupress.org*

CONTENTS

PRÉFACE

Le quarante-neuvième congrès des algonquinistes a été co-organisé par Marie-Pierre Bousquet, anthropologue et directrice du programme en études autochtones de l'Université de Montréal, et Jimena Terraza, linguiste, de l'Université du Québec à Montréal. Il s'est tenu du 27 au 29 octobre 2017 dans la ville de Montréal. Ce congrès fut très diversifié puisqu'il y avait une grande variété de disciplines telles que l'anthropologie, la linguistique, l'éducation, l'archéologie, l'histoire et les sciences de l'activité physique couvertes par les communications, qui étaient présentées non seulement en anglais mais aussi en français et en atikamekw. De plus, les nombreux peuples algonquiens du Québec étaient représentés dans les communications et par les membres de ces nations également.

Marie-Pierre et Jimena aimeraient remercier Nicole O'Bomsawin, pour sa présence à la cérémonie d'ouverture, au cours de laquelle la reconnaissance territoriale a suivi le protocole des Premières Nations. Notons que les peuples algonquiens suivants sont les premiers habitants de la province de Québec: les Innus, les Cris, les Algonquins, les Atikamekw, les Abénakis, les Mi'kmaq, les Malécites et les Naskapis. Les organisatrices remercient également le traiteur Les Trois Sœurs qui a pris soin de tous les services de restauration pendant la conférence, Terry Awashish pour ses services en tant que photographe et la coopérative Migona pour les beaux sacs.

Elles sont particulièrement reconnaissantes envers les étudiants qui se sont portés volontaires pour aider avant, pendant et après la conférence: Michelle Tremblay, David Daines, Priscylla Monteiro, Diane Tenneroni, Rachel Jordan, Mireille Trudelle, Jade Brais, Alexandra Coutu, Janie Cameron et sa fille Alyssa Dumont, Gabriel Roldan, Chloë Leduc, Floriane Padoan, Maryse Meunier, Matisse Nadeau-Décarie, Isabelle Touchette, Anne-Sophie Gignac, Juliane Vandal et Emile Moreault.

La conférence était commanditée par la Faculté des Arts et des Sciences et le Département d'anthropologie de l'Université de Montréal, le CIERA-Montréal (Centre interfacultaire d'études et de recherches autochtones) et l'Institut des sciences cognitives de l'Université du Québec à Montréal (UQAM).

Enfin, nous avons tous été honorés par la visite d'un linguiste qui faisait partie du groupe enthousiaste des fondateurs du congrès des algonquinistes, Don Deblois.

PREFACE

The Forty-Ninth Algonquian Conference was co-organized by Marie-Pierre Bousquet, anthropologist and director of the Indigenous studies program of the Université de Montréal, and Jimena Terraza, linguist, from the Université du Québec à Montréal. It was held from October 27 to 29, 2017, in the city of Montreal. This conference was a quite diverse one as there was a great variety of disciplines such as anthropology, linguistics, education, archaeology, history, and human kinetics covered by the talks, which were presented not only in English but also in French and Atikamekw. Moreover, the many Algonquian peoples from Québec were represented in the talks and by the members of these nations as well.

Marie-Pierre and Jimena would like to thank Nicole O'Bomsawin for her presence in the opening ceremony, including the territorial acknowledgment following the First Nations protocol. We note that the following Algonquian peoples are the first inhabitants of the province of Quebec: Innu, Cree, Algonquin, Atikamekw, Abenaki, Mi'kmaq, Maliseet, and Naskapi. The organizers would like to thank as well Three Sisters catering, who took care of all the catering services during the conference, Terry Awashish for his services as a photographer, and the Migona cooperative for the beautiful bags. They are especially grateful to the students who volunteered to help before, during, and after the conference: Michelle Tremblay, David Daines,

Priscylla_Monteiro, Diane Tenneroni, Rachel Jordan, Mireille Trudelle, Jade Brais, Alexandra Coutu, Janie Cameron and her daughter Alyssa Dumont, Gabriel Roldan, Chloë Leduc, Floriane Padoan, Maryse Meunier, Matisse Nadeau-Décarie, Isabelle Touchette, Anne-Sophie Gignac, Juliane Vandal, and Emile Moreault.

The conference was sponsored by the Faculté des Arts et des Sciences and Département d'anthropologie of the Université de Montréal, the CIERA-Montréal (Centre interfacultaire d'études et recherches autochtones), and the Cognitive Science Institute of Université du Québec à Montréal (UQAM).

Finally, we were all honored by the visit of a linguist who was part of the enthusiastic group of founders of the Algonquian conference, Don Deblois.

Additional Conference Papers

Outre les articles des communications publiés dans ce volume, les communications suivantes ont été présentées au congrès.

In addition to the papers published in this volume, the following papers were presented at the conference:

Sauvane Agnès (Université de Paris IV Sorbonne): Le système "direct-inverse" des langues algonquiennes: un type d'alignement

Véronique Audet (Centre d'innovation des Premiers Peuples): Le mouvement des pow wow chez les Innus au Québec: Algonquiens contemporains, enjeux identitaires et échanges culturels

Sarah Babinski (Yale University): A New Approach to Stress in Southern East Cree

Peter Bakker (Aarhus University): Eastern Algonquians and the Basque Country in the 21st Century

Anne Bertrand (Marist College), Violet Birdstone (University of British Columbia), and Martina Wiltschko (University of British Columbia): Verbal Obviation in Ktunaxa

Heather Bliss (University of Victoria), Inge Genee (University of Lethbridge), Marie-Odile Junker (Carleton University), and Dan O'Donnell (University of Lethbridge): "Credit Where Credit Is Due": How to Handle Attribution, Copyright, and Intellectual Property in Online Digital Resources for Algonquian Languages

Nathon Breu (University of Wisconsin–Milwaukee): Aanji'zaagibagaa: Changing Blooms

Robert Brightman (Reed College): Ontologies of Domestication: Reindeer, Dogs, and Tamed Bears

Chantale Cenerini (University of Manitoba): The Prominence of Speech-Act Participants: A Study of Diachronic Change in Algonquian Person Agreement

Cecil Chabot (Concordia University): Rediscovering Our Shared Humanity: Insights from a Foreign Medical Doctor's Mid-Twentieth-Century Encounter with Northern Algonquian People and Stories

Véronique Chachai (Conseil de la Nation Atikamekw), Marie-Odile Junker (Carleton University), Nicole Petiquay (Conseil de la Nation Atikamekw), and Katie Martunizzi (Carleton University): La langue atikamekw aujourd'hui / Anotc nehirowimowin

Mélanie Chaplier (Université catholique de Louvain / McGill University) and Colin Scott (McGill University): From Beavers to Land: Building on Past Debates to Unpack the Contemporary Entanglements of Algonquian Family Hunting Territories / Des castors au territoire: faire le point sur le débat entourant les territoires de chasse familiaux algonquiens pour comprendre leurs enchevêtrements contemporains

Rose-Marie Dechaine (University of British Columbia): Derivational Paradigms: A Tool for Learning Vocabulary (and Epistemology)

Rose-Marie Dechaine (University of British Columbia), Monique Dufresne (Queen's University), and Charlotte Reinholtz (Queen's University): (Ir)realis Dubitative in the Cree Dialect Continuum

Rose-Marie Dechaine (University of British Columbia) and H. C. Wolfart (University of Manitoba): What Plains Cree Teaches Us about Negation

Émile Duchesne (Université de Montréal): Maîtres des animaux et changements chez les Innus d'Unamen Shipu

Dianne Friesen and Arlene Stevens (Cape Breton University / SIL International / TLE): Obstruent plus Resonant Clusters in Mi'kmaq

Joseph Friis and Jacques Wabanonik (Université d'Ottawa): Résurgence autochtone et réconciliation "autocritique": Séjours de sensibilisation à la culture anicinape et à la pédagogie de la terre—Kitcisakik?

Inge Genee (University of Lethbridge), Myles Shirakawa (University of Lethbridge), and Heather Bliss (University of Victoria): Building a Catalogue of Variation in Contemporary Blackfoot (VCB)

Laurence Hamel-Charest (Université de Montréal): "Range ton baloney, il y a de l'orignal!": regard sur l'alimentation en contexte anicinabe

Christopher Hammerly (University of Massachusetts, Amherst): The Structure of VOS/VSO Alternations in Ojibwe

Atticus G. Harrigan and Antti Arppe (University of Alberta): Conjunct(ion) Junct(ion): What's Your Function

Ryan Henke (University of Hawai'i at Mānoa): Acquiring Possessive Constructions in Northern East Cree

Leila Inksetter (Université Laval): The Trouble and Expense of Holding an Election: Algonquin Selection of Representatives at the Turn of the 20th Century

Marie-Odile Junker (Carleton University), Marguerite Mackenzie (Memorial University of Newfoundland), Yvette Mollen (Université du Québec à Montréal), Nicole Petiquay (Conseil de la Nation Atikamekw), Véronique Chachai (Conseil de la Nation Atikamekw), Bill Jancewicz (University of North Dakota), Nicole Rosen (University of Manitoba), Antti Arppe (University of Alberta), Arok Wolvengrey (First Nations University of Canada), Jean Okimasis (University of Regina), Inge Genee (University of Lethbridge), Mary-Ann Corbiere (Université de Sudbury), Rand Valentine (University of Wisconsin–Madison), Heather Bliss (University of Victoria), and Delasie Torkornoo (Carleton University): Algonquian Dictionaries and Linguistic Atlas Project: Progress Report 2 / Projet des dictionnaires algonquiens et d'atlas linguistique: deuxième rapport

Grant Karcich (Ontario Archaeological Society): Archaic and Historic Population Clusters in Eastern North America

Jacques Leroux (Université de Montréal): À propos de marqueurs du temps et de l'aspect dans la langue algonquine (Anicinabemowin)

Ben Levine (Speaking Place, Inc.): New Approaches for Aiding Fluent Comprehenders to Regain the Ability to Speak Their Language

Robert Lewis Jr. (University of Chicago): The Potawatomi Particle *na:* How and Where to Use It

Anny Morissette (Université Saint-Paul): "Ces Indiens se plaignent pour rien": Les agents indiens et la gestion des écoles de jour indiennes à Kitigan Zibi (1879–1953)

Will Oxford (University of Manitoba) and Graham Still (University of Washington): Developing a Database of Algonquian Language Structures

Robert Papen (Université du Québec à Montréal): On Confirming the Split Phonology Hypothesis for Michif

David Pentland (University of Manitoba): The Earliest Records of the Montagnais Language: A Reassessment

Anne-Marie Reynaud (Université de Montréal): Mitchikanibikok Inik Sense of Self and Remembering in the Context of the Indian Residential Schools Settlement Agreement
Richard Rhodes (University of California, Berkeley): A Civil War Soldier's Letter
Nicole Rosen (University of Manitoba) and Carrie Gillon (Quick Brown Fox Consulting): An Examination of Michif Gender
Olivia Sammons (University of Alberta): Nominal Classification in Michif
Olivia Sammons (University of Alberta) and Katie Grant (Sac and Fox Nation): Developing Corpora for Endangered Languages: An Example from Sauk
Katherine Schmirler (University of Alberta), Antti Arppe (University of Alberta), Trond Trosterud (University of Tromsø), and Lene Antonsen (University of Tromsø): Computational Modelling of Plains Cree Syntax: A Constraint Grammar Approach to Verbs and Arguments in a Plains Cree Corpus
Judy Shepard and Conor Quinn (University of Southern Maine): Morphosyntax in Algonquian and ASL: Insights from Comparison
Daniel Paul Stoltzfus (Université du Québec à Chicoutimi): Exploratory Study on Verbal Morphological Frequency in Northwestern Ojibwe
Lucy Thomason (Smithsonian Institution): Space/Time Parallelism in Meskwaki
Şükran Tipi (Université Laval): Entre Nuhtshimit et Nitassinan: Narrer et nommer le territoire chez les Pekuakamiulnuatsh, Innus du Lac Saint-Jean
Susan Wade and Patricia T. Nájera (University of Wisconsin–Milwaukee): Perspectives from Ganawandemaw: Protection of Language Revitalization and Language Ideologies in the Great Lakes Region
Paul Wattez (Université de Montréal): "It Never Disappeared": Analysis of the Nature and the Status of the Knowledge Involved in the Current and Historical Practice of the Shaking Tent among the Eenouch of Waswanipi
Roy Wright (independent scholar): Wolf Fangs, Flint Points: A Study in the Ethnosemiotics of Algic Myths and Place Names

A Morphosyntactically Tagged Corpus for Plains Cree

Antti Arppe, Katherine Schmirler, Atticus G. Harrigan, and Arok Wolvengrey

This paper presents the underlying resources that comprise a morphologically and syntactically tagged corpus of Plains Cree. Morphosyntactically tagged corpora contribute to linguistic descriptions and language maintenance in a variety of ways. Corpora can be used to supplement online dictionaries with examples of forms in natural language use and allow for systematic quantitative analyses to be performed on much larger scales than previously possible, without extensive experience in computational techniques. Such analyses can then further inform qualitative analysis and benefit descriptions overall.

For Plains Cree, the tagged corpus involves a number of resources; these include the texts, the computational models, the hand-verified "gold standards," and the corpus search interface. Together, these form a morphosyntactically tagged corpus of Plains Cree. The texts included in the present iteration of the corpus are described here as the Ahenakew-Wolfart corpus and represent a selection of Cree texts collected in the late 20th century. Two levels of computational linguistic analysis are briefly described in this paper; these are the morphological model, which allows for automatic analysis of inflectional morphology and morphophonology, and the syntactic model, which currently disambiguates word forms with multiple analyses (based on contextual information) as well as identifies the arguments of verbs and demonstrative-noun pairs. For each of these models, portions of the texts have been hand-verified for evaluation and further development of the models; we describe here the process of annotation and present the coverage statistics for each model. Finally, the online corpus interface is briefly described.

The Texts

The collection of texts presently available in the morphosyntactically tagged corpus for Plains Cree are drawn from those collected and edited by Freda Ahenakew and H. C. Wolfart from the 1970s to 1990s. Published versions of these texts are available in the following volumes: Ahenakew 2000; Bear et al. 1992; Kâ-Nîpitêhtêw 1998; Masuskapoe 2010; Minde 1997; Vandall and Douquette 1987; and Whitecalf 1993.[1] This collection contains various genres, including dialogues, personal narratives, retold stories, lectures, and speeches.

Altogether, these texts currently contain 142,192 tokens (20,503 types), of which 80,221 are word tokens of Plains Cree (16,532 word form types), with an additional 761 Plains Cree word fragments (436 types, typically initial parts of Cree words which are not finished, or restarted after hesitation, explicitly transcribed in the versions of the texts that we have); 8,791 non-Cree word tokens (1,253 types) including English, French, Michif, Arabic and Roman numerals, proper names, and so on; 3,293 yet unanalyzed tokens (2,255 types all from Ahenakew 2000); as well as 49,127 punctuation mark tokens (26 punctuation types).[2] Compared to available corpora for a number of majority languages, a corpus of this size is rather small. However, more comparable corpora are those for Indigenous languages, which, where available, may range from several thousands of words to several million (e.g., Inuktitut). Additionally, the present Plains Cree corpus does not yet include all available texts of substantial size; the corpus will be bolstered by texts collected by Bloomfield in the early 20th century (Bloomfield 1930, 1974 [1934]), the Cree Prayer Book (Demers, McIlwraith, and Thunder 2010, collected in the late 19th century), as well as multiple Bible translations from different time periods. Together, these texts offer a corpus of at least 200,000 words, and potentially several hundreds of thousands. However, even with the smaller present corpus, meaningful analyses can be undertaken and tools can be made available to communities and researchers alike.

The Two Levels of Linguistic Analysis

The corpus is automatically tagged by means of two computational models, one for the inflectional morphology and related morphophonology and one for disambiguation and the assignment of syntactic relationships. Both models are continually under development and the tagging will thus be improved as the models improve. Descriptions for earlier versions of each of these models are available in Snoek et al. 2014; Harrigan et al. 2017; and Schmirler et al. 2018.

The Morphological Model

The morphological computational model for Plains Cree is based in Finite State Transducer (FST) technology (e.g., Beesley and Karttunen 2003a) and is able to both analyze and generate word forms. The current iteration of the Plains Cree morphological model is able to analyze word class, person, number, animacy, obviation, tense, possession, and direction, as well as identify preverbs, reduplication, and two derivational processes, the formation of diminutive nouns and comitative verbs.

The inflectional component makes use of information drawn from grammars of Plains Cree such as Wolfart 1973 and Okimâsis 2004, as well as the expertise of one of the authors, A. Wolvengrey. The lexicon of nouns, verbs, pronouns, and particles is drawn primarily from the database underlying Wolvengrey 2001, a bilingual dictionary of Plains Cree and English. An example input and its analyzed output are given in (1). The model recognizes *ê-* and *nitawi-* as preverbs, *wî-* as the future intentional prefix,[3] *nîmihitow* as the lemma form of the verb stem which is animate intransitive, and *-yân* as the first person conjunct suffix.[4]

(1) ê-wî-nitawi-nîmihitoyân
PV/e+PV/nitawi+nîmihitow+V+AI+Cnj+Fut+Int+1Sg
'I will go and dance'

Morphophonological changes are also covered at specified junctures. These make use of the TWOLC (TWO-Level Compiler) formalism, which applies the set of morphophonological rules in parallel, in comparison to rewrite rules that are applied in an ordered sequence (e.g., Beesley and Karttunen 2003b). Due to their parallel nature, larger numbers of TWOLC rules can become difficult to specify without rule conflicts, though this can be applied rather straightforwardly to the relatively regular phonology of Cree. The TWOLC rules used in a former version of the model are detailed in Harrigan et al. 2017; though we have since simplified and restructured these rules, they still represent the basic sound changes required for Plains Cree inflectional morphology.[5]

The output of the morphological model results in a string of morphological tags, as in (1), which then become tags accessible in the corpus interface. These tags can then be searched individually, or as groups of features, such that a researcher may investigate a feature or group of features of interest using straightforward search capabilities, outlined in greater detail below.

The Syntactic Model

The syntactic computational model for Plains Cree uses the Constraint Grammar formalism (e.g., Karlsson 1995a, 1995b) to (1) disambiguate word form analyses and (2) identify relationships between words in a phrase. The Constraint Grammar version used is the VISLCG-3 compiler (e.g., Bick and Didriksen 2015). Constraint Grammar operates on principles similar to those in more theoretical dependency-based frameworks, using the morphological feature tags output by the morphological model and the syntactic context in which they occur to select the appropriate analysis and to determine the relationships between words in a sentence.

The syntactic model operates in two stages: first, disambiguation constraints are applied to the results of the morphological analysis, and second, function constraints are then applied to label syntactic roles. A form that is ambiguous for animacy or number, for example, may be disambiguated by looking at adjacent demonstratives or nearby verbs: an animate demonstrative or animate intransitive verb may allow for the ambiguous form to be identified as animate. Similarly, an animate nominal in the same phrase as an animate intransitive verb would be tagged as the actor of that verb (depending on number, obviation, and person agreement features), while an inanimate noun in the same phrase would not be marked as an argument of the same verb.[6] An example sentence is given in (2). Here, the ambiguous demonstrative *ôhi* (either inanimate plural or animate obviative) is determined to be inanimate because it is immediately adjacent to an inanimate plural noun (its context). Then, the transitive inanimate verb allows for an animate actor and an inanimate goal,[7] both of which can be found within the sentence. These are tagged appropriately, with arrows pointing towards the verb that allowed the syntactic feature/tag to be assigned. The goal is not explicitly marked on the verb, and so any inanimate nominal, regardless of number, may be selected as the goal of a transitive inanimate verb. However, the features of the verb and actor must agree—in this sentence, the animate singular noun agrees with the third person singular marking on a verb that selects animate actors. Verbs are also tagged for reference in the corpus interface.[8]

(2) iskwêw ayamihtâw ôhi masinahikana.

iskwêw	ayamihtâw	ôhi
iskwêw+N+AN+Sg	ayamihtâw+V+TI+Ind+Prs+3Sg	ôma+**Dem+IN+Pl**
		~~awa+DEM+AN+OBV~~
woman	s/he reads s.t.	these, this
@ACTOR>	**@PRED-TI**	**@N>**

masinahikana
masinahikan+N+IN+Pl
books
@<GOALgoal
'The woman is reading these books.'

The current version of the model identifies relationships between verbs and their nominal arguments and between nouns and associated demonstrative pronouns. The focus of the current model is on identifying relationships rather than maximizing disambiguation. These goals are achieved using only morphological features at present, though lexical semantic and other features can also be made use of within the Constraint Grammar formalism. Further development of each of these aspects is underway.

Syntactic tags can be used in tandem with morphological tags in corpus searches to investigate patterns of both (groups of) morphological features and the basic word order patterns with which they occur. Examples of corpus search results are discussed below.

The Gold Standards

Both models have undergone some degree of testing using hand-verified portions of the corpus. These are referred to as "gold standards" for each model. This section details the annotation process, the coverage of each model after the first stage of development, and the types of errors that were encountered.

The Morphological Gold Standard

For the morphological gold standard, 18,646 unique word types (not individual tokens) were verified. One text (Ahenakew 2000) was not included in the gold standard in order to allow for testing later, though over 86% of the tokens of that text were represented by forms in the gold standard and so had otherwise already been verified. These types were evaluated using the morphological model, resulting in correct analyses, incorrect analyses, and unanalyzed forms. For each of these 18,646 types, two researchers, the second and third authors, then hand-verified the analyses, correcting, removing, and adding analyses where possible. At this stage of verification, forms were analyzed in isolation, and so ambiguous analyses are included and no disambiguation is attempted.

The verification process served two main purposes. One, the verified and corrected analyses are those included in the corpus, resulting in much higher accuracy rates than would be supplied by the morphological model alone, as it is still under development. Two, the corrections and additions allowed us to determine shortcomings and errors in the model. Issues we encountered primarily included differences in vowel length marking, lemmas missing from our lexicon, minor or archaic morphological features not yet implemented in the model (e.g., inanimate actor, *h*-preterit, initial change), vowel sandhi altering preverbs and stems, and errors that arose in the model, particularly the model's overzealous application of morphophonological rules.

A detailed analysis of the coverage of the model at the time the morphological gold standard was first performed is available (for verbs) in Harrigan et al. 2017. However, the morphological gold standard is frequently reviewed by the annotators and so has improved considerably. In the current version, 437 of the 18,646 word form types remain unanalyzed; these include partial words (i.e., due to hesitation), speech errors, or word forms with stems that could not be satisfactorily identified (e.g., for verb class) without context provided by translation, and so require further consideration. Inter-annotator agreement was assessed using two overlapping portions of 200 types from the corpus which had been evaluated by both annotators, and for which, after discussion, a consensus was reached for all analyses; a full account of the inter-annotator agreement can be found in Harrigan et al. 2017. The morphological gold standard is of great benefit not only to an online corpus of Plains Cree and all analyses drawn from it, but also to the further development and improvement to the morphological model for the analysis of more texts for addition to the corpus and for development of additional tools, such as the syntactic model.

The Syntactic Gold Standard

Unlike the morphological gold standard, which arose after significant development of the morphological model, the syntactic gold standard was developed as a testing tool for both building and testing the syntactic model.[9] A much smaller portion of the overall corpus (one text, Vandall and Douquette 1987, approximately 3,200 words) was tagged for selected syntactic functions having a central role in Plains Cree: these are actors and goals associated with verbs and demonstratives associated with nouns; other syntactic functions were not yet tagged. Where possible, disambiguation based on context and translation was also performed. However, as the model cannot make use of translations and only grammatical feature tags are used at this point, much of the disambiguation that can be performed by hand cannot be replicated by the model. The syntactic gold standard will be further expanded as constraints for more syntactic relationships are added to the syntactic model.

Fortunately for modeling, however, the corpus contains a considerable number of word forms that are assigned only one analysis by the morphological model, and so do not require disambiguation in the syntactic model. Before the disambiguation constraints were applied, 65,046 (77.2%) of word form tokens in the entire corpus had a single analysis; after the disambiguation constraints were applied, 75,134 (89.2%) of the tokens had a single analysis.[10] This means that disambiguation reduced 10,088 word tokens (12.0%) that previously had multiple analyses to just a single analysis (which may be correct, or not). While these numbers are promising, it is a feature of Constraint Grammar that at least one analysis will always remain after disambiguation, so these numbers are no guarantee that the correct analysis is selected. Therefore, the model's disambiguation can be compared to the manual disambiguation performed in the syntactic gold standard. This comparison returns a recall rate of 62% and a precision rate of 90%. First, this means that, in the syntactic gold standard, the constraints removed 62% of those multiple alternative analyses that were removed by hand, leaving 38% of the originally ambiguous word form tokens with either more than one analysis (which may include the contextually correct analysis, or not), or with a single but incorrect analysis. Secondly, this entails that of those analyses the constraints removed, 90% matched those removed manually in the syntactic gold standard; thus, for 10% of the word form tokens with ambiguous analyses, an analysis that should have been removed was not, or the analysis that was removed by the constraints would in fact have been the correct one (one per each word form token, based on context). For further details, see Table 1 in Schmirler et al. 2018. Following automatic disambiguation, we make use of a crude heuristic to reduce all remaining tokens to a single analysis; this heuristic selects the analysis with the fewest morphological feature tags (i.e., the simplest analysis), resulting in one analysis per word form in the corpus.

The Corpus Interface

For the online corpus, we make use of the Korp interface. This interface is based on the open-source tools for corpus search and indexing in the IMS Open Corpus Workbench (Evert and Hardie 2011). The Korp interface is a concordance search tool used by the Språkbanken (Swedish Language Bank) research group at the University of Gothenburg (Borin, Forsberg, and Roxendal 2012; https://spraakbanken.gu.se/korp/). It is used to manage the large Swedish language corpus and integrates the IMS Open Corpus Workbench tools with a web interface. This was adapted by our Norwegian collaborators, the Giellatekno and Divvun research teams at UiT Arctic University of Norway, for the morphologically rich indigenous Sámi languages, and thus we have found it suitable for languages such as Cree and Odawa.

For our Plains Cree version, we have incorporated the morphological feature tags, syntactic disambiguation, and syntactic function tags to create a morphosyntactically tagged online corpus. These analyses are supplemented with English glosses for the Plains Cree lemmas, where available, from Wolvengrey 2001. These glosses are also found in an intelligent online dictionary (http://altlab.ualberta.ca/itwewina/) based on the same resource; dictionary entries are linked to the corpus so that the lemmas may be seen in context as well as in the dictionary. Full sentence translations are not yet available, though the inclusion of the translations available in the Ahenakew-Wolfart text corpus to create a parallel Plains Cree–English corpus is among our development plans for the near future.

Here, we briefly detail some of the search capabilities of this corpus interface. However, as this publication format is not conducive to screenshots, examples are instead available on the Alberta Language Technology Lab website (http://altlab.artsrn.ualberta.ca) as well as the PAC website (https://algonquianconference.atlas-ling.ca/eng/supplementary-materials). The Korp interface (http://altlab.ualberta.ca/korp) has three levels of search capabilities: simple, extended, and advanced. Simple search allows for whole words or sequences of characters at the beginning or end of a word form to be searched. Extended search includes drop-down menus that allow a researcher to search for a form containing a sequence of characters, a particular morphological feature or set of features, a particular syntactic function tag, a sequence of words with particular features, or combinations thereof. Advanced search is similar, though it makes use of CQP (corpus query protocol) search format, which includes regular expressions and therefore allows for more precision in the searches. A CQP tutorial is linked directly from the search page, and, combined with basic understanding of regular expressions, the protocol allows for reasonably powerful searches.

The interface is able to display search results in a number of formats. The default setting is the Key Word In Context (KWIC) concordance display, which shows the words that fit the search criteria in the center of each line with the sentential context on either side. The results may also be displayed in paragraph context. On the right-hand side of these results, details of the corpus, the text, and the word attributes (morphological feature tags, syntactic functions, lemma gloss) are given when a word is selected. Results may also be displayed in terms of frequency in the corpus. Further refinement of search capabilities is under development.

These search capabilities and display functions allow researchers to explore features or syntactic relationships of interest in the corpus before extracting data for a quantitative study. A morphosyntactically tagged corpus within a user-friendly corpus interface simplifies and streamlines such investigations.

Results

In this section, we present some of the results we have drawn from our morphosyntactically tagged corpus of Plains Cree to exemplify the types of straightforward

TABLE 1.

WORD CLASS	TYPES	% OF 18,646	TOKENS	% OF 73,189
Nouns	**2,285**	**12.3**	**9,707**	**13.3**
Animate	1,055	5.7	5,658	7.8
Inanimate	1,230	6.6	4,049	5.5
Verbs	**3,207**	**17.2**	**20,726**	**28.3**
II	364	2.0	1,913	2.6
AI	1,470	7.9	9,118	12.5
TI	586	3.1	4,047	5.5
TA	786	4.2	5,648	7.7

Noun and verb (sub)class frequencies in the Ahenakew-Wolfart corpus

quantitative investigations made possible by the corpus, though far more complex questions can also be explored. Simple frequency searches for word classes or subclasses are possible; examples of these using earlier versions of the morphological model and gold standard were presented in Harrigan and Arppe 2015 and Schmirler and Harrigan 2016. Frequencies for different noun and verb classes and subclasses are given in Table 1.

Morphological complexity has also been investigated using the Plains Cree corpus. Wolvengrey (2015) and Arppe et al. (2019) investigated the complexity of preverbs, Schmirler et al. (2019) explored the complexity of derivational morphology, and Harrigan et al. (2017) discussed the complexity of inflectional morphology. As these are generally more recent investigations using versions of the corpus quite close to its present state, these statistics are not repeated here. However, the results of these studies lean toward one key conclusion: there is some upper limit to the maximum complexity (e.g., number of preverbs) at any level of Plains Cree morphology, and this is considerably less than the maximum that can be theoretically constructed.

The syntactic model, developed more recently, has been used in fewer investigations. Results can be found, along with more details regarding the development of the Constraint Grammar parser, in Schmirler et al. 2018. General trends, which align well with previous descriptions of Plains Cree sentences (e.g., Dahlstrom 1991, 1995), include the high frequency of verbs that occur with no lexical items as arguments (~50%), and the fact that obviative arguments (e.g., less topical) are more likely to appear as lexical items than proximate arguments, though proximate arguments are more likely to occur earlier as lexical items in a clause than obviative arguments. The clause structures in the Ahenakew-Wolfart corpus can be summarized in broader terms as well: the syntactic function tags indicate that there are 20,726 clauses containing verbs; in these, there are 4,418 actors manifested as lexical items, 3,709 goals manifested as lexical items, and 2,341 demonstratives associated with adjacent nouns.

The corpus interface also allows for searches of morphological features and their syntactic relationships. For example, one can search for animate nouns tagged as actors immediately preceding transitive animate verbs (VTAs)—this results in 11 examples. However, a more complex search using regular expressions allows one to search for (1) animate nouns tagged as actors that are (2) followed by a VTA in the same clause allowing for (3) any intervening material that is neither punctuation nor another verb. This search results in 24 clauses, and lets us see that where intervening material occurs, this is either a demonstrative or a particle. Further searches into features of nouns or verbs in such clauses may return interesting results for further investigation. For example, nearly all of the 11 clauses of actors immediately followed by their VTA governors were instances of dependent kinship nouns—a coincidence, or is there something else at play?

Conclusion

The morphosyntactically tagged Ahenakew-Wolfart Plains Cree corpus is the first step in a larger corpus of Plains Cree that will include over a century of Plains Cree texts collected across Alberta and Saskatchewan. The corpus represents four major components: the texts themselves, the morphological model and gold standard, the syntactic model and gold standard, and the online corpus interface. The morphosyntactic tags and the user-friendly corpus interface make exploration of Plains Cree texts much easier than previously possible, offering a starting point for the much more in-depth quantitative analysis also made possible by this tagged corpus. The gold standards for both the morphological and syntactic models allow for testing and further development of the models themselves, but the morphological gold standard, as it represents most of the Ahenakew-Wolfart texts, ensures that the current morphological feature tags are more accurate than is possible with the current model.

The online corpus is also linked with an intelligent online dictionary for Plains Cree, giving speakers, teachers, and students the opportunity to make use of both tools to explore natural language use in educational and everyday contexts. Though currently restricted to researchers during the development phase, the tagged corpus will soon be available for such applications. Additionally, the search capabilities in the online interface, as well as the models and gold standards underlying the tagged corpus, will be further developed and improved. Other existing and new texts will be morphologically and syntactically analyzed and implemented in the corpus, and available English translations will be implemented to create a parallel corpus of Plains Cree and English, further increasing the usefulness of the corpus resources.

NOTES

1. We are indebted to Dr. Wolfart for access to digital versions of these texts for our purposes of modeling and corpus development.
2. The digital versions of texts that constitute our corpus follow the conventions of Standard Roman Orthography (SRO) for Cree. Following general corpus linguistics practice, word tokens were defined as character strings separated by white space, and punctuation characters other than word-internal hyphens are considered word tokens as well. Thus, verbal/nominal prefixes, preverbs/prenouns, stems, and suffixes are considered to together form single word tokens. Moreover, the counts presented here may vary somewhat from ones we have presented earlier, in part due to us including now the Ahenakew (2000) text (which was reserved for testing previously), for those words in this particular text which occur elsewhere in the corpus and for which we consequently already have a hand-verified morphological analysis, as well as tokens that we had not been earlier able to analyze as Plains Cree words, but now can. Therefore, as we are revising our morphological and syntactic models, the exact counts may yet change slightly.
3. This prefix could also be considered a preverb as well, incorporating in one morpheme elements of both tense and aspect, and in future development we might treat it as such.
4. Abbreviations: 1Sg = first person singular, 3Sg = third person singular, AI = animate intransitive, AN = animate, Cnj = conjunct, Dem = demonstrative, Fut = future, II = inanimate intransitive, IN = inanimate, Ind = independent, Int = intentional, N = noun, Obv = obviative, Pl = plural, Prs = present, PV = preverb, Sg = singular, TA = transitive animate, TI = transitive inanimate, V = verb, @ACTOR> = actor of verb to the right, @<GOAL = goal of verb to the left, @N> = demonstrative dependent on a noun to the right, @PRED-TI = syntactic tag marking a transitive animate verb. Note: these are tags

output by the morphological and syntactic models, rather than those of traditional glosses.

5. The source code for the Plains Cree morphological model can be found online at https://victorio.uit.no/langtech/trunk/langs/crk/src/.
6. Such an inanimate noun may of course be an adjunct to such a verb, or in the case of a phrase containing a VTA, the second object of a benefactive, for example; these relationships which require the addition of lexical semantic features to verbs and nouns will be implemented in a later version of the model.
7. We have chosen to use *actor* and *goal* over *subject* and *object* for a number of reasons; primarily, we look to Algonquian tradition (e.g., Bloomfield 1946) and to theoretical argumentation for the lack of grammatical relations in favor of semantic ones (e.g., Wolvengrey 2005).
8. The tags in this example serve several different purposes. @ACTOR and @GOAL tags are assigned to nominal elements depending on their features and those of nearby verbs; the position of the verb relative to the argument is indicated with < or >. Verbs are tagged as @PRED for predicate, and specified as II, AI, TI, or TA on the basis of the feature tags output by the morphological model. Finally, demonstratives, when associated with adjacent nouns, are marked @N for "dependent on a noun" and the relative position of the noun with respect to the demonstrative is indicated.
9. The source code for the syntactic model can be found online at https://victorio.uit.no/langtech/trunk/langs/crk/src/syntax/.
10. The yet not analyzed tokens from Ahenakew 2000 were included in the overall token count in the calculation of these disambiguation performance figures.

REFERENCES

Ahenakew, Alice. 2000. *âh-âyîtaw isi ê-kî-kiskêyihtahkik maskihkiy / They Knew Both Sides of Medicine: Cree Tales of Curing and Cursing Told by Alice Ahenakew*, ed. by H. C. Wolfart and Freda Ahenakew. Winnipeg: University of Manitoba Press.

Arppe, Antti, Katherine Schmirler, Miikka Silfverberg, Mans Hulden, and Arok Wolvengrey. 2019. Insights from Computational Modeling of the Derivational Structure of Plains Cree. *Papers of the 48th Algonquian Conference,* ed. by Monica Macaulay and Margaret Noodin, pp. 1–18. East Lansing: Michigan State University Press.

Bear, Glecia, Minnie Fraser, Irene Calliou, Mary Wells, Alpha Lafond, and Rosa Longneck. 1992. *kôhkominawak otâcimowiniwâwa / Our Grandmothers' Lives as Told in Their Own Words,* ed. by Freda Ahenakew and H. C. Wolfart. Regina, Saskatchewan: Canadian Plains

Research Center, University of Regina.

Beesley, Kenneth R., and Lauri Karttunen. 2003a. *Finite State Morphology.* Stanford, CA: CSLI Publications.

Beesley, Kenneth R., and Lauri Karttunen. 2003b. Two-Level Rule Compiler. Xerox PARC. https://web.stanford.edu/~laurik/.book2software/twolc.pdf.

Bick, Eckhard, and Tino Didriksen. 2015. CG-3—Beyond Classical Constraint Grammar. *Proceedings of the 20th Nordic Conference of Computational Linguistics, NODALIDA,* no. 109, pp. 31–39. Vilnius, Lithuania: Linköping University Electronic Press.

Bloomfield, Leonard. 1930. *Sacred Stories of the Sweet Grass Cree.* New York: AMS Press.

Bloomfield, Leonard. 1974 [1934]. *Plains Cree Texts.* American Ethnological Society Publications 16. New York: AMS Press.

Bloomfield, Leonard. 1946. Algonquian. *Linguistic Structures of Native America,* vol. 6, pp. 85–129. New York: Viking Fund Publications in Anthropology.

Borin, Lars, Markus Forsberg, and Johan Roxendal. 2012. Korp—the Corpus Infrastructure of Språkbanken. *Proceedings of the 8th International Conference on Language Resources and Evaluation (LREC 2012),* pp. 474–478. Istanbul: ELRA.

Dahlstrom, Amy. 1991. *Plains Cree Morphosyntax.* New York: Garland.

Dahlstrom, Amy. 1995. *Topic, Focus and Other Word Order Problems in Algonquian.* Winnipeg: Voices of Rupert's Land.

Demers, Patricia, Naomi L. McIlwraith, and Dorothy Thunder (eds.). 2010. *The Beginning of Print Culture in Athabasca Country: A Facsimile Edition & Translation of a Prayer Book in Cree Syllabics by Father Émile Grouard, OMI, Prepared and Printed at Lac La Biche in 1883.* Edmonton: University of Alberta Press.

Evert, Stefan, and Andrew Hardie. 2011. Twenty-First Century Corpus Workbench: Updating a Query Architecture for the New Millennium. *Proceedings of the Corpus Linguistics 2011 Conference.* Birmingham: University of Birmingham. https://www.birmingham.ac.uk/research/activity/corpus/publications/conference-archives/2011-birmingham.aspx.

Harrigan, Atticus G., and Antti Arppe. 2015. oswêw êkwa ê-tipiskâk, mâka mâcîw âhpô ê-mâcît? Paper read at the 47th Algonquian Conference, Winnipeg, Manitoba.

Harrigan, Atticus G., Katherine Schmirler, Antti Arppe, Lene Antonsen, Trond Trosterud, and Arok Wolvengrey. 2017. Learning from the Computational Modelling of Plains Cree Verbs: Analysis and Generation Using Finite State Transduction. *Morphology* 27(4):565–598.

Kâ-Nîpitêhtêw, Jim. 1998. *ana kâ-pimwêwêhahk okakêskihkêmowina / The Counselling Speeches of Jim Kâ-Nîpitêhtêw,* ed., trans., and with a glossary by Freda Ahenakew and H. C. Wolfart. Publications of the Algonquian Text Society. Winnipeg: University of Manitoba Press.

Karlsson, Fred. 1995a. Designing a Parser for Unrestricted Text. *Constraint Grammar: A*

Language-Independent System for Parsing Unrestricted Text, vol. 4, ed. by Fred Karlsson, Atro Voutilainen, Juha Heikkilae, and Arto Anttila, pp. 1–40. New York: Walter de Gruyter.

Karlsson, Fred. 1995b. The Formalism and Environment of Constraint Grammar Parsing. *Constraint Grammar: A Language-Independent System for Parsing Unrestricted Text,* vol. 4, ed. by Fred Karlsson, Atro Voutilainen, Juha Heikkilä, and Arto Anttila, pp. 41–88. New York: Walter de Gruyter.

Masuskapoe, Cecilia. 2010. *piko kîkway ê-nakacihtât: kêkêk otâcimowina ê-nêhiyawastêki,* ed. by H. C. Wolfart and Freda Ahenakew. Winnipeg: Algonquian and Iroquoian Linguistics.

Minde, Emma. 1997. *kwayask ê-kî-pê-kiskinowâpatihicik / Their Example Showed Me the Way: A Cree Woman's Life Shaped by Two Cultures,* ed. by Freda Ahenakew and H. C. Wolfart. Edmonton: University of Alberta Press.

Okimâsis, Jean. 2004. *Cree: Language of the Plains / nēhiyawēwin: paskwāwi-pīkiskwēwin.* Regina, Saskatchewan: Canadian Plains Research Center.

Schmirler, Katherine, Antti Arppe, Trond Trosterud, and Lene Antonsen. 2018. Building a Constraint Grammar Parser for Plains Cree Verbs and Arguments. *Proceedings of the Eleventh International Conference on Language Resources and Evaluation (LREC 2018),* ed. by Nicoletta Calzolari, Khalid Choukri, Christopher Cieri, et al., pp. 2981–2988. Miyazaki, Japan: LREC. https://www.aclweb.org/anthology/L18-1472.

Schmirler, Katherine, and Atticus G. Harrigan. 2016. Word Class Frequencies According to Corpora. Paper read at the Third Prairie Workshop on Language and Linguistics, Regina, Saskatchewan.

Schmirler, Katherine, Atticus G. Harrigan, Antti Arppe, and Arok Wolvengrey. 2019. Plains Cree Verbal Derivational Morphology: A Corpus Investigation. *Papers of the 48th Algonquian Conference,* ed. by Monica Macaulay and Margaret Noodin, pp. 239–254. East Lansing: Michigan State University Press.

Snoek, Connor, Dorothy Thunder, Kaidi Lõo, Antti Arppe, Jordan Lachler, Sjur Moshagen, and Trond Trosterud. 2014. Modeling the Noun Morphology of Plains Cree. Paper read at ComputEL: Workshop on the use of Computational Methods in the Study of Endangered Languages, 52nd Annual Meeting of the Association for Computational Linguistics, Baltimore, Maryland.

Vandall, Peter, and Joe Douquette. 1987. *wâskahikaniwiyiniw-âcimowina / Stories of the House People, Told by Peter Vandall and Joe Douquette,* ed. by Freda Ahenakew. Winnipeg: University of Manitoba Press.

Whitecalf, Sarah. 1993. *kinêhiyawiwininiwaw nêhiyawêwin / The Cree Language Is Our Identity: The La Ronge Lectures of Sarah Whitecalf,* ed. by H. C. Wolfart and Freda Ahenakew. Winnipeg: University of Manitoba Press.

Wolfart, H. Christoph. 1973. *Plains Cree: A Grammatical Study.* Transactions of the American Philosophical Society, n.s., vol. 63, pt. 5. Philadelphia: American Philosophical Society.

Wolvengrey, Arok. 2001. *nēhiyawēwin: itwēwina / Cree: Words.* 2 vols. Regina, Saskatchewan: Canadian Plains Research Center.

Wolvengrey, Arok. 2005. Inversion and the Absence of Grammatical Relations. *Morphosyntactic Expression in Functional Grammar,* ed. by C. de Groot and K. Hengeveld, pp. 419–446. Berlin: Walter de Gruyter.

Wolvengrey, Arok. 2015. Preverb Combinations, Co-occurrences, and Sequences: Preliminary Findings from a Preliminary Plains Cree Corpus. Paper read at the 47th Algonquian Conference, Winnipeg, Manitoba.

Clause Combining in Michif

Peter Bakker and Robert A. Papen

In this paper, we study clause combining in Michif and compare it with Plains Cree, one of its source languages. Michif is a bilingual mixed language in which, roughly, the verbs come from Cree and most of the noun phrases from French (Rhodes 1977; Bakker 1997; Papen 1987, 2005), although there are some dissenting voices about the mixed nature (Rosen 2007 for phonology, Gillon and Rosen 2018 for the structure of the noun phrase).

In Plains Cree and in Michif, there are two sets of verbal paradigms with no overlap in the forms of the person-marking affixes. One set is, roughly, used in main clauses (called the independent order) and the other is used in subordinate clauses or when a nominal element is focused (called the conjunct order). Subordinating prefixes are used in the conjunct order, in which person marking is exclusively suffixing, and combinations of person prefixes and suffixes are used in the independent order.

There are only a few distinct prefixed conjunct order markers, and they have a fairly general meaning. More concrete meanings can be created by additional markers, placed either between the prefixed conjunct markers and the verb (e.g., *-mêkwâ-* 'while,' as in *kâ-mêkwâ-mâyi-kîsikâk* 'while it was bad weather'), or by a separate particle: *mêkwâc êkosi ê-totahk* 'while she was doing this').

The independent and conjunct verb classes are also found in Michif, as well as additional markers specifying the semantic relations. Such specifying particles are more common in Michif than in Cree, and infixed markers are more common in Cree than in Michif. In addition, Michif also uses a number of subordinators from French, and this has an impact on the structure of the language.

This is the first study of clause combining in Michif. We take as our point of departure the example sentences in a Michif dictionary compiled by two native speakers (Laverdure and Allard 1983, henceforth L&A), and compare those with Michif and Cree narratives. Previous research by Bakker (2005) had led to the conclusion that direct speech was virtually absent in spontaneous texts, but not uncommon in the L&A dictionary, and we decided to study clause combining by making an inventory. In Algonquian languages, reported speech is typically presented in a direct manner rather than in an indirect manner. In English, one can say, "He says (that) he is happy" (indirect) or "He says: 'I am happy'" (direct). In L&A, we find embedded phrases equivalent to "He claims that he owns a car," rather than direct speech as in "He claims: 'I own a car.'" (1) provides an example of such an embedding:[1]

(1) Itwayw wiya etipaymawt li shawr.

itwee-w	wiya	ee-tipeeyim-aat	li	shaar
say-3	3	SUB-own.TA-3>3	the	car

'He claims he owns the car.' (L&A: 62)

In Michif narratives, on the other hand, such utterances are exclusively expressed as direct speech acts, often accompanied by quotatives, notably *itweew,* as in (2):

(2)

la	fiy	ashay	**itew:**
the	girl	already	**say.TA.3>3**
'wiipach	ka-peekiiwee-wak	ookik,'	**itwee-w**
soon	FUT-come.home-3PL	they	**say-3**

'The girl already says to him: 'Soon they will come home.' (Norman Fleury, speaker)

We are not aware of spontaneous texts in Plains Cree in which indirect speech is used. In Michif oral narratives, like in Plains Cree, no indirect speech has been observed in these contexts. Michif in L&A seems to be different, as the dictionary does contain examples of indirect speech.

For this paper, we investigate other types of clause combining in Michif and include comparisons with Plains Cree and Michif oral narrative texts. For almost all of the approximately 8,500 English lemmas in L&A, one or more phrases or sentences exemplify the entry word; it therefore constitutes the most extensive published data set of the language. Thus, one can make an inventory of the data and assess the extent to which L&A adequately reflects the spoken language.

Background

It is well known and uncontroversial that verb paradigms in Michif are virtually identical to those of Plains Cree, with only a few minor differences (see e.g., Rhodes 1981; Bakker 2004, 2006; and Gillon and Rosen 2018:179–185). For more details on Plains Cree verbs, see Wolfart 1996 and Wolvengrey 2011.

In Cree, as in Algonquian languages generally, there are two sets of verbal paradigms, called independent and conjunct orders, where the first is generally used in main clauses and the latter in subordinate clauses or sentences with a focused noun phrase. All verbs are finite, with overt inflection for person, and there is only one verb per clause. The so-called subjunctive order can be derived from the conjunct order and is one of several ways to express conditional clauses, at least in Plains Cree.[2] Whereas the independent order makes use of person prefixes and suffixes, person inflection in the conjunct order is exclusively suffixing. Conjunct order verbs will have one of a small set of prefixes *ê-*, *kâ-*, *ci-*, *ta/kita-*, which add temporal, aspectual, discursive, and other semantic nuances to the meanings of the verbs. However, there is one exception to the claim above, that subordinate clauses are always in the conjunct order: conditional sentences preceded by *kîspin* 'if' are usually followed by a clause in the independent order rather than the conjunct order. In more recent recordings, however, *kîspin* is sometimes followed by conjunct order verbs.[3]

There are several ways in which Plains Cree clauses can be connected with each other.[4] Verbal inflection can be sufficient by itself, as in example (3) from Bloomfield's *Plains Cree Texts,* collected in the 1920s. Both verbs have person inflection, and one is in the independent order, the other in the conjunct order, and the first verb is part of a matrix clause and the second verb constitutes an embedded clause. In example (3) it is clear that the second clause relates to a future event related to a current event referred to in the first clause.

(3)	êko	ki-miy-iti-n-âwâw	kita-pimâtisi-*yêk*
	this	2-give-INV-1-PL	SUB.FUT-live-*2PL*

'This I give to you, to be for you a source of life.' (Bloomfield 1934:20–21)

The semantic connection between the two clauses is most often underspecified, in the sense that the exact meaning has to be inferred by the listener. In the Plains Cree sentence (4), there is one main clause ('they are eager'), and two subordinate clauses ('they dance' and 'they eat dog'), without any specifying particles, and it is not explicit that the dancing is the reason for their eagerness, and whether the consumption of dogs just happened simultaneously or was also an object of desire.

(4)	êkwa	tapwê	cîhkêyihtamw-ak	ê-nimihito-*cik,*
	then	truly	be.eager-3PL	SUB-dance-*3PL*
	nayêstaw	atimw-a	ê-mowê-*cik*	
	only	dog-*OBV*	*SUB*-eat.TA-*3PL*	

'Then truly did they put their heart into the dance, and only dogs they ate.' (Bloomfield 1934:8–9)

Not all connections are underspecified: various particles can be used to add semantic precision. In example (5), the subordinating particle *mêkwâc* specifies that the actions of the main clause and the subordinate clause take place at the same time, and *nam êskw* indicates a non-simultaneous temporal relation:

(5)	**mêkwâc**	ê-wiyinihtâkê-*cik,*	**nam êskw**	ê-nawacî-*cik,*
	while	SUB-cut.up-*3PL*	**before**	SUB-roast-*3PL*
	âsay	pâskis-ok-wak	ôki	nêhiyaw-ak
	already	shoot-INV-3PL	these	Cree-PL

'**While** they were cutting up the game, **before** they had begun the roasting, the Blackfoot fired at the Cree.' (Bloomfield 1934:92–93)

There are around a dozen such particles in Cree (see (8) below), and they differ somewhat from dialect to dialect, also within Plains Cree. Occasionally, such particles are integrated in the conjunct verb, between the subordinator and the verb stem, for example *-mêkwâ-*:

(6)	kîtahtawê,	ê-**mêkwâ**-pimiskâ-*cik*	sipi-hk,	
	suddenly	SUB-while-sail-*3PL*	river-LOC	
	kîtahtawê	kâ-pê-nokwani-*yik*	nipiy	ê-pê-cimatê-*yik*
	suddenly	SUB-come-visible-*3OBV*	water	SUB-come-stand-*3OBV*

'Presently as they were canoeing along the river, there suddenly appeared an upright wall of water.' (Bloomfield 1934:194–195)

The type exemplified in (3) and (4) (no particle) is by far the most common in Plains Cree narratives, and (5) (with particle) is fairly common as well. The type illustrated in (6) is much less common. This threefold taxonomy provides the background for our discussion of clause combining in Michif in the following sections.

Clause Combining in Michif: An Inventory from L&A

L&A is a Michif dictionary compiled by two native speakers of Michif. As we indicated above, it contains some constructions that have not otherwise been found in spontaneous speech, but apart from that, it is a landmark in the documentation of Michif, with a wealth of example sentences. It is possible, however, that the unexpected constructions that we referred to above and that are found in the dictionary could be instigated by the possibility that some sentences were first formulated in English and thus influenced by English. In compiling the dictionary, an English dictionary was taken as a point of departure (Patline Laverdure, personal communication to Papen), and this yielded Michif example sentences, or word explanations, for less commonly used English words such as (p. 364): *zany, zephyr cloth, zilch, zing, zinnia.*

In the dictionary, around a dozen coordinators and subordinators from French and Cree are found, listed in (7a) and (7b), whereas (8) lists subordinating particles from Bloomfield's Plains Cree lexicon (n.d.).

(7a) Conjunctions from French (forms that are used as subordinators in Michif that are not used as such in French are underlined)[5]

- ubendon 'or' (French *ou bien donc* 'or' (emphatic))
- pi 'and' (French *puis* 'and then, and')
- enku 'as soon as,' 'once' (Laurentian French *un coup*)
- afors 'because,' 'by dint of' (French ***à force***)
- akuz, akooz 'because' (French ***à cause (que)***)
- apree 'after' (French *après* 'behind,' 'after,' cf. *après que* 'after')
- avan 'before' (French *avant* 'in front of' (P), cf. *avant que* 'before')
- dabor 'provided,' 'as long as' (French *d'abord* 'first')
- par 'by' (French *par* 'by')
- pur 'for, in order to' (French *pour* 'for')
- pur li tan 'as long as' (French *pour le temps*)
- zeusk (a tan) 'until' (French *jusqu'* (*à temps*)) 'until the time')

(7b) Subordinate conjunctions from Cree:

- **âta** 'although,' aspihci 'than,' aspin 'after,' ispî 'when,' kîspin 'if,' mêkwât 'while,' tânisi 'how,' tânitê 'where'

As (7b) shows, the Cree particle *aspin* 'away' has a new function as a subordinator meaning 'after.'

(8) Plains Cree subordinate conjunctions (from Bloomfield's Plains Cree dictionary, n.d., 1984)

- ayis 'for, because, so it is, cannot be changed'
- âhci piko 'more the less, in spite of it, despite'
- âta 'in vain, although'
- awasi- 'before, beyond'
- ici 'afterward, then'
- ispî 'when'
- kîspin 'if'
- mekwâ 'while, in the act or place'
- mekwâc 'during the time, at present'
- mwehci 'exactly then, just after'
- osâm, osâmi 'too much, because of excess, for'
- pâmayas 'before'
- tânisi 'when'

Alice Ahenekew (2000) uses the following particles in the 12 Plains Cree narratives in her book: *ayis(k)* 'for, because', *âta* 'although, on the other hand', *ispî* 'at such time, then; when', *kîspin* 'if', *mayaw* 'as soon as', *mêkwâ(c)* 'while, during, in the course of, in the midst of', *osâm* 'because, for', *pâmwayês* 'before', *tânisi* 'when', *wîya* 'because, for'. The text frequency is low. In the first three stories, covering some 14 pages, six types with ten tokens were counted (*âta* 2, *mêkwa* 1, *ayisk* 4, *ispî* 1, *osâm* 1, *tânisi* 1), showing that the exact semantic relationship between clauses is mostly unspecified, or indicated with relative roots.

We discuss clause combining on the basis of the semantic relations between the two clauses, and relate them to several parameters: the type and source of the verb in the subordinate sentence (Cree conjunct order, Cree independent order, French with subordinator) and the presence or absence of a particle, integrated into the verb or separate from it (see also note 5).

We discuss the following semantic relations between clauses: time 'when, while, after, before', location 'where', manner 'how, like', purpose 'in order to', reason 'because, for', conditional (hypothetical, counterfactual, concessive) 'if, even if', concessive 'although', substitutive 'instead of', additive 'in addition to'.

Temporal Relations

Temporal relations can be simultaneous ('while, when'), or nonsimultaneous ('before,' 'after'). Nonsimultaneous relations can be posterior or anterior. Simultaneous relations can be expressed with a simple conjunct verb, as in (9) or with the particle *meekwat* (Cree: *mêkwâc*) as in (10).

(9) Kicheeskastam see dawn kawnipawt.

kichiiskast-am	sii	dan	<u>kaa</u>-nipaa-*t*
gnash.TI-3	3PL.POSS	tooth	<u>SUB</u>-sleep-*3*

'She gnashes her teeth while sleeping.' (unspecified, simultaneous) (L&A: 112)

(10) Kenawayhchikay a la maezoun maykwawt eshipwayhtayyawn.

Kenawee-hchikee	a	la	mezon
take.care.of-INDEF.OBJ.IMPER	in	the.F	house

meekwaat	ee-shipweehtee-*yaann*
while	<u>SUB</u>-leave-*1CONJ*

'Keep the house while I'm gone.' (specified, simultaneous) (L&A: 153)

If the subordinate clause has a French predicate, French particles and subordinators are used, such as *kant ki* (Laurentian French *quand que*) or *sii* (French *si* 'if'; see (25) below), as in (11) and (13) below. An anterior temporal relation is expressed with French *avan* (French *avant* 'before') (14) and a posterior relationship with French *apree* (French *après* 'after') as in (12) and (13) or *en koo* (Laurentian French *un coup* 'once . . .'; no example provided here), or Cree-origin *ashpin* 'after,' as in (15).

(11) Li kor i sipawr lee zheu kawnt ki foo.
Li kor i sipaar lii zheu **kant** ki *foo*
the.M body 3 secrete PL fluid **when** SUB *need*
'The body secretes fluids when it needs to.' (specified, simultaneous) (L&A: 285)

(12) Pat tet la poul apree aykeemanikwaykanawmist.
Pat tet la pul **apree** ee-kii-manikweekanaam-*ist*
no head the.F chicken **after** SUB-PAST-cut.head-*INDEF.ACTOR*
'The chicken was headless after decapitation.' (specified, anterior) (L&A: 128)

(13) Si taen braev la feey apray ki la soovee li baybee.
Siten braav la fii **apree** ki la soovii li beebii
is.a courageous the.F girl **after** that she.has saved the.M baby
'The girl was a heroine **after** she saved the baby.' (specified, anterior) (L&A: 132)

(14) Keewawpahtem avawn kawshpayik.
Kii-waapaht-em **avan** kaa-ishpayi-*k*
PAST-see.TI-3 **before** SUB-happen-*3*
'He foresaw it before it happened.' (L&A: 101)

(15) Kishkayistam shiamishchikayt pi shiushipayhikayt ashpin a l'ikol kawitoustayt.
Kishkeeyist-am shi-amishchikee-t pi shi-ushipeehikee-*t*
know.TI-3 SUB.FUT-read-3 and SUB.FUT-write-*3*
ashpin a likol kaa-itustee-*t*
away/after in the.school SUB-go-*3*
'He has become literate since he went to school.' (L&A: 164)

In short, only *meekwaat* continues a Cree construction, and *ashpin* is an innovation. French particles are more common than Cree ones in temporal relations.

Location

In locative expressions, the subordinate clause contains information about a place in the main clause, as in the following.

(16) En pchit beut ashtayw ita kawkawtawyawn.

enn	pchit	beut	ashtee-w	**ita**	<u>kaa</u>-kaataa-*yaann*
a.F	little.F	hill	be-3	**where**	<u>SUB</u>-hide.TI-*1SG*

'There's a knoll where I hid it.' (L&A: 157)

(17) Mashinaha li pakay tawnday <u>chitishahamen</u>.

mashinah.ti-a	li pakee	**taandee**	<u>chi</u>-tishaham-*enn*
write-IMPER	the.M package	**where**	<u>SUB.FUT</u>-send.TI-*2SG*

'Label the package for where it will go.' (L&A: 158)

Locative clauses may contain no particle, or one of the Cree particles *taandee* (from the Cree question word *tânitê* 'where?') as in (17) or *ita/itee* (from the Cree locative connector) as in (16), where its function is limited to a clause-connecting particle. Both are found with these functions in Plains Cree as well.

Manner

When clauses refer to the manner in which an action is performed, the Cree particle *taanshi* 'how' (< Cree *tânsi*) is used.

(18) Marii kishkayhtem tawnshi chi-keeshtaypout.

Marii	kishkeeht-em	**taanshi**	<u>chi</u>-kiishteepu-*t*
Mary	know.TI-3	**how**	<u>SUB.FUT</u>-cook.AI-*3*

'Mary learned how to cook.' (L&A: 152)

Purpose

Purpose clauses indicate a way in which a goal is reached, translatable as 'in order to.' Purpose clauses are indicated with a conjunct verb with the future subordinator (*chii-*, *shii-*). No particles are used. Except for the shape of the conjunct markers, the constructions are identical in Michif and Plains Cree. In Plains Cree, the equivalent of *chii/shii* is *kita-* (Bakker 1997:262).

(19) Geeshawpoustawnawn li roond port shi-peestikwayyahk la shawnbr.

gii-shaap-ust-aanaann li rond port
1.PAST-through-go.AI-1PL the.M round gate
shi-piistikwee-*yaahk* la shanbr
SUB.FUT-enter.AI-*1PL* the.F room

'We walked through the archway to enter the room.' (L&A: 25)

A second construction parallels English, where the particle 'if' can be used in a purpose clause. This is what we find in (20) with *kiishpinn* 'if,' which is followed by an independent order verb.

(20) Dawn li sawsii pashpawpi keeshpin apiw.

dan li saasii pashpaap-i **kiishpinn** api-w
in the.M window peep.through.AI-IMPER if be.home.AI-3.INDEP

'Look in the window to see if she's home.' (L&A: 166)

In Cree, this particle is only used in conditional sentences, but it clearly has no conditional meaning in (20). This use of *kiishpinn* could be due to influence from English, where 'if' is used both for a condition and for a purpose clause.

Reason

There are several ways of indicating a clause which expresses a reason: a clause without a particle or with the French particle ***akuz/akuuz*** 'because' (21), which can be followed by a Cree verb in conjunct order, or a French verb introduced by *ki* (French *que* 'that') as in (22). The connector *akuz* is optional; inclusion specifies the meaning relation between the two clauses.

(21) Ispray weechihow (a kouz) aypwawtuwschikayt.

ispre wiichih-aaw **(akooz)** ee-pwaatawischikee-*t*
specific help.TA-INDEF.ACTOR **(because)** SUB-fail.things.AI-*3*

'He gets special help because of his disability.' (L&A: 74)

(22) Li polis ka-ootiniwaywuk a kooz ki la rawbee en bawnk.

li polis ka-ootin-iwee-wak **akooz** ki *la-raabii* enn bank
the.M police FUST-take-INDEF.OBJ-3PL **because** SUB 3.*has-robbed* a.F bank

'The police will arrest one for robbing a bank.' (L&A: 26)

Conditional

Clauses with conditional meanings can have a verb in the conjunct order without a particle (as in 23), in what Bloomfield calls the subjunctive order (as in 24); that is, a conditional clause with a suffix *-i/-u* after the person inflection of the conjunct order. Alternatively, a clause (most often in the independent order) may start with *kiishpinn* 'if,' as in (30). The conditional particle *sii* 'if' (French *si*) is only used in L&A when the predicate is from French, as in (25).

(23) Ta vee il i awn dawnzhee kawshoohkaychahikayyen.

ta	vii	il-i	an	danzhii	kaa-shoohkeechahikee-*yenn*
your.F	life	3-be	in	danger	SUB-drive.fast.AI-*2SG*

'Your life is in peril when you drive too fast.' (L&A: 223)

(24) Meetshoohkan noostayhkatayyani.

miitshoo-hkann	noosteehkatee-*yan*-i
eat.AI-DELAYED.IMPER	be.hungry.AI-2-COND

'If you're hungry, eat.' (L&A: 137)

(25) Papaw-itawpi see ti veu.

papaw-itaap-i	**sii**	*ti*	veu
here.there-look.AI.IMPER	if	2SG.be	want

'Browse around if you want.' (L&A: 52)

Concessive

Concessive phrases are introduced by the particle *aata* (< Cree *âta*), and followed by a Cree conjunct verb, or by a French predicate, which is then introduced by *ki* (< French *que* 'that'):

(26) Papawmoustayw awta ayyawhkoushit.

papaam-ustee-w	**aata**	ee-aahkushi-*t*.
about-go-3	**although**	SUB-be.sick-*3*

'Although sick, she's ambulatory.' (L&A: 22)

(27) Il i vif awta kil i katraven senk.

Il-i	vif	**aata**	kili	katraven	senk.
3-be	lively	**although**	that.3.be	eighty	five

'He has a lot of zip **even though** he is eighty-five years old.' (L&A: 362)

Substitutive

In substitutive clauses, an alternative action is presented. This is done with a Cree particle *ashpiishchi* (< Cree preposition *aspisci* 'than' as in 'bigger than') followed by a Cree conjunct verb.

(28) Kapimbastow ashpeeshchee shioutawpawshout.

ka-pimbasta-w	**ashpiishchi**	shi-utaapaashu-*t.*
3FUT-run.AI-3	than	SUB.FUT-drive.AI-3

'She'll run instead of riding.' (L&A: 277)

Quantity

A clause indicating quantity can be expressed with a subordinate clause preceded by the particle *taamaykuhk* (< Cree *tânimayikohk* 'how far').

(29) Saprawn kakishkayist-ahk tawmuykouhk aykeemaenshtinikayt.

sapran	kaa-kishkeeyist-ahk	**taamayikuhk**	ee-kiimenshtinikee-*t*
necessary	SUB-know.TI-3	how.much	SUB-spend.AI-*3*

'She has to account for the expenses.' (L&A: 17)

Generalizations about Michif Clause Combining in L&A

On the basis of the above observations, and additional examples not listed here, one can formulate a number of generalizations. Each subordinate clause contains a subordinator, either from French (e.g., *ki*) or from Cree (e.g., *kaa-, ee-/en-, chii-, -i/-u*). Cree subordinators (verbal prefixes) can be used with or without specifying particles. If the verb is Cree, the subordinator usually has the form of a verbal prefix *kaa-, ee-/en-, chii-*. If the French subordinator *ki* is used, it is always preceded by a specifying particle from French or Cree such as *avan* 'before' or *aata* 'although'; *ki* is not used as the sole subordinator. French particles are more frequent before *ki.* If no particles are used, the meaning relations between the main clause and the subordinate clause are usually open for interpretation, and the subordinate clause can be called circumstantial. Specifying particles indicate a more narrow and explicit meaning relationship between the two clauses.

The choice between a French or a Cree particle appears largely determined by the intended meaning. Particles for reason and nonsimultaneous time are always from French, and particles for manner, location, and so on, are always from Cree.

If the predicate of the subordinate clause is French (e.g., an adjective, a copula, or a verb), the subordinator is always the French particle *ki.* This subordinator is virtually always preceded by a French particle (cases such as (27) are less common).

Discussion

Clause combining in Michif, based on L&A, appears virtually identical to clause combining in Plains Cree, except, obviously, for the addition of French particles and predicates. Almost all subordinate clauses contain conjunct verbs, but the continuation from Cree is obvious in conditional sentences with *kiishpinn/kîspin,* as they are followed by independent order verbs in both Cree and Michif. In addition, they can also be created with what Algonquianists call the subjunctive order. Examples (30) and (31) from Michif narratives illustrate both (Norman Fleury, speaker).

(30) **Kiishpinn** ki-wiiweew-inn,
if 2-marry.AI-2
sapran enn mesaazh kaa-shipwee-tishaham-*aahk* ota
necessary a.F.message SUB-away-send.TI-*1PL* here
'If you want to take a wife, we will have a message to be sent away here.'

(31) mishkaaw-ach-i ana la fiy chi-teepish-*aahk* uma li suyii
find.TA-2>3-**COND** this the.F girl SUB-fit-*3* this the.M shoe
ka-wiikim-aaw
2.FUT-marry.TA-3
'If you find the girl who fits this shoe, you will marry her.'

Examples in Michif oral narratives appear to be quite similar to those found in L&A (except, apparently, in indirect speech with *verba dicendi*), but space prevents us from providing extensive examples. We have examples of *aata, avan, apree, kan ki, meekwaat, ita,* and of course sole Cree subordinators, in functions similar to those above.

The only ones that warrant additional discussion are the subordinators derived from question words. One could suspect that constructions like the ones in (17) and (18), where the question words *taandee* and *taanishi* (< Cree *tânitê* 'where' and *tânisi* 'how') are used as conjunctions, would be an influence from English, where the conjunctions and question words have the same form, in contrast to Cree, where the subordinators are *itâ* for locations and *isi* for manner (usually as a relative root). The conjunctions *taansi* and *taandee* are also found in Michif narratives. (32) provides an example from Michif that contains both.

(32) namoya gii-kakweechim-aaw son non,
NEG 1.PAST-ask.TA-3 3.POSS name
taandee ee-wiiki-*t,* **taanishi** ee-ishinihkaa-shu-*t*
where SUB-live.AI-*3* how SUB-call-REFL-3
'I did not ask her her name, where she lives, how she is called.' (Norman Fleury, speaker)

However, this appears not to be a Michif innovation, as both *tânitê* and *tânisi* are also present in Cree texts from the 1920s, as in (33) and (34) below, which are less common than *itâ* and *isi:*

(33) wâpahkih pita nka-ntunaw-âw-ak mustusw-ak,
tomorrow first 1.FUT-seek-3-PL buffalo-3PL
tantê ihta-*twaw*-i, êkuta tay-is-pici-*yêk*
where be.present-*3PL*-COND there FUT.SUB-RR-camp-*2PL*
'Well now, Chiefs, tomorrow I shall go look for buffalo, so that you may move camp to wherever they are.' (Bloomfield 1934:166–167)

(34) âcimustaw-êw **tanisi** kâ-tôta-*hk*
narrate-3>3 **how** SUB-do-*3*
'He told them how he had done.' (Bloomfield 1934:114–115)

English influence in the Michif sentences (33) and (34) cannot be excluded, but such early attestations in Cree make contact influence less likely.

In short, subordination strategies in Cree and Michif are remarkably similar.

The introduction of French particles and French predicates has not changed the grammar significantly, except obviously in the lexicon: a different range of particles is available, especially the ones from French. In Michif, however, in contrast to Cree, no particles are integrated into the verb in our data set.

Further, there seem to be two types of change in frequency, although we did not do a thorough quantitative study. First, in Bloomfield's texts from the 1920s, independent particles are clearly more frequent than such elements that form part of the verb (as exemplified in (6)): independent particles are roughly four times more frequent than those integrated in the verb. For instance, in Bloomfield (1934) we find *atah* 'although' 16 times in independent use versus four times integrated in the verb, and *mêkwâ(c)* 23 times independent versus five times integrated. Second, there also seems to be a diachronic development within Plains Cree texts, when comparing Cree as documented by Bloomfield in the 1920s (Bloomfield 1931, 1934) with Cree documented in the 1980s and later, in that later speakers use more particles than earlier ones, who rely more on conjunct forms. In a similar vein, Wolfart (1973:44) observes that the evidential particle *êtokwê* 'I wonder' was ten times as frequent in his recordings from the late 1960s in comparison to Bloomfield's texts from the 1920s, correlating with a decrease of the dubitative evidential verb forms, in which a cognate morpheme *-ikwê-* is part of the verb morphology, during the same time period.

Outlook

We began with an observation that complementation after verbs of speaking is different from Cree in Laverdure and Allard's (1983) Michif dictionary. The statement about indirect speech being absent from Cree must be modified. There are exceptions, as in Ellis (2004:22, 141, 147) in his Moose Cree teaching book: *tâpwê, n'titikawin ê-mîcisocik* (indirect) beside *tâpwê, mîcisowak, n'titikawin* (direct) 'They are eating, I am told' (Ellis 2004:22), where the verb in the first example is a subordinate verb in the conjunct order, and in the second example in the direct order. Direct speech is more common: "In running conversation, quoted or recorded speech (or thought) is often represented in Cree by direct quotation" (Ellis 2004:475). Also for Plains Cree (Cook 2014:169) and Swampy Cree, examples can be found in elicited materials:

(35)	cân	kiskênim-êw	tânitê	mêrî-wa	ê-itohtê-ni-*t*
	John-3	knows.TA-3>3'	where	Mary-OBV	SUB-go-OBV-*3*

'John knows where Mary (obv.) went.' (Long 1999:85; Swampy Cree)

Data on other forms of clause combining, as surveyed here, do not show much divergence between Cree and Michif. There are a few differences in this realm in that there is a higher frequency of particles in Michif compared to the Cree of the 1920s. In Michif, the intended meanings greatly influence the choice of French or Cree particles in that some meanings seem to require a Cree particle (e.g., concessives), while other meanings will require a French particle (e.g., anterior and posterior temporals), and some meanings allow particles from both languages (simultaneous temporal, conditional). One can speculate about reasons why some meanings yield French particles and others Cree ones. We want to suggest two paths for possible explanations. Even though Cree subordinate particles are less used than just conjunct verbs, some of the Cree particles (*aata, meekwat, kiishpinn*) are more frequent in Cree than other particles, and those are the ones used in Michif. A second reason may be in line with Matras's (2008) work on language contact, where meaning contrasts tend to trigger elements to be borrowed from other languages. His hierarchy (2008:187) on subordination is that concessive, conditional, causal, and purpose are more likely to be borrowed than other subordinators, due to more insecurity on the part of the speaker. In Michif, these four are mostly from Cree. Different temporal reference in main and subordinate clause would work, but concessives would be a counterexample, as these are from French as well. On the other hand, Matras (2008) also considers mixed languages such as Michif an exceptional category, where special conditions apply.

NOTES

1. The first line in the examples is from L&A, where we provide the English-inspired spelling as given in that source. The second line is the same example in a standardized spelling. We have adapted the spelling of the dictionary examples to the Flamand-Papen system (Papen 2004–5), where long vowels are indicated by a double vowel rather than by a circumflex accent, as is done in writing Plains Cree. Affixes are not separated from their base by a hyphen in L&A, but they are in the second line. For examples not from the dictionary, the first line is lacking. The following abbreviations are used in the glosses: COND = conditional, F = feminine, FUT = future, IMPER = imperative, INDEF = indefinite,

INDEP = independent, INV = inverse, M = masculine, OBV = obviative, PL = plural, POSS = possessive, REFL = reflexive, RR = relative root, SG = singular, SUB = subordinator, SUBJ = subject, TA = transitive animate, TI = transitive inanimate.

2. This traditional Algonquianist term is misleading in that the same term is used for very different phenomena in other traditions; in Romance philology, for instance, the subjunctive refers to a type of mood referring to what is imagined or desired.
3. Blain (1997:200) has one example with *kîspin* followed by a conjunct order verb, which is clearly elicited having an English equivalent like 'who is it that John asked you if Bill married?' Cook (2014:44, 112, 184) has several examples, also from spontaneous speech, where *kîspin* is followed by a conjunct verb.
4. We use the following visual aids in the examples: conjunct order person inflection is indicated in *italics,* French subordinator *ki* and subordinating prefixes in conjunct verbs are indicated with underscore, and particles are indicated in **bold**, also when they are integrated in the verbal complex.
5. It should be said that some are not used in all varieties of French: *akuz ki/à cause que, dabor/d'abord* as well as *enku/un coup* (also with the meaning 'in case') are used in Laurentian (Canadian) French, but not in European French. Also, the forms *par* and *pur li tan/pour le temps* 'as long as' do not exist as clause-connecting particles in any French variety that we know of.

REFERENCES

Ahenekew, Alice. 2000. *Âh-âyîtaw isi ê-kî-kiskêhihtahkik maskihkiy / They Knew Both Sides of Medicine: Cree Tales of Curing and Cursing Told by Alice Ahenekew,* ed. and trans. by H. C. Wolfart and Freda Ahenekew. Winnipeg: University of Manitoba Press.

Bakker, Peter. 1997. *"A Language of Our Own": The Genesis of Michif—the Mixed Cree-French Language of the Canadian Métis.* New York: Oxford University Press.

Bakker, Peter. 2004. The Verb in Michif. *La Lawng: Michif Peekishkwewin. The Heritage Language of the Canadian Metis,* vol 2: *Language Theory,* ed. by Lawrence Barkwell, pp. 63–80. Winnipeg: Pemmican Publications / Manitoba Metis Federation Michif Language Program.

Bakker, Peter. 2005. Direct and Indirect Speech in Cree and Michif. Paper read at Research Centre for Linguistic Typology, La Trobe University.

Bakker, Peter. 2006. Algonquian Verb Structure: Plains Cree. *What's in a Verb?* LOT Occasional Series 5, ed. by Grazyna Rowicka and Eithne Carlin, pp. 3–27. Utrecht: LOT.

Blain, Eleanor M. 1997. Wh-constructions in Nêhiyawêwin. Ph.D. thesis, University of British

Columbia, Vancouver.

Bloomfield, Leonard. 1930. *Sacred Stories of the Sweetgrass* Cree. Ottawa: F.A. Acland.

Bloomfield, Leonard. 1934. *Plains Cree Texts.* New York: G. E. Stechert.

Bloomfield, Leonard. n.d. [1984]. *Cree-English Lexicon.* New Haven, CT: Human Relations Area Files.

Cook, Clare. 2014. *The Clause-Typing System of Plains Cree: Indexicality, Anaphoricity, and Contrast.* New York: Oxford University Press.

Ellis, C. Douglas. 2004. *Spoken Cree, Level II.* Edmonton: University of Alberta Press.

Gillon, Carrie, and Nicole Rosen. 2018. *Nominal Contact in Michif.* New York: Oxford University Press.

Laverdure, Patline, and Ida Rose Allard.1983. *The Michif Dictionary: Turtle Mountain Chippewa Cree,* ed. by John C. Crawford. Winnipeg: Pemmican Publications.

Long, Michelle Anne. 1999. Adverbial and Argument-Doubling Clauses in Cree. MA thesis, Department of Linguistics, University of Manitoba.

Matras, Yaron. 2008. *Language Contact.* Cambridge: Cambridge University Press.

Papen, Robert A. 1987. Le Métif: Le Nec Plus Ultra des Grammmaires en Contact. *Revue Québecoise de Linguistique Théorique et Appliquée* 6(2):57–70.

Papen, Robert A. 2004–5. On Developing a Writing System for Michif. *Linguistica Atlantica* 26:75–97.

Papen, Robert A. 2005. Le Michif: Langue Franco-Crie des Plaines. *Le Français en Amérique du Nord: État Présent,* ed. by Albert Valdman, Julie Auger, and Deborah Piston-Hatlen, pp. 327–347. Saint-Nicolas, QC: Presses de l'Université Laval.

Rhodes, Richard. 1977. French Cree—a Case of Borrowing. *Actes du Huitième Congrès des Algonquinistes,* ed. by W. Cowan, pp. 6–25. Ottawa: Carleton University.

Rosen, Nicole. 2007. Domains in Michif Phonology. PhD thesis, University of Toronto. http://twpl.library.utoronto.ca/index.php/twpl/article/view/6495.

Wolfart, H. Christoph. 1973. *Plains Cree: A Grammatical Study.* Transactions of the American Philosophical Society, n.s., vol. 63, pt. 5. Philadelphia: American Philosophical Society.

Wolfart, H. Christof. 1996. Sketch of Cree, an Algonquian Language. *Handbook of North American Indians,* vol. 17: *Languages,* ed. by I. Goddard, pp. 390–439. Washington, DC: Smithsonian Institution.

Wolvengrey, Arok Elessar. 2011. *Semantic and Pragmatic Functions in Plains Cree Syntax.* Utrecht: LOT.

Referring to a Deceased Person in Plains Cree

Vincent Collette

The aim of this article is to describe and analyze distinct sets of social deictics used when referring to the dead in Plains Cree, an Algonquian language spoken in Saskatchewan and Alberta.[1] As mentioned by Stivers, Enfield, and Levinson (2007:1), person reference stands at an interdisciplinary crossroad between anthropology, psychology, cognitive neuroscience, and social theories. They remark that, paradoxically, even though person reference is a central topic in the humanities, it is also one that has been quite neglected so far. According to Brown (2007:173), "referring to persons, unlike referring to inanimate objects and animals, is a socially delicate operation, since persons are circumscribed by social identities, hierarchical status, and taboos in ways that are highly variable across cultures." Thus, if we assume that referring to a living person can require tact in certain contexts, this will prove even more acute when referring to a deceased person. We also expect that referring to a deceased person will vary considerably cross-culturally and even within a single culture (Frazer 1922: section 3; Granger 1961:34–35). For instance, Malay speakers drop the name of a deceased person and use instead the title *marhum,* an Arabic word meaning 'that has found mercy' (Needham 1954). In French, the adjective *feu, feue* (from Vulgar Latin *fatutus* 'who has such a destiny') is normally used in the case of a person who has recently passed away (*feu mon père disait* 'my late father said'), while *défunt, défunte* is reserved for somebody who passed away long ago (*mon défunt père disait toujours que . . .* 'my late father always said that . . . '), although these adjectives are now mainly used in highly formal contexts or for fun. Other nominal attributive expressions like *paix à son âme* (lit. 'peace to his/her soul') are even more reverential and deferential (*mon père, paix à son âme, disait toujours que . . .* 'my father, peace to his soul, always said that . . . ') than expressions like *le/la regreté(e)* 'the regretted', which are more affective in nature.

In this paper, I examine alternative ways of referring to the deceased in Plains Cree in order to find the semantic and pragmatic principles that guide the choices of strategies. More precisely I try to answer the following questions: (1) What is the conventional way(s) to refer to a deceased person in Plains Cree? (2) Are there some nearly synonymous options and what motivates the choice between these options? (3) Do speakers of Plains Cree make use of unmarked terms to indicate close intimacy with the person referred to? (4) Are there name avoidance rules? I use data taken from my fieldwork, as well as from Plains Cree literature. Many of the insights provided here stem from discussions with speakers of Plains Cree. The starting point of my data collection and analysis was to search for contrastive pairs, which I define as the use by a speaker in the span of a sentence, paragraph, or story of different strategies to refer to a deceased person. I believe that the unearthing of such contrastive pairs can contribute to a deeper understanding of person reference within a given culture.

Preferences in Person Reference and "Synonymous" Alternatives

One of the most pervasive dimensions surrounding studies of onomastics and person reference revolves around the following questions: Why do speakers choose between alternative means when establishing person reference? How do they do it? How does their choice reflect cultural values? In order to shed some light on these questions, two types of preferences have been suggested by Stivers, Enfield, and Levinson (2007:12–13):

- Preference for achieving recognition via an unmarked term: speakers should use the most efficient way (i.e. the unmarked form, either a name or a kinship term) of establishing recognition of a person with his/her recipient.

- PREFERENCE FOR MINIMIZATION: speaker should use one rather than multiple expressions (name, title, kinship) when referring to a real person.

Although these two types of preference seem natural at first sight, they are nevertheless too simplistic to cover the full range of complexity in human affairs, and languages differ as to what is considered important or not. While it might be assumed that the use of a single expression (a proper name such as *Bob* or *Mary*) would be universal—since after all, the task of the speaker is to provide enough information about *Bob* or *Mary* in order to maintain communication with his/her addressee—this is often not the case in many cultures. In Plains Cree, for example, one can use names to introduce, and then kinship terms to refer to, a deceased person in the rest of a narrative. In Tzeltal (Brown 2007), one may use up to three different referring strategies in a single discourse or story. The data presented here comply with Brown's view that preference for minimization is universal but that there are other cultural parameters (e.g., levels of formality, circumspection, deference, time elapsed since the passing away, level of acquaintance and intimacy) that are equally important, if not more important, in making reference to a deceased person. Because person reference is something that is concomitant with specific cultural values and implicit rules, such as taboos and avoidance of direct reference, two additional preferences have been proposed by Levinson (2007) and Garde (2008:204–205):

- PREFERENCE FOR CIRCUMSPECTION: speakers should use any local constraints surrounding person reference (e.g., cultural taboos, prohibition of unmarked referring expressions, etc.).
- PREFERENCE FOR ASSOCIATION: speakers will associate a referent with a conversation participant (e.g., *I spoke to your uncle today*).

In what follows, I show that speakers of Plains Cree follow the preferences for recognition and minimization (i.e., use of a proper name or a bare kinship noun) and especially so when introducing relatives for the first time in a story, while in other contexts, they avoid proper names despite the fact that names refer more directly than titles and kinship terms. In Plains Cree, direct reference to a deceased person is often avoided by cultural circumspection, and indirect association strategies are used instead when living relatives are present. Plains Cree constructions used to refer to deceased people are referentially synonymous (Leech 1974; Murphy 2003), in the sense that one expression could be substituted by another without losing the truth value of the sentence. However, I assume that superficial synonyms, even though they do not violate the truth conditions of a sentence, have different pragmatic extensions attached to them (e.g., deference, reverence, circumspection), and thus serve different rhetorical purposes. The types of preferences seen above and the interplay between them, as well as culturally embedded nuances of meaning, will help us understand the motives underlying Plains Cree speakers' use of one expression over another in referring to deceased people.

Linguistic Strategies of Referencing the Dead

There are three basic ways to refer to a deceased person in Plains Cree: (*a*) use of personal names (*Bob*) or a single kinship noun (*nimosôm* 'my grandfather'); (*b*) a relative clause built on a kinship noun (i.e. 'periphrastic constructions' as labeled by Wolfart and Ahenakew 1998:204) such as *ana kâ-kî-omosômiyân* 'my late grandfather'; (*c*) a dependent or independent noun onto which is added the absentative -(*i*)*pan* 'late' (e.g., *nimosômipan* 'my late grandfather'). Other morphosyntactic devices such as attributive plurality are also used to speak about the dead when a relative is present. In this section, I analyze the distribution and use of these four strategies by Plains Cree storytellers. The objective is to circumscribe in which contexts and about whom these strategies are generally employed.

Personal Names and Single Kinship Nouns

Personal names (either Christian or traditional) and single kinship nouns like *nôhkom* 'my grandmother' are used, often together, to refer to a deceased person in Plains Cree. In written literature personal names usually occur at the beginning of a narrative to introduce a person (kin or not) who may not be known to the reader. If personal names have no referential ambiguity, they normally appear at the beginning of a story, but they are often accompanied by a kinship or deferential term in the rest of the story. For instance, in (1–2) Alice Ahenakew introduces her adopted grandfather (Thomas Charles) and her father-in-law (Louis Ahenakew) with their Christian names and the appropriate kinship terms. Note that in many cases personal names of deceased people often occur with the verb *kî-isiyîhkâsow* 's/he was called' as in (1–3). The preverb *kî-* 'perfective' signals the fact that the person is no longer alive.[2]

(1) **'Thomas Charles'** kî-isiyîhkâso-w an[a] â- ~, **ana** **kisêyiniw,**
Thomas Charles perf.be.named.ai-3 dem.sg old.man.na
kâ-kî-ohpih-icik w-îw-a asici (. . .)
cj-perf-raise.ta-3pl/1 3-spouse.nad-3' along
'Thomas Charles was the name of that old man who raised me along with his wife.' (Ahenakew 2000:40)

(2) êkos êkwa (. . .) **'Louis Ahenakew'** kî-isiyîhkâso-w ana
then so 'Louis Ahenakew' perf-be.named.ai-3 dem.sg
kâ-kî-osisi-yân, êkwa w-îw-a anihi, aya . . .
cj.rel-perf- father.in.law.nad-1 so 3-spouse.nad-3' dem.3' euh . . .
Catherine . . . wâsceyâp
'Then my late father-in-law, his name was Louis Ahenakew, and his wife . . . ' Catherine *wâsceyâp*' (Ahenakew 2000:40)

Personal names can also be used with living people, but again they appear exclusively in the initial sentences of a text sometimes with the corresponding kinship term. For example, in (3) Alice Ahenakew introduces her sister-in-law by her full name and title ('Mrs.'), while using the appropriate kinship noun *nicâhkos* 'my sister-in-law' in the rest of the story.

(3) êkwa awa **ni-câhkos** kêyapic ê-pimâtisi-t,
and dem.sg 1-sister.in.law.nad still cj-live.ai-3sg
'Mrs. Minnie Fraser' kî-isiyîhkâso-w (. . .)
Mrs. Minnie Fraser perf-be.named.ai-3sg
'And my sister-in-law was still alive, her name was Mrs. Minnie Fraser (. . .)' (Ahenakew 2000:70)

Although Mandelbaum (1979:142) mentions that traditional names may not be used after somebody has passed away (except for prominent chiefs or war leaders), or even with living people, Darren Okemaysim (personal communication 2017) indicates that nowadays it is a matter of time: some speakers use personal names again when the grieving period is over, that is, after roughly four years, or even one year. The use or not of personal names is a matter of style, spiritual allegiance, or whether the person discussed was a public figure or not. For instance, Cecilia Masuskapoe (2010) makes heavy use of personal names (plus *kî-isiyîhkâsow* 's/he was named') or single kinship terms, while Alice Ahenakew (Ahenakew 2000) uses personal names to introduce someone, then turns to marked strategies, although she uses single kinship terms with her female relatives and grandparents in many circumstances.

Lastly, in order to avoid mentioning directly the name of the recently deceased, some speakers modify the personal name with a speech verb in the conjunct order which is preceded by the preverbs *kâ-kî-* 'CONJUNCT PERFECTIVE', as in *Aileen kâ-kî-itiht* 'She was called Aileen'. This strategy is mostly used with nonkin and is culturally and cosmologically appropriate since by using *kâ-kî-itiht* the speaker does not invoke directly the name of the deceased person but relegates the responsibility to others who "called her Aileen."

Form and Distribution of the Relative Clause Kinship Terms in kâ-kî

In Plains Cree one can also refer to a deceased person with a periphrastic construction. Wolfart and Ahenakew (1998:204) identify this as the conventional way of referring to a deceased person with circumspection and deference in Plains Cree culture. For example, with the dependent noun stem *-ôhkom-* 'grandmother' one can derive an animate intransitive verb of being *ôhkomiwi-* 'to be a grandmother' and also a verb of possession by adding the animate intransitive verb final *-i* and a root extension (*oy-*) as in *oyôhkomi-* 'to have X as a grandmother'. In Plains Cree, a periphrastic construction like *ana kâ-kî-oyôhkomiyân* 'my late grandmother' contains a conjunct verb which bears the inflection *-yân* 'first sg. (possessor)', and the preverbs *kâ-* 'conjunct subordination' and *kî-* 'perfective aspect, state of completion', which indicate that a person is no longer alive at the time of speech.[3] The conjunct verb that acts as a relative clause is often headed by a demonstrative like *awa* 'this one' as in (4) or no demonstrative at all (5). Relative clauses headed by a demonstrative behave syntactically like nouns and are often translated as such in English.

(4)

(. . .)	'tânis	ôma	k-êsi-nipâ-yâhk	êkwa?'	ê-it-ak	**awa**
	how	then	CJ-IC.thus-sleep.AI-13	now	CJ-say.to.TA-1/3	DEM.SG

kâ-wîkim-ak.
CJ.REL-live.with.TA-1/3
'"How will we sleep now," I said to my husband.' (Ahenakew and Wolfart 1998:214)

(5)

ni-kî-it-ik	**kâ-kî-oyohtâwî-yân**
1-PERF-say.TA-3/1	CJ.REL-PERF-father.NAD-1

'My late father had said to me.' (Ahenakew and Wolfart 1998:204)

In (4) we see that 'my husband' is expressed by a relative clause *awa* 'demonstrative singular' *kâ-wîkimak* ('I live with him/her') which can be translated as 'this one whom I live with'. Thus, the third person referent is the goal of the nominalized verb but that third person is an unmarked goal within the verbal relative clause.

Relative kinship clauses also occur alongside personal names:

(6)

kâ-kî-omisi-yân	ê-kî-miy-it	**âniy**,	mihcet
CJ-PERF-older.sister.NAD-1SG	CJ-PERF-give.TA-3/1	Annie	a lot

ê-kî-miy-it (. . .)	êwakw	ân[a]—	wîsta	mâna
CJ-PERF-give.TA-3/1	FOCUS	DEM.SG	over	habitually

kâ-kî-oyôhkom-iyân,	**'osâwisip'**	kî-it-âw (. . .)
CJ-PERF-grandmother.NAD-1SG	osâwisip	PERF-be.called.AI-IMPERS.3SG

'My late older sister, *âniy*, gave them to me, she gave me a lot (. . .) That's the one—my late grandmother, her name was osâwisip (. . .).' (Wolfart and Ahenakew 1998:335)

In her personal reminiscences (2010), Cecilia Masuskapoe makes a heavy use of single kinship nouns and personal names for all her close relatives (mother, father, sons, uncle, and grandparents) and allies (sister-in-law and mother-in-law), but uses relative kinship clauses to introduce her late father-in-law and her husband, as seen in (7):

(7) niyanân oti, awa **kâ-kî-wîkim-ak** Tommy,
we in.fact DEM.SG CJ.REL-PERF-to.live.with.TA-1/3 Tommy
ê-kî-kaskihtamâso-yâhk (. . .)
CJ.PERF.earn.it.for.onself.AI-13
'As for us, we earned it for ourselves with my late husband Tommy (. . .).'
(Masuskapoe 2010:10)

She refers to her late husband with his personal name ('Tommy') or *niwîkimâkan* 'my spouse' throughout. She does not use the absentative -*(i)pan* on kinship terms. Some personal names followed by a verb of speaking occur such as *Frank Hillard kî-isiyîhkâsow, môy pimâtisiw ana nîtim* 'Frank Hillard he was named, my (female possessor) cross-cousin passed away' (Masuskapoe 2010:43).

One of the most culturally salient details about reference to a deceased person in Plains Cree occurs when reference is made to a person in an indirect manner, through their kinship relationship with living people (Wolfart 1999:169–170). Here, the preference for association takes precedence over the preference for unmarked terms (recall the person reference preferences described above) and this is observed when the living relatives in question are present, as in (8), which is taken from a speech where respected elders were mentioned in the presence of some of their relatives.

(8) mihchêt ki-kî-kiskêyim-â-wâw, Allan Ahenakew mîna kahkiyaw
a lot 2-PERF-know.TA-DIR-2PL Allan Ahenakew more more
w-îtisân-a, êkota ohci wiyawâw êkotê
3-sibling.NAD-OBV right.there from 3PL over.there
ê-ohcî-cik aniki wiyawâw.
CJ-be.from.AI-3PL DEM.PL 3PL
'Many of you used to know him, the father of Allan Ahenakew and his siblings, he was their father.' (Wolfart 1990:377)

(9)

Louis,	êkwa,	â (. . .)	'pacîs'	pêyak	kî-isiyîhkâso-w,	êkwa	kotak
Louis	and	euh	Baptiste	one	PERF-be.named.AI-3SG	and	other

(tânisi	kotak	kâ-kî-isiyîhkâso-t,	Adam	ôki
what	other	CJ-PERF-be.named.AI-3SG	Adam	DEM.PL

kâ-kî-opâpâ-cik) (. . .)
CJ-PERF-father.NAD-AI.3PL

'Louis, then, well (. . .) the name of one of them was Baptiste, and the other (what was the other one's name, the late dad of Adam and his siblings).' (Ahenakew 2000:40)

In (9) Alice Ahenakew identifies two of the Ahenakew brothers by name, but refers to the third one indirectly through his children: *Adam ôki kâ-kî-opâpâ-cik* means 'the one Adam and his siblings (*ôki*) used to have as a dad' (Wolfart 2000:170). This type of oblique reference is deeply embedded with the culturally recognized practice of circumspection and deference towards deceased persons in Plains Cree culture.

The Pragmatics of -(i)pan

The nominal suffix -(*i*)*pan,* found throughout the Cree-Innu-Naskapi-Atikamekw dialect continuum, is known as 'preterit' or 'past tense' in the Algonquianist tradition. James (1991) says that the Cree and Ojibwa reflexes of Proto-Algonquian *-(*e*)*pan* indicate some sort of reference to the past, but they also indicate imperfective aspect, which she defines as the means of making reference to "the internal portion of a situation only, with no reference being made to its beginning or end" (1991:283). Unlike Moose Cree, where *-pan* is still used on verbs and nouns, in Plains Cree -(*i*)*pan* can only be added to nouns and to *awîn-* which is the root for *awîna* 'who (SG)', *awîniki* 'who (PL)'. It does not indicate imperfective aspect, but rather mirativity or irrealis, as in ***awînipan*** *oma!* 'Where is he?' (implying that the subject is supposed to be here now) (Darren Okemaysim, personal communication 2016). Note, for example, that the verb is marked with *ta-* 'future' but co-occurs with the so-called nominal "preterite" -(*i*)*pan* in (10).

(10) ohci ta-pê-kîwê-cik ni-sîmis-Ø **awîn-ipan**
source FUT-TOWARDS-come.home.AI-3PL 1-grandson.NAD-SG who-ABS
ta-takohtê-cik (. . .)
FUT-arrive.by.foot.AI-3PL
'My grandson [and his associates] will come home. When will my grandson [and his associates] ever arrive? (. . .)' (Masuskapoe 2010:121)

More commonly the absentative -(*i*)*pan* is attached to referentially animate nominal lexemes, mostly dependent kinship terms as in (11), but it also appears on a handful of independent nouns like *nôtokwêsiw* 'old woman' and *kisêyinîw* 'old man', as seen in (12–13):[4]

(11) n-ôhkom-**ipan**-ak
1-grandmother.NAD-ABS-PL
'My late grandmothers'

(12) — kisêyinî-**pan** mân nêtê wîsta kî-wîcihiwê-w
old.man.NA-ABS too over.there beyond PERF-participate.AI-3SG
ayisk nêma nête.
because isn't.it over.there
— âha, kâ-kî-opâpâ-yan.
yes CJ-PERF-father.NAD-AI-2SG
— kâ-kî-opâpâ-yân pâsîl, êkon-ik.
CJ-PERF-father.NAD-AI-1SG Basile FOCUS-PL
'— The old man, too, was always over there because (he played at Françoise's place).
— Yes, your late dad.
— My late dad, pâsîl, and those others.' (Ahenakew and Wolfart 1998:290)

(13) kisêyinî-**pan**-ak kayâs, kisêyinî-**pan**-ak êkon-ik
old.man.NA-ABS-PL long.ago old.man.NA-ABS-PL FOCUS-PL
kâ-kî-atâwâkê-cik anim âskiy (. . .)
CJ-PERF-sell.AI-3PL DEM.SG land.NI
'Old men long deceased, it was the old men long deceased who sold the land (. . .).' (Ahenakew and Wolfart 1998:292)

As can be seen in the examples, the nominal suffix -*(i)pan* does not indicate imperfective aspect or past tense per se, but conveys the idea that the denotatum is temporarily absent or that it no longer exists (Wolfart 1973:31). In other words, -*(i)pan* means 'spatio-temporal remoteness from Ego' and this is why it is more properly glossed as absentative (ABS), a term that encompasses both the 'late' and irrealis meanings seen above. Since it has restricted productivity and often an unpredictable meaning, some Algonquianists consider it derivational (see Oxford 2010:36 n. 5). This is supported by the fact that -*(i)pan* does not turn a noun into a past tense predicative noun, nor does it trigger past tense/perfective aspect agreement on the verb. The concatenation of the absentative -*(i)pan* can modify, rather unpredictably, the meaning of certain nouns, and change their nominal class. These are properties not usually associated with prototypical grammatical categories. For example, *-ôhtâwiy-* 'father' is known as a "dependent" stem in Algonquian linguistics (along with body parts and some intimate possessions). This means that it cannot be used without a possessor prefix, as in *nôhtâwiy* 'my father', *kôhtâwiy* 'your father', *ôhtâwiya* 'his/her father(s)', or *niskât* 'my leg', *kiskât* 'your leg', *oskât* 'his/her leg'. If the speaker wants to convey the idea of a relative or a body part without referring to the possessor, then an unspecified nominal suffix *-imâw* is used for kinship nouns, as in *ôhtâwîmâw* 'a father', and an unspecified possessor prefix *mi-* for body parts as in *miskât* 'a leg'. However, in some Algonquian languages like Plains Cree and Northern Algonquin the dependent stem *-mosôm-* 'grandfather' also has an independent counterpart *mosômipanak* which contains the absentative -*(i)pan*.[5] No possessive affixes can be used with this independent stem and it cannot be used alone as in **mosômak* 'grandfathers'. Moreover, the meaning of *mosômipanak* differs from that of its dependent counterpart, since it does not necessarily refer to one's grandfathers but to the Grandfathers' Spirit, or to one's male/female ancestors. As indicated by Westman (2008:209), *mosômipanak* is "a term of respect for spiritually powerful persons that does not necessarily imply kinship or even humanity." This interpretation is motivated by the fact that *mosômipanak* seems to be a phonologically contracted form of *nimosômipanak* 'my grandfathers'. Other related ceremonial terms where -*(i)pan* is linked to immaterial entities include *nôtokwêw âtayôhkanipan* 'Old Woman's Spirit', a noun phrase used in the four directions prayer.

Because of its rare occurrence on nouns (independent and dependent), the absentative -*(i)pan* is considered archaic by some younger speakers who see it as pertaining to a higher style of Cree which is mostly heard in traditional ceremonies, as is *mosômipanak*. However, it is still used by older speakers, as seen in Plains Cree literature.[6] In my survey of two Plains Cree books (Ahenakew and Wolfart 1998; Ahenakew 2000) I have found only 26 instances of morphologically marked references to deceased persons. Of these, nine used the absentative -(*i*)*pan,* and 17 used relative kinship clauses with *kâ-kî-*.

Although the relative kinship clauses and the nouns in -(*i*)*pan* refer to the same entity, their pragmatic extensions are distinct. The analysis of contrastive pairs (i.e., when two linguistic strategies are used to refer to one or two persons in a sentence or a whole narrative but with differing pragmatic and rhetorical effects) shows that speakers who still use -(*i*)*pan* usually do so in contexts where deference, reverence, or even circumspection are needed, as when talking about somebody who is recognized as spiritually powerful, or when reporting or quoting what a respected person has said or done. Some storytellers, like Alice Ahenakew, follow these rhetorical guidelines quite thoroughly, while others do not. It is important to note that the use of the marked and the unmarked strategies sometimes differs from speaker to speaker and especially between younger and older speakers and even between older speakers altogether.[7]

In (14), Alice Ahenakew introduces her grandparents and her mother, who died when Alice was around six years of age, with single kinship nouns. She introduces them first with nouns in -(*i*)*pan,* then specifies the identity of her late grandfather with both his English and traditional Cree names. Alice also refers to her grandparents with personal names for initial reference, but in the rest of this particular story she switches to single kinship nouns, a strategy that seems to reflect the speaker's intimacy and respect for her grandparents.

(14) kî-âpihtawikosisân-iskwê-wi-w **ni-kâwiy,** mâka **n-ôhkom-ipan**
PERF-half-woman-AI-3SG 1-mother.NAD COOR 1-grandmother.NAD-ABS
wiya kî-nî-, nîhiyaw mitoni, apâskwêyâ-hk ohci
3SG . . . Cree.NA real apâskweyâw-LOC SOURCE
n-ôhkom-ipan; êkwa **ni-mosôm-ipan,**
1-grandmother.NAD-ABS and 1-grandfather.NAD-ABS
wêmistikôsiw-âpihtawikosisân. niyânan it-itwêwin-a
French-half five thus-language.NI-PL
isi-pîkiskwewin-a ê-kî-kaskihtâ-t **ni-mosôm-ipan,**
thus-language.NI-PL CJ-PERF-use.TI2–3SG 1-grandfather.NAD-ABS
ê-kî-âh-itwêstamâkê-t mâna; o-nîhiyawi-wîhowin
CJ-PERF-REDUP-translate.AI-3SG usually 3-Cree-name.NI
'cimikwayâs' kî-isiyîhkâso-w, êkwa o-kayâsîwi-wîhowin,
Cimikwayâs PERF-be.named.AI-3SG and 3-English-name.NI
'Alexân Landry' kî-it-âw
Alexandre Landry PERF-be.called.AI-INDEF.3SG
'My mother was a half-breed woman, but my late grandmother had been a real Cree, my late grandmother was from *apâskwêyâhk;* and my late grandfather was a French half-breed. He spoke five languages, and he used to be interpreter for these languages; his Cree name was *cimikwayâs,* and as for an English name he was called Alexandre Landry.' (Ahenakew 2000:32)

In (3) above we saw that Alice Ahenakew introduces Thomas Charles (and his wife) with their personal names. Later in the same narrative she refers to them, affectionately, as "grandparents" and uses the single kinship nouns *nôhkom* 'my grandmother' and *nimosôm* 'my grandfather', which convey a certain degree of intimacy. However, since the old couple were also powerful traditional healers, she later switches to -(*i*)*pan* when her adopted grandfather is the subject of verbs describing traditional activities (e.g., smudging, weeping, and praying):

(15) awa **ni-mosôm-ipan** kâ-kî-ohpikih-icik,
DEM.SG 1-grandfather.NAD-ABS CJ.PERF-raise.TA-3PL/1
iyikohk ê-kî-miyw-âyisiyinîwi-t, wîpac mân
to.such.a.degree CJ-PERF-good-person.AI-3SG early then
ê-kî-waniskâ-t ê-pônah-k, êkwa êkota
CJ-PERF-wake.up.AI-3SG CJ-light.fire.AI-3SG then there
ê-miyâhkasah-k wîhkaskw-a, sweetgrass, ê-ayamihâ-t
CJ-smudge.it.TI-3SG sweetgrass.NI-OBV sweetgrass CJ-pray.AI-3SG
ê-mawimoscikê-t wêpac kâ-kîkisêpâyâ-k (. . .) piyis mân
CJ-worship.AI-3SG early CJ.REL-morning.II-0SG at.last usually
ê-kî-ati-mâto-t awa **ni-mosôm-ipan**.
CJ.PERF-start-cry.AI-3SG DEM.SG 1-grandfather.NAD-ABS
'My late grandfather who with his wife had raised me, he was such a good person, he would make a smudge of sweetgrass and would pray and worship early in the morning (. . .) at last my late grandfather would go on to weep.' (Ahenakew 2000:78)

Alice Ahenakew provides other contrastive pairs when referring to her father-in-law, Louis Ahenakew, a highly respected and influential man. The relative kinship clause in *kâ-kî-* is used at the beginning of the narrative to introduce him (16), while the kinship noun in -(*i*)*pan* occurs later in the narrative to introduce an ancient story, which was passed on to her by this traditional healer (17).

(16) êkos êkwa (. . .) 'Louis Ahenakew' **kî-isiyîhkâso-w** ana
then and Louis Ahenakew PERF-be.named.AI-3SG DEM.SG
kâ-kî-osis-i-yân, êkwa w-îw-a anihi,
CJ.REL-PERF-f.in.law.NAD-AI-1 then 3-spouse.NAD-3′ DEM.SG
aya . . . Catherine wâsceyâp
uh . . . Catherine wâsceyâp
'Then my late father-in-law, his name was Louis Ahenakew, and his wife . . . Catherine . . . Wasceyâp' (Ahenakew 2000:40)

(17) mîn êwako tâpwê (. . .) êkî-ispayi-k;
another FOCUS true CJ.PERF-happen.II-0SG
ni-sis-ipan ôm êwak ôm ê-kî-âtotah-k.
1-father.in.law.NAD-ABS DEM.SG FOCUS DEM.SG CJ.PERF-tell.about.it.TI-3SG
'and it also truly happened; my late father-in-law had told this story.' (Ahenakew 2000:108)

The contrastive pair in (16) and (17) indicates that while both the relative kinship clause in *kâ-kî-* and the noun in *-(i)pan* refer to the same person, the latter has an extra pragmatic extension related to the need for deference and circumspection toward important and/or powerful people, especially so when they are the source of the speaker's knowledge. The use of *-(i)pan* is also definitely more reverential and formal in nature than the other strategies seen so far. This is consistent with the fact that in many languages, morphologically marked expressions used to refer to deceased people are often reserved for respected people and this is why "the late Adolf Hitler" sounds awkward but not "the late Leonard Cohen." Alice Ahenakew uses the absentative *-(i)pan* again when referring to an old woman who managed to protect herself from a wendigo by sleeping in the snow:

(18) âna **nôcikwê-s-îpan** ana, kêhtê-aya
DEM.SG old.woman.NA-DIM-ABS DEM.SG oldest-being.NA
ana, kôn-a ômis (gesture) ê-isi-wêpahw-ât (. . .)
DEM.SG snow.NA-OBV in.this.way (gesture) CJ-thus-brushed.TA-3/3′
'(. . .) that old woman who is now dead, the older of the two simply brushed the snow aside like this.' (Ahenakew 2000:106)

The hypothesis that the absentative suffix *-(i)pan* has distinct pragmatic extensions associated with circumspection, deference, and reverence is again clearly illustrated in (19). This excerpt is taken from a collection of narratives by Cecilia Masuskapoe (2010), who tells the secondhand story of an old woman who was said to have had sexual intercourse with her grandson whom she raised. Masuskapoe introduces the story *ê-wî-wiyahkwêw-âcimoyân* 'I will tell a cursing/dirty story', then talks about the old woman in question with coarse vocabulary and contempt (e.g., 'big sow'). While at the beginning of the story she simply refers to the old lady as *awa nôcok(w)êsiw* 'the old lady', in the final sentence (19) she uses the absentative which occurs only twice (see (10) above) in the book:

(19)

mâka	mîn	Alice	ê-pêhtaw-it,	'tâpwê	êsa	mitoni
but	also	Alice	CJ-hear.TA-3/1	truly	REPORT	really

misi-kôhkôsi-nôtokwêw-Ø!'	wahwâ,	miton	êtikwê
big-pig-old.lady.NA-SG	oh my!	really	DUB

ê-kî-môhcowi-c	ana	**nôcokê-sî-pan**,	cî?
CJ-PERF-be.crazy.AI-3	DEM.SG	old.woman.NA-DIM-ABS	TAG.QST

'And then Alice heard me [saying] "She was truly a really big sow!" Oh my! She must have been really crazy, that late little old lady, wasn't she?' (Masuskapoe 2010:102)

I hypothesize that the unexpected occurrence of the absentative in this particular context marks the speaker's circumspection, as a way to protect herself, or at least to reestablish a cosmological balance at the end of a story which combines coarse vocabulary and overt derision for a deceased person, a blatant violation of Plains Cree social norms of respect. To that effect Garde (2008:229) writes that "words [or in this case suffixes] have extralinguistic significance in the sense that they beget creative, protective, preventative, destructive or regenerative cosmological effects." According to Lockwood (2015:4) the use of *-pan* in Potawatomi is "a way to use a person's name or title without summoning their spirit." The parallel of this strategy in Plains Cree is the use a personal name with a speech verb (X was called, X was his/her name).

Conclusion

In this paper I have described different ways to refer to a deceased person in Plains Cree. I have shown that the use of a personal name establishes reference at the beginning of a story, but only if the protagonists are not known to the addressees or readers. In most of the cases reported here personal names occur with *kî-isiyîhkâsow* 's/he was named' or *kâ-kî-itiht* 'the one who was called'. Single kinship nouns are used mainly with relatives with whom the speaker shared a certain level of intimacy: more frequently with female relatives, grandparents, and in-laws than with immediate family members (mother, father, son, or daughter). The relative kinship clause in *kâ-kî-* is the conventional way of referring to deceased people with deference in Plains Cree. In some written texts its occurrence is high compared to other strategies like the nominal absentative *-(i)pan,* which is quite rare orally as well as in published texts.

According to Seiler (1980), the choice between verbs and nouns in person reference is based on semantic and biocultural motivations. He notes that in Cahuilla, kinship verbs are used to refer to a deceased relative, while kinship nouns are reserved for living relatives. This observation finds a parallel in Plains Cree since some storytellers (like Cecilia Masuskapoe) use relative kinship clauses almost exclusively for in-laws. This use of different strategies is consistent with the observation made by Seiler that kinship relations expressed through verbal means are often seen as processes that have to be maintained, unlike blood ties, which cannot be terminated.

In this paper, I have made the assumption that two different but superficially synonymous expressions (e.g., *nimosômipan* 'my late grandfather' versus *ana kâ-kî-omosômiyân* 'the one who I had as a father') may refer to the same person but that they could not have exactly the same meaning and pragmatic extensions. I have analyzed contrastive pairs (nominal and verbal strategies) to show that when they occur in the same sentence, paragraph, or story, the absentative nouns in -(*i*)*pan* index the speaker's overt expression of deference, reverence, affection, or even circumspection toward the person spoken about; while kinship clauses in *kâ-kî-* or even unmarked strategies like single nouns were more neutral pragmatically. The study reveals that absentative nouns occur frequently with verbs related to the spiritual domain (e.g., 'weep, smudge, pray'), with verbs identifying the source of knowledge of Ego (e.g., 'my late grandfather told me'), and with verbs describing the actions of a powerful person (as in the case of cursing and curing). I suspect that the distribution of absentative nouns with such verbs is influenced by the fact that -(*i*)*pan* also occurs with a handful of independent nouns which are highly reverential in nature and used in ceremonial contexts. These nouns refer to figures remote from Ego: *kisêyinîpanak* 'male ancestors', *mosômipanak* 'Grandfather spirits', and *nôtokwêw âtayôhkanipan* 'old woman's spirit'. Thus, Plains Cree speakers seem more concerned with the preferences for circumspection and association then with the preferences for maximization and unmarked terms when referring to a deceased person, although this is not true of all storytellers. The nominal absentative constitutes a marked way to negotiate the delicate balance between the preference for maximization (be as clear as possible) and the preference for circumspection (use indirect ways when speaking about deceased people), and this is especially true in referencing a person in a spiritual or ceremonial context.

In conclusion, it appears that the use of marked or unmarked strategies also depends on the speaker's spiritual allegiance, since some storytellers who are well versed in Christian ideology (as shown throughout Ahenakew and Wolfart 1998) are also the ones who make heavy use of morphologically unmarked strategies (personal names, single kinship terms) to refer to deceased people.

NOTES

1. I want to thank Darren Okemaysim and Jean Okimasis, as well as Arok Wolvengrey and Lynn Cote, for sharing with me their knowledge of Plains Cree and Saulteaux languages and cultures.
2. The abbreviations used are as follows: ABS = absentative, AI = animate intransitive verb, CJ = conjunct order, COOR = coordinator, DEM = demonstrative, DIM = diminutive, DIR = direct marker, DUB = dubitative, IC = initial change, IMPERS = impersonal, INDEF = indefinite subject, II = inanimate intransitive, LOC = locative, NA = animate noun, NAD = dependent animate noun, NI = inanimate noun, OBV = obviative, PERF = perfective aspect, PL = plural, QST = question, REDUP = reduplication, CJ.REL = relative conjunct clause, SG = singular, TA = transitive animate verb, TI = transitive inanimate verb, TI2 = syntactically transitive inanimate verb, 1 = first person, 3 = animate third person, 3′ = animate third person obviative, 0′SG = inanimate obviative singular.
3. In Plains Cree verbs are inflected for person, number, obviation (second third person), direction, and aspect/tense. The morphology of the inflection differs according to verbal orders. Generally speaking, the inflections of the INDEPENDENT ORDER are used in independent clauses (*mîciso**wak*** 'they eat/they are eating'), as well as in main clauses (*kiskêyimâ**wak** tânitê kâ-ihtâyit* 'they know where s/he was'). Those of the CONJUNCT ORDER are used in independent as well as in dependent clauses (*nikiskêyimâwak tânitê kâ-ihtâ**twâw*** 'I know where they were'), and in interrogative sentences (*tânitê kâ-ihtâ**twâw*** 'where were they?').
4. Note that *kisêyinîw+pan* contracts to *kisêyinîpan.*
5. I wish to thank Arok Wolvengrey and Darren Okemaysim for having pointed these details out to me. Cuoq (1886) notes a similar generic meaning for Northern Algonquin; compare *Kawin ningi kikenimasik ni micomisi**ban**ek* 'je n'ai pas connu mes défunts grands-pères' ['I never met my late grandfathers'] with *ni micomisina**ban**ek* 'nos ancêtres' ['our ancestors']. Hallowell (1940:41) indicates for Saulteaux that "since 'grandfather' is commonly used, not only as a term of respect for any old man, but also in addressing, or referring to, spiritual helpers of all types, it has probably a deeper significance in this context." Benedict (1934:64) also provides a striking parallel in Zuni culture: "People say to the children when the summer afternoon rain clouds come up the sky 'your

grandfathers are coming' and the reference is not to individual dead relatives, but applies impersonally to all forbears."

6. In some isolated cases, the English adjective *deceased* (which is the functional equivalent of -(*i*)*pan*) appears in front of a personal Christian name as in *ôtê mân ê-kî-ohtinamân, deceased Françoise* 'I used to learn things from over there, from the late Françoise' (Ahenakew and Wolfart 1998:406).
7. Although more work is needed to shed light on this problem, it seems that with speakers who do not use absentative nouns in -(*i*)*pan* the relative kinship clause in *kâ-kî-* or other marked circumlocutions serve the same function as -(*i*)*pan*. To paraphrase De Saussure (1962:160–161), when a given way to address one's forebears falls out of use, its affective meaning, or "value," will be expressed by a neighboring construction or an equivalent verbal strategy.

REFERENCES

Ahenakew, Alice. 2000. *âh-âyîtaw isi ê-kî-kiskêyihtahkik maskihkiy / They Knew Both Sides of Medicine: Cree Tales of Curing and Cursing Told by Alice Ahenakew,* ed., trans., and with a glossary by H. C. Wolfart and Freda Ahenakew. Publications of the Algonquian Text Society. Winnipeg: University of Manitoba Press.

Ahenakew, Freda, and H. Christoph, Wolfart (eds.). 1998. *kôhkominawak otâcimowiniwâwa: Our Grandmothers' Lives as Told in Their Own Words.* Regina, Saskatchewan: Canadian Plains Research Center, University of Regina.

Benedict, Ruth. 1934. *Patterns of Culture.* Boston: Houghton, Mifflin & Harcourt.

Brown, Penelope. 2007. Principles of Person Reference in Tzeltal Conversation. *Person Reference in Interaction: Linguistic, Cultural, and Social Perspectives,* ed. by Tanya Stivers and Nick J. Enfield, pp. 172–202. Cambridge: Cambridge University Press.

Cuoq, Jean André. 1886. *Lexique de la langue algonquine.* Montréal: J. Chapleau.

Garde, Murray. 2008. Person Reference, Proper Names and Circumspection in Bininj Kunwok Conversation. *Discourse and Grammar in Australian Languages,* ed. by Ilana Mushin and Brett Joseph Baker, pp. 203–232. Amsterdam: John Benjamins.

Granger, Byrd Howell. 1961. Naming: In Customs, Beliefs, and Folk Tales. *Western Folklore* 20(1):27–37.

Frazer, James. 1922. *The Golden Bough.* New York: Macmillan.

Hallowell, A. Irving. 1940. The Spirits of the Dead in Saulteaux Life and Thought. *Journal of the Royal Anthropological Institute of Great Britain and Ireland* 70(1):29–51.

James, Deborah. 1991. Preterit Forms in Moose Cree as Markers of Tense, Aspect, and Modality.

International Journal of American Linguistics 57(3):281–297.

Leech, Geoffrey. 1974. *Semantics.* Middlesex: Penguin.

Levinson, Stephen C. 2007. Optimizing Person Reference-Perspectives from Usage on Rossel Island. *Person Reference in Interaction: Linguistic, Cultural, and Social Perspectives,* ed. by Nick J. Enfield and Tanya Stivers, pp. 29–72. Cambridge: Cambridge University Press.

Lockwood, Hunter Thompson. 2015. Nominal TAM and the Preterit in Potawatomi. Paper read at the 47th Algonquian Conference, University of Manitoba.

Mandelbaum, David G. 1979. *The Plains Cree: An Ethnographic, Historical, and Comparative Study.* Regina, Saskatchewan: University of Regina Press.

Masuskapoe, Cecilia. 2010. *piko kīkway ē-nakacihtāt: kēkēk otācimowina ē-nēhiyawastēki mitoni ē-āh-itwēt māna Cecilia Masuskapoe / There's Nothing She Can't Do: Kēkēk's Autobiography Published in Cree,* ed. H. Christoph Wolfart and Freda Ahenakew. Algonquian and Iroquoian Linguistics Memoir 21. Winnipeg: Algonquian and Iroquoian Linguistics.

Murphy, Lynne M. 2003. Synonymy and Similarity. *Semantic Relations and the Lexicon: Antonymy, Synonymy and other Paradigms,* ed. by Lynne M. Murphy, pp. 133–168. Cambridge: Cambridge University Press

Needham, Rodney. 1954. Reference to the Dead among the Penan. *Man* 54(January):10.

Oxford, Will. 2010. Nominal Predication and Verb Morphology in Innu-aimun. *University of British Columbia Working Papers in Linguistics* 29:30–46.

Saussure, Ferdinand de. 1962. *Cours de linguistique générale,* ed. by Charles Baily, Albert Sechehaye, and Albert Riedlinger. Paris: Payot.

Seiler, Hansjakob. 1980. Two Systems of Cahuilla Kinship Expressions: Labeling and Descriptive. *American Indian and Indo-European Studies: Papers in Honor of Madison S. Beeler,* ed. by Kathryn Klar, Margaret Langdon, and Shirley Silver, pp. 229–236. New York: Mouton.

Stivers, Tanya, Nick J. Enfield, and Stephen C. Levinson. 2007. Person Reference in Interaction. *Person Reference in Interaction: Linguistic, Cultural, and Social Perspectives,* ed. by Tanya Stivers and Nick J. Enfield, pp. 1–20. Cambridge: Cambridge University Press.

Westman, Clinton. 2008. Understanding Cree Religious Discourse. PhD thesis, University of Alberta.

Wolfart, H. Christoph. 1973. *Plains Cree: A Grammatical Study.* Transactions of the American Philosophical Society, n.s., vol 63, pt. 5. Philadelphia: American Philosophical Society.

Wolfart, H. Christoph. 1990. 1001 Nights: The Orient and the Far Northwest. *Papers of the 21st Algonquian Conference,* ed. by William Cowan, pp. 370–395. Ottawa: Carleton University Press.

Wolfart, H. Christoph. 2000. Commentaries and Notes. *âh-âyîtaw isi ê-kî-kiskêyihtahkik maskihkiy / They Knew Both Sides of Medicine: Cree Tales of Curing and Cursing Told by Alice Ahenakew,* ed. by Christoph H. Wolfart and Freda Ahenakew, pp. 141–196. Winnipeg: University of Manitoba Press.

Instrumental Nouns in Miami-Illinois

David J. Costa

Miami-Illinois has a very common nominalization construction taking the ending *aakan.* Hundreds of *-aakan* nouns are attested in Miami-Illinois, from the oldest Illinois records up through the early 20th-century records of Miami, Peoria, and Wea. While there are matches for this construction elsewhere in Algonquian, it is far more common in Miami-Illinois than in its sister languages, indicating that it has been greatly expanded within Miami-Illinois. Nouns with *aakan* are most often used to form instruments, though they also sometimes form simple abstract or verbal nouns, and other times something that might be described as either results or undergoers of actions. They are very frequently used to name new objects of European-American technology, though they are also common for items of precontact technology. The exact morphological environment of this construction is somewhat complicated; most *aakan* nouns are straightforwardly formed off TI stems, though they also can be formed off TA stems, AI stems, and even noun stems. This paper will examine the *aakan* construction in Miami-Illinois, looking especially at its morphological and phonological conditioning and its semantics, with a few glances at how it compares with analogous constructions elsewhere in Algonquian.

A sign that the class of *-aakan* nouns has been greatly expanded in Miami-Illinois is the fact that *-aakan* nouns derived from TI stems often have cognates in the sister languages consistently showing the ending *-ikan.*[1] The ending *-ikan* is very commonly seen with quasi-instrumental nouns in other Algonquian languages, though this ending is almost totally absent from Miami-Illinois. Table 1 shows some clear sets showing this correspondence, where all the cognates in the sister languages take *-ikan.*[2]

The only *-ikan* noun found in Miami-Illinois is the word in Table 2, which has no corresponding verb stem in the language, and which strongly looks as though it is borrowed from a neighboring Algonquian language.[3] Of the various words translated as 'bread' in Miami-Illinois, this word is actually rather uncommon;[4] the usual deletion of the initial *pah-* syllable by the late 19th century (and its occasional appearance as apparent *mah-*) is irregular. Moreover, this word is absent from the Jesuit Illinois records, which seems to indicate that its borrowing postdated the Illinois mission period; perhaps it was borrowed from Kickapoo when the Miami and Kickapoo lived near each other in northern Indiana in the early 1800s (see Costa 2013a:201–202).

Formation of *-aakan* Nouns

The great majority of *-aakan* nouns are straightforwardly formed off TI stems, so commonly so that the construction is probably completely productive for such stems. To form *aakan* nouns from TI stems, the theme signs *-am* and *-oo* delete before *-aakan.*[5] Table 3 illustrates typical *-aakan* nouns are derived from Type 1 TI stems.

Nouns with *-aakan* are also productively formed off Type 2 TI stems (Table 4).

Though they are considerably less common, there are also *-aakan* nouns formed off TA stems; the examples in Table 5, all animate dependent nouns, usually do not quite designate instruments so much as undergoers of the action designated by the verb.

Many *-aakan* nouns formed off TA stems also have alternates formed off their corresponding TI stems. Sometimes there is a discernible semantic difference with these pairs (as in the last two pairs in Table 6), while other times the glosses given in the sources are basically identical (as in the first two pairs). In cases where the TA- and TI-derived forms are semantically identical, usage of one form versus the other may represent dialectal variation (Table 6).

It is quite common, especially in the modern language, for *-aakan* nouns formed off stems with the TI1 final *-aham* 'by tool' to contract the expected *ahaa* sequence to *aa.* Such nouns do not appear with the expected *-ahaakani* ending, but simple *-aakani.* These nouns usually preserve the full *-ahaakani* ending in the Illinois records (Table 7).[6]

There are several notable *-aakan* nouns where the stems from which they are presumably derived happen not to be attested anywhere as verbs (Table 8).

Miami-Illinois *-aakan* nouns are also freely formed from AI stems. When forming *-aakan* nouns from AI stems, stem-final *aa* and *ii* regularly delete before *-aakan* (Table 9).

AI stems ending in long *ee* vary in their treatment; about half the time, stem-final *ee* deletes before *-aakan,* but about an equal amount of the time stem-final *ee* is retained and the *aa* deleted, yielding an ending *-eekan.* The instrumental nouns in Table 10 take *-eekan* and sometimes are attested with *-aakan* as well; given that *-eekan* nouns seem to be extremely rare in the modern language, they are presumably the older forms, with the *aakan* forms created by analogy.

The *ee*-final AI stems in Table 11 take *-aakan* only.

In a few unpredictable cases (especially stems containing *-iinkwee-* 'face'), AI stems ending in *ee* give endings in *-iaakan.* The stem *kimote* 'steal' takes this ending in the derived noun as well, though as a rare AI stem ending in short *-e,* this might actually be regular for such nouns (Table 12).

Much like with TAs, a handful of *-aakan* nouns formed from AI stems are also attested with dialect variants derived from TI stems, though without any discernible semantic distinction (Table 13).

And finally, a handful of *-aakan* nouns in modern Miami-Illinois are not derived from verb stems at all, but from noun stems (Table 14).

Unpredictably, as shown in Table 15, several *-aakan* nouns in modern Miami-Illinois undergo initial change, often optionally or perhaps simply varying with dialect.

Semantics of *-aakan* Nouns

Most *-aakan* nouns straightforwardly form instruments; that is, nouns designating things used to do the action denoted by the verb stem (Table 16).

However, many *-aakan* nouns do not exactly form instruments; in some cases, they form something more like abstract nouns, essentially nominalizations of the verbs from which they are derived (Table 17).

Sometimes *-aakan* nouns denote something more like the undergoer or result of the action of the verb, as in Table 18.

Given the rather vague semantics of *-aakan* nouns, it is not surprising that several of them are variously glossed in different sources as either straight instruments, verbal nouns, or as results (Table 19).

Actually, many *-aakan* nouns must be seen as lexicalized, since their meanings are not predictable from the semantics of their verb stems (Table 20).

It is instructive to compare the *-aakan* nouns deriving from the semantically very similar TI stems *ehkisam-* 'boil it down to evaporation' versus *paankosam-* 'boil it down, let it become dry'; the noun *iihkisaakani* (Table 15) gives a straightforward instrument, glossed by Jacob Dunn as 'vessel for boiling down something,' whereas *paankosaakani* (Table 20), glossed in all sources as 'sugar', gives a noun representing something more like a result. This indicates that even though the formation of *-aakan* nouns is probably completely productive at least for TI stems, the MEANINGS of these nouns are unpredictable enough that semantically they must be viewed as at least partially lexicalized.

Conclusion

It is clear that the *-aakan* construction is extremely important in Miami-Illinois. It has become much more common in Miami-Illinois than in its sister languages, not merely in generalizing the actual *-aakan* ending beyond what is seen in the other languages, but also in its deployment as a crucial strategy for naming objects, not least items of European-American technology. However, the *-aakan* construction is not simply a nominalizer: even though the ending appears to be entirely productive for TI stems and possibly AI stems as well, its semantics cannot be easily summarized. While there are obviously patterns to the meaning of *-aakan* nouns, in many cases their meanings cannot be predicted.

What still remains to be done is to place *-aakan* nouns within a framework of Algonquian in general: that is, a comparative study of analogous *-aakan* and *-ikan* constructions across the sister languages, to discover how their semantics and morphological construction vary from language to language. Hopefully this paper will both assist and spur such future research.

TABLE 1. Miami-Illinois *-aakan* nouns with *-ikan* cognates

MIAMI-ILLINOIS FORM	GLOSS	UNDERLYING STEM	ORIGINAL MIAMI-ILLINOIS FORM(S)	COGNATES
ahtehsaakani	‘paint, dye’	*ahtehsam-* ‘paint it’	LB/P ‹atessagane› ‘teinture’/‘teinture in gre.’	Oj *atisigan,* K *ahteϑikani,* Mn *atɛ·hsekan,* C *atisikan,* ‘dye’
mahsinahaakani, mahsenaakani	‘paper, book, writing’	*mahsenaham-* ‘owe it, buy it on credit’	Gr/P ‹massinahagane›, LB ‹massinaagane›, Gt ‹ma’senakáni›	Oj *mazinahigan,* F *mesenahikani,* Mn *mase·nahekan,* C *masinahikan,* ‘book, paper’
sakahaakani	‘nail (metal), screw’	*sakaham-* ‘nail it, fasten it’	Gr ‹sacahagane›, LB ‹sacaacane›, Gt ‹sakahakáni›	Oj *zagahigan,* Sh *ϑakhika,* K *ϑakahikani,* Mn *saka·hekan,* C *sakahikan,* ‘nail’
sakahaakana	‘button’		Gt ‹sakahakána›	
šaaponaakani	‘pin, needle’	*šaaponam-* ‘push it through’	Gr/P ‹chab8nagane›, Hk ‹shabunakani›, Gt ‹shapûnakani›	Oj *žaabonigan,* Sh *saaponika,* F *ša·ponikani,* Mn *sa·ponekan,* C *sa·ponikan*
tipahaakani	‘measure, payment’	*tepaham-* ‘pay for it’	Gr/P ‹tipahagane›, LB ‹tepahagane›	Oj *dibahigan,* K *tepahikani,* Mn *tepa·hekan,* C *tipahikan,* ‘hour, mile, measure’

TABLE 2. Probable loanword

MIAMI-ILLINOIS FORM	GLOSS	ORIGINAL MIAMI-ILLINOIS FORMS	COGNATES
(pah)kweešikani	‘bread’	E ‹pahcoisican›, Tr ‹pukwaashēēkunee› ‘bread’, Th ‹mhkuaishekeneh› ‘bread’, Gt ‹kweshikáni› ‘bread’, D ‹kwäcĭkáni›, ‹m’kwäcíkun› ‘light bread, wheat bread’	Oj *bakwežigan* ‘bread, flour’, K *pahkweesikani* ‘bread, flour’, Mn *pahki·sekan* ‘wheat, flour, bread’, C *pahkwe·sikan* ‘bannock, bread, flour’

TABLE 3. Instrumental nouns from Type 1 TIs

MIAMI-ILLINOIS FORM	GLOSS	UNDERLYING STEM	ORIGINAL MIAMI-ILLINOIS FORM(S)	COGNATES
kipenaakani	'(beaver) dam'	*kipenam-* 'block it, obstruct it'	Gr ‹amec8a akipinagane› 'chaussee de castor'	Ms ‹kupponnonk› 'milldam'
kwaantinaakani	'portage'	*kwaantinam-* 'carry it (a canoe) on a portage'	Gr/LB ‹c8antinagane›, Tr ‹kwaundēēnukarn›	—
laapinaakani, naapinaakani	'coat, shirt, garment'	*laapinam-~ naapinam-* 'wear it, put it on'	Gr/LB/P ‹rapinagane›, Hk ‹napinakani›, Gt ‹lapínakan›, D ‹napínakánĭ›	—
paahpahaakani	'key'	*paahpaham-* 'lock it'	Gr/LB ‹papahagane›, Gt ‹pa'hpáhakáni›	—
pakantaakani	'hammer, pestle for pounding corn'	*pakantam-* 'hit it, beat it'	Gr/LB ‹pacantagane›, Gt ‹pakandakáni›, D ‹pakándakánĭ›	K *pakačikani* 'hammer'
poohkaanaakani	'sieve, sifter'	*poohkaanam-* 'sift it, winnow it'	Gr ‹p8canagane›, Gt ‹puxkanakáni›	Po *boškangən* 'winnowing tray'
sahkahaakani	'torch, match'	*sahkaham-* 'light it, set fire to it'	Gr ‹saccahagane›	Oj *zakahigan* 'lighter'
teehsinaakani	'travois'	*teehsinam-* 'carry it on a travois'	Gr/LB ‹tessinagane›	Oj *desinang* 'he spreads it out'

TABLE 4. Instrumental nouns from Type 2 TIs

MIAMI-ILLINOIS FORM	GLOSS	UNDERLYING STEM	ORIGINAL MIAMI-ILLINOIS FORM(S)	COGNATES
akotaakani	'pot hook'	*akotoo-* 'hang it'	Gr/LB ‹ac8tagane› 'cremaillere'	C *akota·w* 'he hangs it'
ansiwataakani	'seed of a plant'	*ansiwatoo-* 'plant it'	Gr/P/LB ‹assi8atagane› Gt ‹a^{n}ziwatakáni›, D ‹zĭwatakani›	Mn *ase·wataw* 'he sows, plants it'
kiihkihpotaakani	'hand saw'	*kiihkihpotoo-* 'saw it crosswise'	D ‹kĭkpótákánĭ›	K *kiiskipotoo-* 'saw it apart'
kiintaakana	'whetstone'	*kiintoo-* 'sharpen it'	Gt ‹kindakána›, D ‹kíndakána›	Sh *nikiito* 'I grind it sharp'
kocimotaakani	'question'	*kocimotoo-* 'ask it'	Gt ‹kutchimutakáni›	Mn *koce·motam* 'he asks it'

TABLE 5. Instrumental nouns from TA stems

MIAMI-ILLINOIS FORM	GLOSS	UNDERLYING STEM	ORIGINAL MIAMI-ILLINOIS FORM(S)	COGNATES
nintaloolaakana	'mon employe'	*alool-* 'hire him, order him'	LB ‹nitar8ragana›	Sh *haloolaaka* 'chauffeur'
nimpawaalaakana	'my dream-spirit'	*pawaal-* 'dream of him'	Gr ‹nipa8aragana› 'mes manitous qui me parlent dans mes resves', LB pl. ‹nipa8araganaki› 'mes dieux des songes'	Oj *nimbawaanaa* 'I dream of him'
Nintaweemaakana[1]	'my cousin, relative'	*aweem-* 'be related to him'	LB ‹nita8emagana› 'mon allié', WP ‹dʊuamʊkʊnʊ› 'cousin'	F *netawe·ma·wa* 'my brother' (woman speaking)
nintentalaakana	'my slave'	*ental-* 'own him, enslave him'	Gr ‹nitintaragana›, LB ‹nitentaragana›	Mn *tanɛ·w* 'he has, keeps, owns him'

1. See also *aweemaakani* in Table 17 below.

TABLE 6. Instrumental nouns from TI and TA stems

MIAMI-ILLINOIS FORM	GLOSS	UNDERLYING STEM		ORIGINAL MIAMI-ILLINOIS FORMS	COGNATES
kitahswaakani	'parched corn'	**kitahsw-*	TA	Gt ‹kitasswakáni›	Oj *ningidasaan* 'I parch it (e.g., wild rice)', F *ketasa·ni* 'parched corn'
kitahsaakani		*kitahsam-* 'roast it, parch it, as corn or coffee beans'	TI1	Gr/LB ‹kitassagane›, Gt ‹kitássakani›, D ‹kĭtássakánĭ›	
moošwaakani	'scissors, sickle, scythe, reaper'	*moošw-* 'cut his hair'	TA	Gr ‹m8nch8agane›, Gt ‹muzhuakáni›, D ‹mónjwakánĭ›	Ot *moožwaagan* 'scissors'
moošaakani		*moošam-* 'cut it (hair)'	TI1	Gt ‹mužakáni›, D ‹mónjakáni›	
kiihkahwaakani	'sword'	*kiihkahw-* 'cut him, break him'	TA	Gr ‹kiscah8agane›, Gt ‹kíkahuákani›	K *kiiskaham* 'cut it apart by tool'
kiihkahaakani	'saw, cutter, cutting instrument'	*kiihkaham-* 'break it open, cut it'	TI1	D ‹kikáhakánĭ›	
pimwaakani	'ammunition'	*pemw-* 'shoot him'	TA	LB ‹pim8agane›, Gt ‹pimuákani›	F *pemwe·wa, pemotamwa* 'he shoots at him/it'
pimotaakani	'gunpowder'	*pemotam-* 'shoot it'	TI1	D ‹pimótakanĭ›	

TABLE 7. Instrumental nouns changing *ahaa* to *aa*

MIAMI-ILLINOIS FORM	GLOSS	UNDERLYING STEM	ORIGINAL MIAMI-ILLINOIS FORMS	COGNATES
kaahkahaakani, *kaahkaakani*	'scraper'	*kaahkaham-* 'dress it (as of game), scrape it out'	Gt ‹kakákani›, D ‹kakahakani›	Sh *kakhika* 'pumpkin scraper'
kipalwahaakani, *kipalwaakani*	'lid, cover of a pot'	*kipalwaham-* 'cover it with a lid'	Gr ‹kipar8agane›, Gt ‹kipalwakáni›, ‹kipalwahakáni›	F *kepanohikani* 'lid'
poohkahaakani, *poohkaakani*	'gimlet, chisel, lance'	*poohkaham-* 'cut a hole in it by tool'	Gr ‹p8cahagane› 'vrille, tairier', Gt ‹pukakáni›, D ‹pokahakanĭ›	F *po·hkahamwa* 'he pokes a hole in it, pierces it'
siinipiikahaakani, *siinipiikaakani*	'soft Indian corn, the juice still in the corn'	*siinipiikaham-* 'squeeze juice from it (by tool)'	Gt ‹sinípikáhakani›, ‹sinipikákani›	C *si·nipe·kinam* 'he wrings it out'
šoohkwahaakani, *šoohkwaakani*	'sled, wagon'	*šoohkwaham-* 'drag it'	LB ‹ch8c8ahagane› Gt ‹shú'hkwakani›, D ‹cókwakánĭ›	C *so·skwaham* 'he irons it', *so·skwahikan* 'iron'
teehsahaakani, *teehsaakani*	'support, strut, brace'	*teehsaham-* 'put a support under it'	Gr/LB ‹tessahagane›, Gt ‹tessákan›	C *te·htaha·kan* 'shelf for stored meat'
wiihkapaakani[1]	'salt'	*wiihkapaham-* 'salt it'	Tr ‹weekupaukāūnee›, Gt ‹wixkapákani›, D ‹wikapákanĭ›	K *(w)iiskopaham-* 'salt it', *(w)iiskopahaakani* 'salt'

1. This word never appears as full **wiihkapahaakani,* nor is it found before Trowbridge's Miami notes. Although Miami-Illinois and Kickapoo share an etymon for 'salt', this is not matched by Sauk *θi·wehta·kani* or Meskwaki *si·wahta·kani* (cf. Potawatomi *ziwtagən* and Ottawa *ziiwtaagan*). Borrowing by Kickapoo from Miami-Illinois would seem to be indicated (see Costa 2013a: 201–202).

TABLE 8. Instrumental nouns with unattested verb stems

MIAMI-ILLINOIS FORM	GLOSS	UNDERLYING STEM	ORIGINAL MIAMI-ILLINOIS FORM(S)	COGNATES
ahkihkalaakani	'basket'	?	Gr/LB ‹akicaragane›, Tr ‹kikalaukāūnee›, Gt ‹kíxkalákani›	—
mihkintaakana[1]	'pillow, bundle of furs'	**mehkintam-* (?)	Gr ‹mikintagana›, WP ‹mekendʋkʋnʋ›, Gt ‹mixkindakána›	Oj *mikindaagan* 'a packet or bundle of fur'
poohkihtaakani	'window' (Wea)	**poohkihtam-* 'hear it through a hole' (?)	WP ‹poktʋkʋne›, W/Gt ‹puktakáni›, W/D ‹póktakánĭ›	—
šimaakani	'lance, spear'	?	LB ‹chimagane›, Gt ‹shimágani›	Oj *žimaagan* 'spear'
šiipaakani	'awl'[2]	**šiipaaham-* (?)	D ‹cípakáni›	F *ši·pa·hikani* 'hold and slot heddle for making beadwork'
takahaakani, takaakani	'ax, tomahawk'	**takaham-* (?)	Gr/LB ‹tacahagane›, V ‹takâkané›, Gt ‹takákani›, Mc ‹takā'kani'›	Sh *tekhaaka*
teepantaakani	'barrel'	?	Tr ‹tepaundekāūnee›, Gt ‹täpandakáni›	—
waawiinaakani	'bread, biscuit'	**waawiinam-* (?)	Gr/P/LB ‹8a8inagane›, Gt ‹wawinakáni›, D ‹wawínakánĭ›	—
wiihsakaakani	'pepper'	**wiihsakaham-* (?)	Gt ‹wissakákani›, D ‹wĭssákakánĭ›	K *wiiϑakahaakani* 'pepper'[3]

1. This noun also appears as inanimate *mihkintaakani.*
2. This noun is found only in Jacob Dunn's notes from Miami speaker Gabriel Godfroy; the normal word for a sewing awl for all other speakers and dialects is *ahkanihkwi* (see Costa 2016:393; cf. Menominee *ohka·nɛh*).
3. Given Meskwaki *wi·sakaki,* Sauk *wi·ϑakaki,* Potawatomi *wasgək,* and Ottawa *waasgang* 'pepper', borrowing between Kickapoo and Miami-Illinois seems likely. (See Costa 2013a:201–202.)

TABLE 9. Instrumental nouns formed from AI stems

MIAMI-ILLINOIS FORM	GLOSS	UNDERLYING STEM	ORIGINAL MIAMI-ILLINOIS FORM(S)	COGNATES
ahpwaakana	'pipe'	*ahpwaa-* 'smoke'	Gr ‹ap8agana›, Tr ‹pwaukāūnar›, D ‹pwakana›	PA **ospwa·kana*
ahseehkaakani	'hide scraper'	*ahseehkii-* 'tan, scrape a hide'	Gr ‹assecagane› 'grate pr les peaux', P ‹assekagane› 'petitte gratte'	F *ase·hke·wa* 'she tans hides'
aalhsoohkaakani[1]	'winter story'	*aalhsoohkii-* 'tell a winter story'	Gt ‹halthúkakani›, D ‹alsókakáni›	F *a·teso·hka·kana*
maawihšinaakani	'band, hunting band'	*maawihšin-* 'gather, assemble'	Gr ‹ma8ichinagane›	—
minaakani	'cup, dipper'	*men-* 'drink'	LB/P ‹minagane›, WP ‹menʊkʊne›, Gt ‹minákani›	—
paakicaakani	'belly swelling, ague cake'	*paakicii-* 'have a swollen belly'	Gt ‹pakítchakan›, D ‹pakitcakan›	—
weeweepihsaakani	'cradle, swing'	*weeweepihsaa-* 'swing'	Gt ‹wewepsakáni›, D ‹wäwäpsakanĭ›	F *we·we·piso·ni* 'swing, baby hammock'

1. The alternate *aalhsoohkaani* is significantly more common in Miami-Illinois (cf. Ojibwe *aadisookaan*).

TABLE 10. Instrumental nouns with *-eekan*

MIAMI-ILLINOIS FORM	GLOSS	UNDERLYING STEM	ORIGINAL MIAMI-ILLINOIS FORM(S)	COGNATES
aalhsaalakiinkweekani, later *aalhsaalakiinkwaakani*	'eyeglasses'	*aalhsaalakiinkwee-*	Gr ‹arsaraking8egane›, Gt ‹ál'ssalakingwakáni›	—
apweekani, apwaakani	'grill'	*apwee-* 'broil, roast'	LB ‹ap8egane›, Gr ‹ap8agane›	F *apwa·kana* 'frying pan'
ataawaakani, ataaweekani	'trade'	*atawee-* 'trade'	LB ‹ata8egane›, Gr/P ‹ata8agane›	Oj *adaawaagan* 'fur for trade'
atešiinkweekanemi	'his face'	*ešiinkwee-* 'have one's face be so'	Gr ‹ateching8eganemi›	—
ilweekani	'word'	*elwee-* 'speak so'	Gr/LB ‹ir8egane›	—
kiiyaaskweekani, later *kiiyaahkwaakani*	'wicked-ness'	*kiiyaahkwee-* 'be wicked, foolish'	LB ‹kiasc8egane›, D ‹kíakwakánĭ›	—
kišihšiinkweekani	'washbasin for face'	*kišihšiinkwee-* 'wash one's face'	D ‹kĭcĭcíngwäkanĭ›	—
piiminahkweekani	'wool'	*piiminahkwee-* 'spin cordage'	LB ‹piminac8egane›	Oj *biiminakwed* 'he makes rope, string'

TABLE 11. Instrumental nouns from *ee*-stems

MIAMI-ILLINOIS FORM	GLOSS	UNDERLYING STEM	ORIGINAL MIAMI-ILLINOIS FORM(S)	COGNATES
inohkaatawaakani	'Illinois dictionary'	*inohkaatawee-* 'speak Illinois'	LB ‹atinocata8aganemi› 'son dictionaire illinois'	—
aalahkwahkiink-waakani	'eyeshade for a horse's harness'	**aalahkwahkiinkwee-*	Gt ‹alxkwakingwákani›	—
ciinkwaakani	'drum'	*ciinkwee-* 'thunder, roar'	Hk ‹tschingwakanni›	—
minehkwaakani	cup, glass, 'a deep dish, used for drinking'	*menehkwee-* 'eat soup, liquid'	Gt ‹minä'kwakáni›, D ‹mĭnäkwakánĭ›	C *minihkwa·kan* 'cup, glass'
ilaatawaakani	'language'	*elaatawee-* 'speak such a language'	P ‹kiterata8aganeminani› 'our language'	Ms ‹unnont8wâonk› 'language'
išiteehaakani	'mind'	*ešiteehee-* 'think so'	Tr ‹ndaashītehaukarn› 'my mind'	F *išite·ha·kani* 'thought'
pinaahkwaakani[1]	'comb (noun)'	*penahkwee-* 'comb one's (own) hair'	Gt ‹pinaxkwakáni›	Oj *binaakwaan*

1. The alternate *pinaahkwaani* is more common.

TABLE 12. Instrumental nouns with *-iaakan*

MIAMI-ILLINOIS FORM	GLOSS	UNDERLYING STEM	ORIGINAL MIAMI-ILLINOIS FORM(S)
ahtawaaniinkwiaakani	'wooden false-face mask'	*ahtawaaniinkwee-* 'wear a false face mask, be a shaman'	Gt ‹tawaníngwiakani›
wiihkweetiaakani	'trousers'	*wiihkweetii-* 'wear pants, leggings'	Gt ‹wixkwetiákani›, D ‹awĭ́kwätĭ́akánĭ›
kimotiaakani	'thievery, theft, stolen goods'	*kimote-* 'steal'	Gr ‹kim8tiagane›, Mc ‹kimṓtiyākāni›
kišihšinehkiaakani	'washbasin for hands'	*kišihšinehkii-* 'wash one's hands'	D ‹kĭcĭ́cĭnäkiakanĭ›
naapiinkwiaakani	'bridle, false face mask'	*naapiinkwee-* 'wear a false face mask, a bridle'[1]	Tr ‹naupingweeaukārnee›, Gt ‹nápingwiakani›, D ‹napĭngwĭakanĭ›
poohkihšiikoliaakani[2]	'nose ring'	**poohkihšiikolee-* 'have a hole in one's nose' (?)[3]	Gt ‹pukšikuliakani›

1. Note Illinois *laapiinkweewa* (Gr ‹raping8e8a›) 'il a un masque' and modern *naapiinkwia* 'one who wears a false face, shaman' (Gt ‹napíng-wia›, D ‹napĭ́ngwĭa›). Outside Miami-Illinois, cf. Potawatomi *nabigwagən* 'halter'.
2. Note also Illinois *nimpoohkihšiikolaakani* 'my nostrils' (LB ‹nip8kichic8ragane› 'narines'), showing simple *-aakan.*
3. The only known attestation of this AI verb is Dunn's *poohkihšikoliaani* (‹póqcĭkolyanĭ›), which Dunn's Wea speaker gave as 'my nostrils'. Also related is *poohkihšikolia* 'yoncopin, American lotus (*nelumbo lutea*)' (Tr pl. ‹poakshikwileeārkee›, Gt ‹pukshíkulia›, D pl. ‹pókcĭkolyakĭ›); cf. Potawatomi *bokšəgneyək* 'yuccapans', Oklahoma Ottawa **bookšigəne* 'water or marsh potato' (Gatschet Ottawa ‹pókshikĕnä›) and Kickapoo pl. *poohkisikomeewaki* (Hockett 1938 ‹po·hkišikome·waki›).

TABLE 14. Instrumental nouns from noun stems

MIAMI-ILLINOIS FORM	GLOSS	UNDERLYING STEM	ORIGINAL MIAMI-ILLINOIS FORM(S)
ahtawaanahkisinaakani	'snowshoe'	*ahtawaanahkisin-* 'wooden shoe'	Tr ‹ndohtewaunaukēēsuneekarn› 'my snowshoe'
mahkisinaakani	'ribbonwork moccasin top'	*mahkisin-* 'moccasin, shoe'	Gt ‹makissenakáni› 'moccasins', MRH ‹makĭsanakan›
waapihkolaakani	'white clothing'	*waapihkolayi* 'habit blanc'	LB ‹8apicoragane› 'habit blanc'
wiiwašaakani	'saddle'	*wiiwaš-* 'saddle, pack'	Gt ‹wiwashákani›[1]
kiipihkatwi ahkašaakani	'horseshoe'	*-hkaš-* 'nail, claw' (*kiipihkatwi* = 'metal')	Gt ‹kípkatwi kashakani›

1. Gatschet's informant identified this as a Piankashaw dialect form.

TABLE 13. Instrumental nouns from TI and AI stems

MIAMI-ILLINOIS FORM	GLOSS	UNDERLYING STEM		ORIGINAL MIAMI-ILLINOIS FORMS	COGNATES
aalikoontawaakani	'stairway, ladder'	*aalikoontawee-* 'climb a ladder, staircase'	AI	Gr ‹aric8nta8agane›	—
aalakoontahaakani		**aalikoontaham-* 'use it to climb' (?)	TI	LB ‹aric8ntaagane›, ‹aricontaagane›, D ‹alakóndakanĭ›	
awikaakani, eewikaakani	'pencil, pen'	*awikii-* 'draw, write'	AI	Gr ‹a8icagane›, Gt ‹wikakáni›, ‹äwikakáni›, D ‹wíkakánĭ›	Sh *hawike* 'he writes'
awikaataakani, eewikaataakani		*awikaatam-* 'draw/write on it'	TI	Gt ‹wikatakáni›, ‹äwikatakáni›, D ‹wíkatakánĭ›	Sh *awikaatam-* 'write on it'
kwiihkwiihšaakani	'whistle (instrument)'	*kwiihkwiihši-* 'whistle'	AI	Gt ‹kwixkwixshakáni›	
kwiihkwiihšantaakani		*kwiihkwiihšantam-* 'blow a whistle'	TI	Gt ‹kwikwishandakáni›	

TABLE 15. Instrumental nouns with initial change

MIAMI-ILLINOIS FORM	GLOSS	UNDERLYING STEM	ORIGINAL MIAMI-ILLINOIS FORM(S)	COGNATES
alaamihtaakani, eelaamihtaakani	'belief'	*alaamihtam-* 'believe it'	Gt ‹lam'htakáni›, ‹elam'htakáni›	Ms ‹wunnaumptamooonk› 'faith'
iihkisaakani	'vessel for boiling down something'	*ehkisam-* 'boil it down'	D ‹ĭkĭssakani›	Mn *ehkɛ·sam* 'he boils it down, to dryness'
kiihkaapiišaakani, keehkaapiišaakani	'parallel line drawn by land surveyors to obtain a network for mapmaking'	*kiihkaapiišam-* 'divide (land), cut off in portions, divide land into lots'	Gr ‹kicapishagane› 'marque gravée ou peinte, compas qui grave en rond', Gt ‹kiäkapishakáni›	—
takwahaakani, teekwahaakana	'pounding stone, grindstone, grinder'	*takwaham-* 'grind it to powder'	Gr ‹tac8ahagane›, Gt ‹takwahakáni›, ‹tekwahakána›	Mu *tăkwahá·kan* 'mortar'
wiintaakani, weentaakani	'reading book'	*wiintam-* 'name it, read it'	Gt ‹windakáni›, ‹wendakáni›	Sh *niwiita* 'I name it, read it'
wiiponaakani, weeponaakani	'wrapping'	*wiiponam-* 'wrap it, swathe it'	LB ‹8ip8nagane›, Gt ‹wipûnakani›, ‹wepunakáni›	Sh *niwiipona* 'I squeeze him tightly'

TABLE 16. *-aakan* nouns forming simple instruments

MIAMI-ILLINOIS FORM	GLOSS	UNDERLYING STEM	ORIGINAL MIAMI-ILLINOIS FORM(S)	COGNATES
ahšitisaakani	'glue'	*ahšitesam-* 'glue it'	Gt ‹ashítisakan›	Oj *ašidinan* 'he holds it against something'
kihpitaakani	'string'	*kihpitoo-* 'tie it'	Gr/LB ‹kipitagane›, Gt ‹kpitakáni›, Mi/H ‹ki̲pitakani̲›	Mn *kɛhpe·ta·w* 'he ties it'
kipahaakani	'key, bolt, lock'	*kipaham-* 'block it, shut it'	LB ‹kipahagane›, Gt ‹kipahakáni›	Sh *kiphika* 'lock'
laapihkaakani, naapihkaakani	'necklace'	*laapihkam-, naapihkam-* 'wear it around one's neck'	Gr ‹rabicagane›, LB ‹nabiscagane›, D ‹n'lápkakánĭ› (*sic*)	K *naapihkaakani* 'necklace'
moonahaakani	'hoe, shovel'	*moonaham-* 'dig it, cultivate it'	Gr/LB ‹m8nahagane›	F *mo·naha·kani* 'hoe'
pakitahaakani	'lacrosse stick'	*pakitaham-* 'play lacrosse'	LB ‹pakitahagane›	Ot *nbagdahaan* 'I throw it down (with an instrument)'
piiwahaakani	'brush'	*piiwaham-* 'brush it'	D ‹piwáhakáni›	Ot *biiwhang* 'he brushes dust or crumbs off it'
wilaahkwahaakani	'broadax'	*welaahkwaham-* 'prepare it (wood) with an ax, hew it'	Gt ‹wilaxkwahakáni›	Mn *ona·hkwaham* 'he puts it on a spit or stake'
pootaataakani	'blowpipe'	*pootaatam-* 'blow on it'	Gr/LB ‹p8tatagane›, D ‹pótatakánĭ›	Sh *pootaačika* 'blowgun'

TABLE 17. *-aakan* nouns forming verbal nouns

MIAMI-ILLINOIS FORM	GLOSS	UNDERLYING STEM	ORIGINAL MIAMI-ILLINOIS FORM(S)	COGNATES
alaamweekani, alaamwaakani	'truth'	*alamwee-* 'tell the truth'	Gr/LB/P ‹aram8egane›, Gt ‹lamokáni›, D ‹alamwakani›	Mu *wə̆la·m-we·wá·kan* 'truth'
aweemaakani[1]	'thankfulness'	*aweem-* 'thank him, have him as a relative'	Gt ‹wämakáni›	Ms ‹auwamochek› 'those who are related to him'
miihkweelintaakani	'remembrance, memory'	*miihkweelintam-* 'remember it'	Gt ‹mi'hkwälíndakáni›	Po *nmikwendan* 'I think of it'
mintaakani	'sickness, disease'	*mentam-* 'be sick'	P ‹mintagane›, LB ‹mentagane›	F *metamwa* 'he groans'
šoowaapitaakani	'toothache'	*šoowaapitee-* 'have a toothache'	Gt ‹shuwapitakáni›	—
tapaalaakani	'love'	*tapaal-* 'love him'	D ‹tapálakan›	K *tapaan-* 'love him'

1. See also *nintaweemaakana* in Table 5.

TABLE 18. *-aakan* nouns used to denote undergoers/results

MIAMI-ILLINOIS FORM	GLOSS	UNDERLYING STEM	ORIGINAL MIAMI-ILLINOIS FORM(S)	COGNATES
aapahkwihkiišaakani	'a scalp'	**aapahkwihkiišam-* 'scalp it'[1]	D ‹apakwi̋kĭcakánĭ›	—
palakiinkweesaakani[2]	'lye hominy'	*palakiinkweesam-* 'hull it (corn) in lye'	Gt ‹palakingwesakáni›, P/D ‹pálaki̋ngwäcakánĭ›	F *panakesamwa* 'he scorches it, parches it' Po *bnəgzəgən* 'hominy, hulled corn'
tipilahotaakani	'raft'	*tepilahotoo-* 'tie two things side by side'	Gr/P/LB ‹tepira8tagane›, Tr ‹tipelauhoatukārnee›, D ‹tĭpílahótakánĭ›	—
wilahtookani	'anything put away for preservation'	*welahtoo-* 'put it away, put it in its place'	D ‹wilatokáni›	Mn *ona·ʔtaw* 'he puts it in order, in place'

1. This noun appears to be derived from the TI stem, which is not actually attested, though the corresponding TA stem is commonly found, e.g., *aapahkwihkiišonta* 'one who is scalped' (P ‹apac8ikich8nta›, Hk ‹apaquich-kishónta›, Gt ‹apakwí'hkishonda›).

2. For related terms, note also Wea *palakisaakani* 'lye hominy' (W/Gt ‹palakidakani›), Peoria *palakahaakani* (Gt ‹palakahákani›, ‹palakákan›) variously given by Gatschet as 'crack hominy' and 'rice', as well as old Illinois *pahšakiinkweesaakani* 'bled lexivé' (Gr ‹pchaking8esagane›; cf. Shawnee *nipsakiϑa* 'I scald the peel off it').

TABLE 19. *-aakan* nouns varying in their semantics

MIAMI-ILLINOIS FORM	UNDERLYING STEM	GLOSS	ORIGINAL MIAMI-ILLINOIS FORM(S)	COGNATES
kimotiaakani	*kimote-* 'steal'	'thievery, theft'	Mc ‹kimṓtiyākāni›	C *kimoti-* 'steal'
		'stolen goods'	Gr ‹kim8tiagane›	
waalihkaakani	*waalihkii-* 'dig a hole'	'spade, pickax'	Gt ‹wálxkakani›	F *wa·nehke·wa* 'he digs'
		'hole in the ground'	Gr ‹8aricagane›	
milantaakani	*melantam-* 'vomit'	'emetic'	LB ‹mirantagane›	U *məlántam* 'he vomits'
		'vomit'	Gt ‹milandakáni›	
ahkweetaakani, *eehkwaataakani*	*ahkwaatam-* 'sew it'	'stitching of my shoe'	LB ‹ac8etagane›	—
		'sewing machine'	Gt ‹äxkwatakani›, D ‹äkwátakáni›	
siinipiikiinkweehaakani	*siinipiikiinkweeham-* 'scrape the juice from corn'	'tool for making juice of scraped green corn'	D ‹sĭnĭ́pĭkĭ́ngwähakánĭ›	C *si·nipe·kinam* 'he wrings it out'
		'scraped green corn used for bread or soup'		

TABLE 20. *-aakan* nouns with unpredictable/lexicalized semantics

MIAMI-ILLINOIS FORM	GLOSS	UNDERLYING STEM	ORIGINAL MIAMI-ILLINOIS FORMS	COGNATES
apihkaataakani	'corn plait'	*apihkaatam-* 'braid it'	Gr ‹apicatagane› 'tresse de bled, ou viande, ou citrouilles'	C *apihka·tam* 'she braids it'
ataahpahtaakani	'drawer'	*ataahpahtoo-* 'pull it'	Gt ‹ta'ptakani›, D ‹ataptakanĭ›	F *ata·hpahamwa* 'he draws it in'
kilahkwaakani	'wampum belt'	*kilahkwee-* 'speak, give a speech'	Gt ‹kilaxkwakáni›	—
mahsinahaakani, mahsenaakani	'paper, book, writing'	*mahsenaham-* 'owe it, buy it on credit'	Gr/P ‹massinahagane›, Gt ‹ma'senakáni›, D ‹masänakánĭ›	K *meϑanohamwa* 'he buys it on credit'
mahtohkahaakani	'pestle for grinding hominy'	*mahtohkaham-* 'chop it up, pulverize it'	D ‹p'tokáhakanĭ›	—
niimahaakani, niimaakani	'flag'	*niimaham-* 'carry it aloft, lift it'	Gr/LB ‹nimahagane›, Gt ‹nimakáni›, D ‹nĭmakánĭ›	Sh *niimhhika* 'flag'
paankosaakani	'sugar'	*paankosam-* 'boil it down, let it become dry'	Gt ‹pángussakani›, D ‹pangʊˁakanĭ›, Mc ‹pᴀñgṓ'sᴀᴋᴀni› Mi/H ‹paŋgosakani›	Mu *pé·nkwsəm* 'he dries it by heat'
paahsatoowaakani[1]	'puffball mushroom'	*paahsatoowee-* 'have dropsy, edema'	D ‹pasatowakanĭ›	—
pimohsaakani[2]	'war party'	*pimohsee-* 'walk along, past'	Gr ‹pem8ssagane›, LB ‹pim8sagane›, P ‹pim8ssagane›, D ‹pĭmácakánĭ› [*sic*]	F *pemose·wa* 'he walks along'
poohkišaakani	'window'[3]	*poohkišam-* 'cut a hole in it'	Tr ‹poahkeeshukārnee›, Gt ‹pukishákani›, D ‹pokĭ́cakánĭ›	K *poohkesamwa* 'he cuts a hole in it'
siikahaakani	'batter, dough'	*siikaham-* 'pour it out (by tool)'	WP ‹fekʊʊkʊne›	F *si·kahamwa* 'he pours it out, serves it up'
toohkahaakani	'poison used in curses against people'	*toohkaham-* 'touch it by tool'	Gt ‹tukahakáni›	Mn *to·ckaham* 'he prods it with something'
waalantaakani	'deer lick, buffalo lick'	*waalantam-* 'bite or lick a hole in it'	Gr ‹8arantagane›, Gt ‹walandakáni›, D ‹walándakanĭ›	—

1. Jacob Dunn states that this noun literally means 'it makes dropsy'. This would seem to have the same initial as Meskwaki *pa·sana·mowa* 'he feels bloated, has gastric bloating.'
2. From the same initial, note also *peemohseeta~peemohsia* 'leader of a war party who carries the medicine bundle' (LB ‹pem8sseta› 'celui qui porte la nate le chef du parti', Tr ‹paamooseeāū›) and *nimpemohseeyoma* 'mon capitaine' (Gr ‹nipem8sseï8ma›). Dunn's ‹pimónjakánĭ› 'war headdress made of deer tails' may be misremembered by his speaker.
3. In old Illinois this noun (Gr ‹p8kichagane›) is given as 'lancette, instrument ppre a percer en coupent.'

NOTES

1. For a historical account of **-ikan* and **-a·kan* nouns in Algonquian, see Goddard (1990: 473–474).
2. The abbreviations used in this paper are as follows: AI = animate intransitive, C = Cree, D = Jacob Dunn's notes on Miami-Illinois (Dunn no date (a) and no date (b)), E = the *Elements for a Grammar of Miami-Illinois* vocabulary of Miami-Illinois, from around the late 1700s (see Costa 2013b), F = Meskwaki (Fox), Gr = the Gravier/Largillier Illinois-French dictionary (Largillier no date), Gt = Albert Gatschet's notes on Miami-Illinois (Gatschet no date, 1895a and 1895b), Hk = Heckewelder's notes on Miami-Illinois (Heckewelder no date), K = Kickapoo, LB = LeBoullenger's French-Illinois dictionary (LeBoullenger 1725), Mc = Truman Michelson's notes on Peoria (Michelson 1916), Mi/H = Charles Hockett's notes on Miami (Hockett 1985), Mn = Menominee, Ms = Massachusett, Mu = Munsee Delaware, Oj = Ojibwe, P = Pinet's French-Illinois dictionary (Pinet no date), P/D = Dunn's notes on Peoria (Dunn no date (a) and no date (b), P/H = Charles Hockett's notes on Peoria (Hockett 1985), pl. = plural, Po = Potawatomi, Sh = Shawnee, TA = transitive animate, Th = Thornton's notes on Miami (Thornton 1802), TI = transitive inanimate, TI1 = Type 1 transitive inanimate, Tr = Trowbridge's notes on Miami (Trowbridge 1824–5), U = Unami, V = Volney's Miami wordlist (Volney 1968), W/D = Dunn's notes on Wea (Dunn no date (a) and no date (b)), W/Gt = Gatschet's notes on Wea (Gatschet no date, 1895a and 1895b), WP = the 1837 Wea Primer (Anonymous 1837).
3. Miami-Illinois also has *paankosikani* 'sugar' (Tr ‹pungoaseekārnee›, Mc ‹pᴀñgố'sikᴀni›, P/H ‹pɑŋgósi̱kɑ̀ʔɑ̱ni̱›), a rare dialect variant found alongside the much more common *paankosaakani* (see Table 20).
4. By far the most common Miami-Illinois word for 'bread' is *waawiinaakani,* attested from the old Illinois period up through the early 20th century (see Table 8). It is likely that *waawiinaakani* originally denoted traditional corn bread, while *(pah)kweešikani* was used more for European-origin wheat bread.
5. No *-aakan* nouns have yet been found derived from Type 3 TI stems.
6. There are other scattered examples of original *ahV·* sequences contracting to *V·* in the modern language; for example, Illinois *aapotahooni,* modern Miami-Illinois *aapatooni* 'cane, walking stick' (Gr/LB ‹ap8ta8ni›, Gt ‹apatúni›; cf. Fox *a·pataho·ni*) and Illinois *teehsahooni,* modern Miami-Illinois *teehsooni* 'scaffold, sleeping platform, bed, bench, shelf' (Gr ‹tessah8ni›, Gt ‹tessúni›, D ‹tässóni̊›; cf. Ojibwe *desahon* 'platform, bed in wigwam, bench').

REFERENCES

Anonymous. 1837. *The Wea Primer, Wev Mvs Nv Kv Ne, to Teach the Wea Language.* Cherokee Nation: Mission Press.

Costa, David J. 2013a. Borrowing in Southern Great Lakes Algonquian and the History of Potawatomi. *Anthropological Linguistics* 55:195–233.

Costa, David J. 2013b. On the Elements for a Grammar of Miami-Illinois. *Papers of the 41st Algonquian Conference,* ed. by Karl S. Hele and J. Randolph Valentine, pp. 40–59. Albany: State University of New York Press.

Costa, David J. 2016. Diminutive Nouns in Miami-Illinois. *Anthropological Linguistics* 58:381–410.

Dunn, Jacob P. [n.d.] (a) Miami filecard dictionary. Manuscript at the Indiana State Library, Indianapolis.

Dunn, Jacob P. [n.d.] (b) Various notes on Miami. Manuscripts at the Indiana State Library, Indianapolis.

Gatschet, Albert. [n.d.]. Vocabulary and text (three original Miami and Peoria field notebooks). Manuscript 236, National Anthropological Archives, Smithsonian Museum Support Center, Suitland, Maryland.

Gatschet, Albert. 1895a. Peoria and MiamiEnglish Dictionary. Manuscript 2481, National Anthropological Archives, Smithsonian Museum Support Center, Suitland, Maryland.

Gatschet, Albert. 1895b. Peoria and MiamiEnglish Dictionary. Manuscript 2483, National Anthropological Archives, Smithsonian Museum Support Center, Suitland, Maryland.

Goddard, Ives. 1990. Primary and Secondary Stem Derivation in Algonquian. *International Journal of American Linguistics* 56:449–483.

Heckewelder, John. [ca. 1795]. Vocabulary of the Shawanese Language. Manuscript 3670, American Philosophical Society, Philadelphia.

Hockett, Charles F. 1938. Kickapoo fieldnotes from Shawnee, Oklahoma. Manuscript at National Anthropological Archives, Smithsonian Museum Support Center, Suitland, Maryland.

Hockett, Charles F. 1985. Notes on Peoria & Miami. *Algonquian & Iroquoian Linguistics* 10(4):29–41.

Largillier, Jacques, S.J. [ca. 1700]. IllinoisFrench Dictionary. Manuscript in Watkinson Library, Trinity College, Hartford, Connecticut (manuscript formerly attributed to Gravier).

LeBoullenger, Antoine-Robert, S.J. [ca. 1725]. French and MiamiIllinois Dictionary. Manuscript at the John Carter Brown Library, Brown University, Providence, Rhode Island.

Michelson, Truman. 1916. Notes on Peoria. Manuscript 2721, National Anthropological Archives, Smithsonian Museum Support Center, Suitland, Maryland.

Pinet, Pierre-François. [ca. 1702]. French-Miami-Illinois Dictionary. Manuscript at the Archives des Jésuites au Canada, Montréal, Québec.

Thornton, William. 1802. Vocabulary of the Miami Language taken at the City of Washington. Manuscript at the American Philosophical Society, Philadelphia.

Trowbridge, Charles C. 1824–25. Unpublished notes on the Miami. Manuscripts at the Detroit Public Library, Detroit, Michigan.

Volney, Constantin F. C. de. 1968. *A View of the Soil and Climate of the United States of America.* New York: Hafner.

An Overview of Meskwaki Evidentiality

Amy Dahlstrom

Evidentials are grammatical markers which indicate the warrant for an utterance: for example, whether a reported event was witnessed firsthand, or whether the speaker was told about it by someone else.[1] For Algonquian, Murray (2016) demonstrates that Cheyenne exhibits a striking paradigm for expressing evidential notions. I show below that Meskwaki also encodes a similar set of evidential functions but the organization of the system is quite different from that of Cheyenne. Also discussed are other Meskwaki constructions which bear a resemblance to prototypical evidential constructions in expressing speaker uncertainty.

Preliminaries

Definition of Evidentiality

Brugman and Macaulay (2015), in a long survey article on evidentiality, posit the following definition:

(1) "two properties are criterial: (i) marking source of evidence and (ii) membership in grammatical categories. Other properties vary cross-linguistically: presence

> of epistemic, illocutionary, or mirative meaning; speaker deixis; obligatoriness; complementarity of meaning with other items; and truth-conditionality." (Brugman and Macaulay 2015:201)

Brugman and Macaulay take a fairly conservative position, viewing the issue of SOURCE OF EVIDENCE as criterial, along with stipulating that the evidentials must be expressed as a grammatical category and not, for example, with an optional adverb such as *reportedly* in English. Other properties that have been claimed to be part of evidentiality, such as the parameter of speaker certainty discussed below, are taken to be optional components which may vary cross-linguistically.

Cheyenne Evidential Paradigm

The most striking cases of an evidential opposition are those in which an evidential morpheme appears in a single inflectional slot, creating a paradigm of evidential possibilities. Cheyenne, as described by Murray (2016), is one such language. Consider the following set of examples from Murray 2016:493–494, citing forms from Leman 2011:

(2) a. É–hoo'koho–Ø.
3–rain–WTN
'It's raining, I witnessed.'

b. É–hoo'kȯhó–**nėse.**
3–rain–RPT.SG.INAN
'It's raining, they say.' or 'It's raining, I hear.'

c. É–hoo'kȯhó–**neho.**
3–rain–NAR.SG.INAN
'It rained, it's told.'

d. **Mó**–hoo'kȯhó–**hané**–**he.**
Q+3–rain–NEG_{INAN}–INF
'It's raining, I gather.' or 'It must be raining.'

In (2a) a verb with no overt morpheme in the evidential slot must be interpreted as the speaker having directly witnessed the described event. In (2b) the suffix *-nėse* indicates that the speaker is reporting what the speaker was told. (2c) exhibits a different suffix *-neho,* which marks the assertion as being part of a traditional narrative. (2d) contains an affix complex which marks the assertion as an inference on the part of the speaker.

Background on Verb Inflection

Some of the Meskwaki evidential categories are expressed by inflecting the verb of the clause in a specific paradigm. An explicit description of (part of) the verbal system may therefore be useful.[2] The opposition of INDEPENDENT ORDER and CONJUNCT ORDER inflection is familiar to Algonquianists; this opposition obtains in most of the daughter languages. Independent order verbs, as in (3) and (4) below, use a prefix position to the left of the verb stem to express a person feature for one of the arguments of the verb:[3]

(3) ke-wača·ho-Ø 'you (sg.) cook' [independent indicative]
2-cook-SG

(4) ke-wača·ho-petoke 'you (sg.) probably cook' [dubitative]
2-cook-DUB

The independent indicative verb in (3) bears the second person prefix *ke-*; since no plural marker is present in the suffix position, the second person argument is unambiguously singular. The dubitative paradigm exemplified in (4) likewise belongs to the independent order, as seen by the presence of the second person prefix *ke-*; its use is discussed in a later section of this paper.

Conjunct order verbs use a different set of morphemes to express person and number agreement with the argument(s) of the verb, and no person marker is prefixed to the verb stem. Instead, the left edge of the verb may be prefixed with the aorist prefix *e·h-*, serve as the locus of an ablaut process affecting the vowel of the first syllable of the verb stem (initial change), or have neither an aorist prefix nor initial change ("plain"). Meskwaki conjunct verbs also bear a final affix known as a MODE SUFFIX, which combines with the marking on the verb's left edge to indicate the specific paradigm within the conjunct order.[4] A later section of this paper discusses the use of conjunct verbs bearing the past tense/irrealis mode suffix *-ehe,* so it is necessary to provide some background on the mode suffixes here.

(5) e·h-wača·ho-yan-i 'that you (sg.) cooked' [aorist conjunct]
AOR-cook-2-MODE

(6) we·ča·hoyanini 'whenever you (sg.) cook' [iterative]
IC-wača·ho-yan-ini
IC-cook-2-MODE

(7) wača·ho-yan-e 'if you (sg.) cook' [subjunctive]
cook-2-MODE

In (5)–(7) the second person singular subject is expressed by the suffix *-yan,* completely unrelated to the second person morpheme found in the independent order forms in (3)–(4). The verb in (5) is marked as aorist conjunct by the combination of the prefix *e·h-* and the mode suffix *-i;* aorist conjunct verbs are used in subordinate clauses (and main clauses in narratives, as discussed below). The iterative form in (6) is marked by initial change applying to the first syllable of the stem plus the mode suffix *-ini;* such verbs are glossed 'whenever . . . ' The subjunctive form in (7), used for hypothetical conditional clauses and 'when' clauses referring to future time, requires only the mode suffix *-e;* neither initial change nor the aorist prefix is used in the subjunctive paradigm.

Conjunct participles, which function as relative clauses, fill the mode suffix slot with a suffix agreeing with the head of the relative clause:

(8) a. ke·no·na·ta 'the one (prox.) who spoke to him/her (obv.)'
IC-kano·n-a·-t-a [conjunct participle]
IC-speak.to-direct-3–3.head
b. ke·no·na·čini 'the one (obv.) whom he/she (prox.) spoke to'
IC-kano·n-a·-t-ini [conjunct participle]
IC-speak.to-direct-3–3.'head

The transitive verb forms in (8) are both suffixed with the direct theme sign *-a·,* indicating that the subject outranks the object on a hierarchy of non-third person > third person proximate > third person obviative, plus the person agreement suffix *-t,* encoding third person. In (8a) the final suffix *-a* indicates that the head of the relative clause is the third person proximate singular argument; in (8b) the third person obviative argument is marked as head of the relative clause.

The INTERROGATIVE ORDER in Meskwaki is organized in a fashion similar to that of the conjunct order. The left edge of the verb may undergo initial change, be prefixed with the aorist prefix, or be plain. A suffix *-w* appears in all interrogative paradigms after the theme sign and before the person/number suffix; an additional suffix *-e·n* appears in almost all of the interrogative order paradigms.[5] As in the conjunct order, a mode suffix appears in the final suffix position.

(9) mehkaw-a·-**w**-an-**e·n**-i — 'you (sg.) apparently found him/her'
find-direct-**interr**-2-**interr**-mode — [plain interrogative]

(10) we·ča·hokwe·na — 'whoever cooks'
IC-wača·ho-**w**-k-**e·n**-a — [interrogative participle]
IC-cook-**interr**-3-**interr**-3.head

In (9) the interrogative suffix *-w* occurs after the direct theme sign *-a·*, which indicates that the subject of 'find' outranks the object. The second person singular subject is expressed by the suffix *-an*, which is in turn followed by the interrogative suffix *-e·n*. The mode suffix slot is filled with *-i*. Note that the verb in (9) is plain, neither bearing an aorist prefix nor having undergone initial change. (The evidential function of the plain interrogative is discussed further below.) (10) likewise belongs to the interrogative order: as a participle, its mode suffix slot is filled with a suffix agreeing with the head of the relative clause. Note further that in (10) the suffix sequence of *-w-k* metathesizes to *kw*.

The label of "interrogative" for this set of paradigms dates back at least to Jones 1911:826, motivated by the use of interrogative participles as in (10) to express embedded questions. Embedded questions are described in detail by Dahlstrom (2019). In general, the paradigms belonging to the interrogative order perform various irrealis functions (Dahlstrom 2019); Goddard (2006b:189ff) analyzes the *-w* suffix of the interrogative order as an irrealis suffix which derives ultimately from a Proto-Algonquian negative.[6]

Meskwaki Evidentials

With this background information on the Cheyenne paradigm in (2) and the organization of Meskwaki verb inflection, let us now examine how Meskwaki indicates a speaker's warrant for making a statement. Meskwaki expresses the same range of evidential functions as the Cheyenne system—hearsay/inference/traditional narrative—but Meskwaki exhibits what Brugman and Macaulay (2015:224) term the SCATTERED type of system. That is, the evidential markers are not in a single morphological slot forming a paradigmatic opposition. Instead, the strategies employed in Meskwaki include a second-position enclitic particle, an inflectional paradigm specialized for one of the evidential functions, and appearance of a subordinate clause verbal paradigm in main clause contexts to mark another function. Each of these strategies is explicated below.

Hearsay: Second-Position Enclitic =ipi

Meskwaki exhibits a number of second-position enclitic particles which attach to the first phonological word of the clause, most with pragmatic functions such as emphasis or contrastive focus (Goddard 2015). A particularly frequent second-position enclitic is the hearsay evidential *=ipi.* (Note that the first vowel of this enclitic is frequently deleted by clitic sandhi [cf. Goddard 1991].)

(11) *=ipi* < *ipi* 'one says (thus), people say (thus)'
i- 'say thus' + *-pi* 'X' (unspecified subject, independent indicative)

=ipi is a grammaticalized form of the Animate Intransitive verb stem *i-* 'say thus' inflected with the suffix *-pi,* the independent indicative form of the unspecified subject suffix denoting people in general.

The textual passage in (12), taken from a long text published in Dahlstrom 2003, illustrates the function of *=ipi.* The context of this passage is that the Meskwakis have defeated the Sioux, their traditional enemies, in a battle, killing all but one. The one survivor is sent home to tell the story and given detailed instructions about what to say. The hero ends with, 'As for you, right when you finish talking is when you will die.' The Sioux man goes back home, recounts what happened in the battle and says, 'As for me <HEARSAY EVIDENTIAL> I will die.'

(12) "ki·nake·hwi·na ki·šetone·moyanemeko i·ni wi·hnepo·hiyani," e·hineči,

"ki·na=ke·hi=wi·na ki·šetone·mo-yane=meko
you=moreover=CONTRAST PERF.talk-2/SUBJUNCT=EMPH
i·ni wi·h-nepo·hi-yani," e·h-in-eči,
then FUT-die-2/AOR AOR-say.thus.to-X>3/AOR
'"But as for you, right when you finish talking
is when you will die," he was told,'
[nine clauses intervene]
ki·ša·čimočimeko, "ni·nake·hwi·na**pi** ni·hnepo·hi," e·hišiwe·či.
e·ha·htawa·sa·hiči e·hnepo·hiči.
IC-ki·ša·čimo-či=meko,
IC-PERF.tell.story-3/CH.CONJ=EMPH
"ni·na=ke·hi=wi·na=**ipi** n-i·h-nepo·hi-Ø," e·h-išiwe·-či.
I=moreover=CONTRAST=**HRSY** 1-FUT-die-1/IND AOR-declare.thus-3/AOR
e·h-a·htawa·sa·hi-či e·h-nepo·hi-či.
AOR-suddenly.fall.on.back.DIM-3/AOR AOR-die-3/AOR
'After he had finished the whole story,
"And as for me, **they say** I will die," he declared.
'The poor guy keeled over backward and died.' (Dahlstrom 2003:43–44)

Since the source of the Meskwaki hearsay evidential is a verb of quoting, one might ask if the form in (12) is merely an instance of a quoting verb. The answer to that question is no: the enclitic seen in (12) and elsewhere has undergone grammaticalization to become an evidential particle and is not functioning as a verb. Evidence against analyzing *=ipi* in (12) as an ordinary verb of quoting comes from the shift of person between the two parts of (12). In the represented speech containing the evidential, the subject of *nepo·hi-* 'die' is first person. But if *=ipi* were functioning as a quoting verb framing a direct quotation, we would see a second person subject of 'die,' matching the earlier utterance. Alternatively, if the represented speech were presented as indirect quotation (possible though infrequent in Meskwaki), the verb *nepo·hi-* 'die' would be inflected in the aorist conjunct paradigm, used for subordinate clauses, instead of in the independent indicative paradigm found in main clauses. Since the clause in question exhibits both a shift in person and main clause independent indicative inflection, it is clear that *=ipi* here is not a regular quoting verb but instead a grammaticalized evidential particle.

The passage in (13), taken from the text in Dahlstrom 1996, provides a further example of the use of *=ipi,* here reporting what the subject was told in a vision or dream:

(13) o·ni·na oškinawe·he·ha, "nahi, natawi-po·ni-mahkate·wi·no,"
e·hineči e·hina·hpawa·či.

o·ni=i·na	oškinawe·he·ha	"nahi,	natawi–po·ni–mahkate·wi·-no,"
and.then=that	young.man.DIM	okay,	time.to–stop–fast-2/IMP

e·h-in-eči	e·h-ina·hpawa·-či.	[. . .]
AOR-say.thus.to-X>3/AOR	AOR-dream.thus-3/AOR	.

pye·ya·niči o·sani, e·ha·čimoha·či e·na·hpawa·či. "ni·hpo·ni**pi**–mahkate·wi," . . .

IC-pya·-niči	o·s-ani,	e·h-a·čimoh-a·či	IC-ina·hpawa·-či.
IC-come-3′/CH.CONJ	3.father-OBV	AOR-tell-3>3′/AOR	IC-dream.thus-3/PART/OBL

"n-i·h-po·ni–=**ipi**–mahkate·wi·-Ø," . . .
1-FUT-stop–=**HRSY**–fast-1/IND

'And then that young teenage boy, "Okay, it's time for you to stop fasting," he dreamed that he was told. [. . .]
When his father came, he told him what he had dreamed.
"**They said** I should stop fasting," . . . ' (Dahlstrom 1996:130)

In (13) we again see the hearsay evidential *=ipi* used to report a previous utterance. The original utterance is by the spirits whom the young man sees in a dream; they tell the young man to stop fasting, using an imperative form with second person singular inflection. The young man then reports this to his father, changing the imperative to a statement, shifting the person of the subject of *po·ni–mahkate·wi·-* 'stop fasting' to first person singular, and attaching the evidential enclitic to the right of the first phonological word, the preverb *po·ni–*'stop, cease.'

Inference: Plain Interrogative Inflection

A very different strategy is employed in Meskwaki to indicate that an utterance is an inference: that is, that the speaker is deducing after the fact that something has occurred. Such utterances are marked by inflecting the verb in the plain interrogative paradigm, analyzed in (9). For example, the context for (14) is that the speaker has seen tracks in the snow and signs of a struggle. He infers that a bear has killed his son:

(14) nesekokwe·nima·hi·na mahkwani

nes-**ekokwe·ni**=ma·hi=i·na mahkw-ani

kill-3′>3/**PLAIN.INTERR**=after.all=that.ANIM bear-OBV

'A bear must have killed that guy, after all.' (Dahlstrom 1996:140)

An additional example of plain interrogative verbal inflection marking an utterance as an inference may be seen in (15):

(15) aniwisa·hikwe·ni

aniwisa·hi-**kwe·ni**

run.fast.DIM-3/**PLAIN.INTERR**

'He must have run fast.' (Kiyana 1913:1005)

(15) is from a long text about the culture hero Wisahkeha; the speakers are young women who failed to keep up with a no longer visible Wisahkeha and infer that Wisahkeha must have run so fast that he is out of sight.

The following example illustrates the use of plain interrogative verb inflection with a first person subject:

(16) ki·ša·kotekwa·mo·hiwa·ne·ni

ki·ša·kotekwa·mo·hi-**wa·ne·ni**

sleep.soundly.DIM-1/**PLAIN.INTERR**

'I must have been sound asleep.' (Kiyana 1913:496)

(16) shows that the inferential evidential can be used about one's own previous experiences if one is not conscious at the time.

The expression of the inferential evidential with verb inflection is formally distinct from the use of a second-position enclitic to express the hearsay evidential, illustrating the scattered nature of Meskwaki evidentiality.

Traditional Narratives: Aorist Conjunct Inflection on Verbs in Main Clauses

Like Cheyenne, Meskwaki has a way of indicating that a narrative is a traditional one, rather than a personal story. Aorist conjunct verb inflection, illustrated above in (5), has as its primary function encoding subject and object agreement in subordinate clauses, both complement clauses subcategorized for by the matrix verb and adjunct clauses expressing adverbial notions. In traditional Meskwaki narratives, however, we find aorist conjunct inflection appearing also in the main clauses of the sentences of the story.[7] (17) is one of countless examples that could be provided of this use, here as the very first sentence of a story.

(17) našawaye nekoti neniwa okwisani e·hmahkate·wi·na·či

našawaye	nekoti	neniwa	o-kwis-ani	**e·h**-mahkate·wi·n-**a·či**
long.ago	one	man	3-son-OBV	AOR-make.O.fast-3>3′/**AOR**

'Long ago a certain man made his son fast.' (Dahlstrom 1996:129)

Other examples of main clause aorist conjunct verbs may be seen in the nonquoted segments of (12) and (13) above.

Personal narratives, on the other hand, such as *The Autobiography of a Meskwaki Woman* (Goddard 2006a), use independent indicative inflection in many of the main clauses:

(18) ke·htenameko ke·keya·h nenahiha·wa

ke·htena=meko	ke·keya·hi	**ne**-nahih-**a·wa**
truly=EMPH	eventually	1-know.how.to.make-1>3/**IND**

'I really did learn how to make it [a yarn belt] eventually.' (Goddard 2006a:32)

Here the narrator is telling about her own life, rather than relating a traditional story, so the regular independent indicative inflection for main clauses is used.[8]

Hearsay Enclitics in Narratives

The Cheyenne system makes a clear distinction between the reportative evidential and the narrative evidential: only one can be chosen for the inflectional slot. Since Meskwaki evidentiality is of the scattered sort, there is no paradigmatic blocking preventing a hearsay enclitic being used in narratives, as will be shown in the subsections below.

Shifts to Independent Indicative within the Narrative

A fairly common phenomenon in Meskwaki narrative texts is that the narrator will sometimes step out of the narrative mode, adding background information as a remark in one of the inflectional paradigms typical of face-to-face conversation. Such asides are often accompanied by the hearsay evidential:

(19) aniwe·we·kesiniwanipi pe·hki i·nini ahkohko·ni,

aniwe·we·kesi-**niwani=ipi**	pe·hki	i·nini	ahkohkw-ani,
have.loud.sound-3′/**IND=HRSY**	really	that.ANIM.OBV	drum-OBV

'That drum really had a loud sound, it's said, . . . ' (Dahlstrom 2015:191)

The verb in (19) is inflected in the independent indicative, used for nonnegated main clause assertions.

Negated main clauses express negation with the negative particle *a·kwi* 'not' plus negative inflection on the verb. This pattern is also seen in asides by a narrator, and may be accompanied by a hearsay evidential:

(20) na·hka a·kwipi nahi-mi·hkemehkwe·we·čini,

na·hka	a·kwi=**ipi**	nahi–mi·hkemehkwe·we·-čini,
also	not=**HRSY**	be.given.to–court.women-3/**NEG**

'Also, it's said, he never chased women, . . . ' (Dahlstrom 2015:188)

In contrast to (20), (21) illustrates how narrative clauses marked with the evidential strategy of employing aorist conjunct inflection on main clauses express negation: a negative preverb *pwa·wi–*'not' is added to the verb complex, allowing the aorist conjunct inflection to surround the preverb-verb compound:

(21) e·hpwa·wi–ki·šihto·či na·tawino·ni

e·h-pwa·wi–ki·šiht-**o·či**	na·tawino·ni
AOR-not–fix-3>0/**AOR**	medicine

'He hadn't prepared any medicine.' (Dahlstrom 2003:36)

Another syntactic construction typical of main clauses in face-to-face conversation is an equational sentence with a zero copula. Such equational sentences are also found as asides by a narrator and are likely to include a hearsay evidential:

(22) oškinawe·he·hanipi ke·hekwičini.
oškinawe·he·h-ani=**ipi** IC-kehekwi-čini.
young.man.DIM-OBV=**HRSY** IC-lose.O2.as captive 3/PART/3′
'It was a young teenage boy, it's said, who gave him the slip.' (Dahlstrom 2015:146)

The second word in (22) is a conjunct participle, 'the one who gave him the slip,' equated with the clause-initial noun.

Asides such as (19), (20), and (22) break the sequence of foregrounded clauses advancing the narrative, and thus are not expressed using the aorist conjunct paradigm typical of traditional narratives. At the same time, such asides present information that the narrator does not know from firsthand experience, and the hearsay evidential is therefore appropriate.

Evidential Particles at Episode Boundaries

Besides the use of the hearsay evidential in asides by the narrator, the enclitic *=ipi* may sometimes occur at the start of a new episode of the story (cf. Dahlstrom 1996 for discussion of episode structure):

(23) kaho·nipi e·howi·wiči.
kaho·ni=**ipi** e·h-owi·wi-či.
so.then=**HRSY** AOR-have.wife-3/**AOR**
'So then, it's said, he got married.' (Dahlstrom 2015:187)

The following sentences in the episode typically do not occur with the hearsay evidential, but rather simply use the main clause aorist conjunct inflection to indicate that this is part of a traditional narrative.[9]

Speaker Certainty

Some descriptions of evidential systems include forms marking the extent of speaker certainty (cf. Brugman and Macaulay 2015:205ff). If this parameter is taken to be part of evidentiality, then Meskwaki exhibits even more evidential distinctions, all expressed by the choice of verbal inflectional paradigm, as illustrated in this section.[10]

Dubitative

The DUBITATIVE mode of the independent order is used for speculations, and is often glossed 'probably' or 'must.' Cognate forms of this inflectional paradigm are reported to have evidential functions in Cree dialects (cf. Déchaine et al. 2017).[11]

(24) owiye·ha kekaka·čihekowa·toke

owiye·ha	ke-kaka·čih-**ekowa·toke**
someone	2-joke.with-3>2P/**DUB**

'Probably someone was playing a joke on you two.' (Kiyana 1913:103)

(25) i·nina·hwe·na na·hkači ki·hka·nena·naki šawesi·toke·hiki

i·nina·hi=we·na	na·hkači	ki·hka·nena·naki	šawesi-·**toke·hiki**
then=rather	again	our.friends	be.hungry-3P/**DUB**

'By this time our friends must be hungry again.' (Kiyana 1913:298)

Utterances expressed with dubitative inflection are based upon the speaker's general knowledge of what is likely and may refer to past, present, or future events. In contrast, utterances expressed with plain interrogative inflection are specific deductions about a past event based upon present evidence, typically visual evidence.

Remote Past

Some paradigms within the conjunct order form a remote past by replacing the regular mode suffix for that paradigm with the mode suffix *-ehe*. The resulting forms may be used for events in the past or to express speaker uncertainty, or both (cf. Thomason 2003:71). Example (26) illustrates the PAST AORIST CONJUNCT on a complement clause:

(26) šewe·na ayo·hmeko ki·hpya·ya·ni,
e·hkehke·netama·ni e·hkemo·temiwa·tehe aša·haki.

"šewe·na	ayo·hi=meko	IC-ki·h-pya·-ya·ni,
but	here=EMPH	IC-PERF-come-1/CH.CONJ

e·h-kehke·net-ama·ni	**e·h**-kemo·tem-iwa·**tehe**	aša·h-aki."
AOR-know-1>0/AOR	AOR-steal.O2.from-3P>1/**PAST.AOR**	Sioux-PL

'But after I came back here,
I realized that the Sioux had stolen it [a canoe] from me.' (Dahlstrom 2015:162)

In (26), the use of *-ehe* on the complement clause makes it explicit that the time of the theft was earlier than the time of the speaker's realization.

(27) illustrates the use of the suffix–*ehe* with negative inflection, producing a PAST NEGATIVE:

(27) a·kwiča·hye·toke nana·ši mešotehe i·niya nemešo·ha
     a·kwi=ča·hi=ye·toke nana·ši mešw-et**ehe**
     not=so=it.seems ever hit.with.shot-X>3/**PAST.NEG**
     i·niya nemešo·ha
     that.ABSENT my.grandfather
     'My late grandfather was never hit in battle, it seems.' (Michelson 1927:70)

Both (26) and (27) describe past events that were not witnessed directly by the speaker, illustrating the close connection between past tense and speaker uncertainty. Relatedly, Murray (2016:496) observes that the Cheyenne remote past co-occurs with the narrative evidential.

Changed Unreal: Mirative/Surprise

The CHANGED UNREAL occurs with the particle *keye·hapa* 'it turned out that . . . ' and displays the same suffix *-ehe* that occurs in the remote past. Mirative marking (i.e., marking of unexpected or surprising information) is closely connected to evidentiality in a number of languages (cf. Brugman and Macaulay 2015:209ff).

(28) keye·hapake·hwi·na išemeko e·šimikehe . . .
     keye·hapa=ke·hi=wi·na iše=meko IC-išim-ik**ehe**
     it.turned.out=moreover=but just=EMPH IC-speak.thus.to-X>1/**CH.UNR**
     'Actually, though, I was just being told that . . . ' (Goddard 2006a:18)

(29) keye·hapake·hipi i·nini mahkwani a·wahki·kwe·sahekotehe
     keye·hapa=ke·hi=ipi i·nini mahkw-ani
     it.turned.out=moreover=HRSY that.OBV bear-OBV

     IC-a·wahki·kwe·sah-ekot**ehe**
     IC-scratch.O.face-3′>3/**CH.UNR**
     'But it turned out, they say, that the bear had scratched her face.' (Kiyana 1913:122)

Note that the hearsay evidential =*ipi* also appears in (29). (29) is hearsay from the point of view of the narrator speaking to the audience. The surprise is in the world of the story.

Conclusion

Using the conservative definition of evidentiality proposed by Brugman and Macaulay 2015, we may say that Meskwaki distinguishes three types of indirect evidence: hearsay, inference, and traditional narratives. These are the same distinctions made in the Cheyenne system and ones frequently found crosslinguistically in languages with evidential marking. A significant difference between the Cheyenne system and that of Meskwaki is that the Cheyenne morphemes indicating evidentiality occur in a single slot of the inflectional template, forming a neat paradigm, while evidential morphology in Meskwaki is realized in a "scattered" fashion. The scattered nature of Meskwaki evidentials permits an overlap in the distribution of the hearsay enclitic and the inflectional marking of a story as a traditional narrative. We may further conjecture that Meskwaki clauses with no overt evidential morphology are simply unmarked for source of evidence, rather than being explicitly marked as "witnessed," as in the Cheyenne system (cf. Brugman and Macaulay 2015:226ff on obligatoriness and complementarity).

Meskwaki also exhibits a number of inflectional verb paradigms specialized for indicating the extent of speaker certainty, a semantic parameter often included in discussions of evidentiality, including strategies for indicating speculation, uncertainty due to an event occurring in the remote past, and a mirative inflection indicating surprise.

NOTES

1. Thanks to Ives Goddard, Lucy Thomason, and others in the audience at the 49th Algonquian conference for their comments, and thanks also to Adam Singerman and the two anonymous reviewers for this paper.
2. See Goddard 1994:187–207; 1995 for full listings of the Meskwaki inflectional paradigms.
3. Abbreviations in the Meskwaki examples: 3′ = obviative, 0 = inanimate, ABSENT = absentative demonstrative, ANIM = animate, AOR = aorist prefix; aorist conjunct inflection, CH.CONJ = changed conjunct, CH.UNR = changed unreal, CONTRAST =

contrastive, DIM = diminutive, DUB= dubitative, EMPH = emphatic, FUT = future, HRSY= hearsay evidential, IC = initial change (ablaut rule), IMP = imperative, INAN = inanimate, IND = independent indicative, NAR = narrative evidential, NEG= negative inflection, O = (first) object, O2 = second object, OBL = oblique head of relative clause, OBV = obviative, PART = conjunct participle, PAST.AOR = past aorist conjunct, PAST.NEG = past negative inflection, PERF = perfective, PLAIN.INTERR = plain interrogative inflection, RPT = reportative evidential, SUBJUNCT = subjunctive, WTN = direct/witness evidential, X = unspecified subject. Subject and object features in verb inflection are separated by > and are followed by identification of the verbal paradigm. The head of a relative clause is identified following the label PART (participle). Vowel length is marked by a raised dot.

4. Most of the daughter languages have lost the Proto-Algonquian final vowels, with concomitant loss of many of the mode suffixes.
5. The prioritive paradigm, used to express that one event took place before another, lacks the *-e·n* suffix.
6. In this regard, note that the Cheyenne inferential evidential includes a negative morpheme in its complex of affixes (example (2d)).
7. Evidence that a particular clause is the main clause includes the clause being the only one in a given sentence; containing a matrix verb subcategorizing a complement clause; being the clause that advances the action of the narrative. See Dahlstrom 2006 for more detailed discussion.
8. See Cook 2014:92ff. for a discussion of the evidential function of main clause conjunct verb forms in Plains Cree.
9. But see Thomason 2015:329 for a writer who uses the hearsay evidential throughout.
10. Two more inflectional paradigms may be mentioned here, both archaic and rare. The CONCLUSIVE (e.g., *-hapa* third singular) is used for definite conclusions, often in exclamations, and the ASSERTIVE is used for strong assertions (e.g., *-·pani* third singular). See Goddard 1995 for discussion and examples; cognate forms are used as evidentials in Mi'gmaq (Inglis 2003) and in the Cree-Innu dialect continuum (James et al. 2001; Déchaine et al. 2017).
11. See also the discussion of dubitative forms in Nishnaabemwin in Valentine 2001:832ff.

REFERENCES

Brugman, Claudia, and Monica Macaulay. 2015. Characterizing Evidentiality. *Linguistic Typology* 19(2):201–237.

Cook, Clare. 2014. *The Clause-Typing System of Plains Cree: Indexicality, Anaphoricity, and*

Contrast. Oxford: Oxford University Press.

Dahlstrom, Amy. 1996. Narrative Structure of a Fox Text. *nikotwâsik iskwâhtêm, pâakihtêpayih! Studies in Honour of H. C. Wolfart,* ed. by J. D. Nichols and A. C. Ogg, pp. 113–162. Algonquian and Iroquoian Memoir 13. Winnipeg: Algonquian and Iroquoian Linguistics.

Dahlstrom, Amy. 2003. Warrior Powers from an Underwater Spirit: Cultural and Linguistic Aspects of an Illustrated Meskwaki Text. *Anthropological Linguistics* 45:1–56.

Dahlstrom, Amy. 2006. The Syntax of Algonquian Ethnopoetics. *Actes du Trente-Septième Congrès des Algonquinistes,* ed. by H. C. Wolfart, pp. 131–147. Winnipeg: University of Manitoba.

Dahlstrom, Amy. 2015. Highlighting Rhetorical Structure through Syntactic Analysis: An Illustrated Meskwaki Text by Alfred Kiyana. *New Voices for Old Words: Algonquian Oral Literatures,* ed. by David J. Costa, pp. 118–197. Lincoln: University of Nebraska Press.

Dahlstrom, Amy. 2019. Embedded Questions in Meskwaki. *Papers of the Forty-Eighth Algonquian Conference,* ed. by Monica Macaulay and Margaret Noodin, pp. 69–85. East Lansing: Michigan State University Press.

Déchaine, Rose-Marie, Monique Dufresne, and Charlotte Reinholtz. 2017. (Ir)realis Dubitative in the Cree Dialect Continuum. Paper read at the 49th Algonquian Conference, Montreal.

Goddard, Ives. 1991. Observations Regarding Fox (Mesquakie) Phonology. *Papers of the Twenty-Second Algonquian Conference,* ed. by William Cowan, pp. 157–181. Ottawa: Carleton University.

Goddard, Ives. 1994. *Leonard Bloomfield's Fox Lexicon: Critical Edition.* Algonquian and Iroquoian Linguistics, Memoir 12. Winnipeg: Algonquian and Iroquoian Linguistics.

Goddard, Ives. 1995. Notes on Fox (Mesquakie) Inflection: Minor Modes and Incompletely Described Morphemes. *Papers of the Twenty-Sixth Algonquian Conference,* ed. by David H. Pentland, pp. 124–150. Winnipeg: University of Manitoba.

Goddard, Ives. 2006a. *The Autobiography of a Meskwaki Woman.* Winnipeg: Algonquian and Iroquoian Linguistics.

Goddard, Ives. 2006b. The Proto-Algonquian Negative and Its Descendants. *Actes du Trente-Septième Congrès des Algonquinistes,* ed. by H. C. Wolfart, pp. 161–208. Winnipeg: University of Manitoba.

Goddard, Ives. 2015. The Twenty-Nine Enclitics of Meskwaki. *Papers of the Forty-Third Algonquian Conference,* ed. by Monica Macaulay and J. Randolph Valentine, pp. 72–116. Albany: SUNY Press.

Inglis, Stephanie. 2003. The Deferential Evidential in Mi'kmaq. *Papers of the Thirty-Fourth Algonquian Conference,* ed. by H. C. Wolfart, pp. 193–200. Winnipeg: University of Manitoba.

James, Deborah, Sandra Clarke, and Marguerite MacKenzie. 2001. The Encoding of Information Source in Algonquian: Evidentials in Cree/Montagnais/Naskapi. *International Journal of American Linguistics* 67:229–263.

Jones, William. 1911. Algonquian (Fox). *Handbook of North American Languages,* pt. 1, ed. by Franz Boas, pp. 735–834. Bureau of American Ethnology Bulletin 40. Washington, DC: GPO.

Kiyana, Alfred. 1913. *wisakea osani okyeni osimeani okomeseani* [Wisahkeha, his father, his mother, his younger brother, his grandmother]. Manuscript 2958-a, National Anthropological Archives, Smithsonian Institution, Washington, DC.

Leman, Wayne. 2011. *A Reference Grammar of the Cheyenne Language.* n.p.: Lulu Press.

Michelson, Truman. 1927. *Contributions to Fox Ethnology.* Bureau of American Ethnology Bulletin 85. Washington: GPO.

Murray, Sarah E. 2016. Evidentiality and Illocutionary Mood in Cheyenne. *International Journal of American Linguistics* 82:487–517.

Thomason, Lucy. 2003. *The Proximate and Obviative Contrast in Meskwaki.* PhD dissertation, University of Texas.

Thomason, Lucy. 2015. On Editing Bill Leaf's Meskwaki Texts. *New Voices for Old Words: Algonquian Oral Literatures,* edited by David J. Costa, pp. 315–452. Lincoln: University of Nebraska Press.

Valentine, J. Randolph. 2001. *Nishnaabemwin Reference Grammar.* Toronto: University of Toronto Press.

The Paradox of Partial Similarity

Unami Secondary-Object Marking and Other Clones of the N-Endings

Ives Goddard

The Eastern Algonquian language Unami has a great deal of morphological complexity, apparently distinguishing a greater number of grammatical categories than any other Eastern language, though the rather divergent Micmac may challenge this claim.[1] It is assumed here that morphology, the grammatical structure of words, repays study in its own right, separate from, though of course linked to, syntax. Inconveniently, however, Unami morphophonemic rules are extremely complex, and the resulting variation in the surface shapes of morphemes often makes the parsing of words challenging. The phonological rules that convert underlying forms (given here between bars) into surface phonemic transcriptions are in Goddard 1979: Foreword, revising pp. 20–26).

The data presented are specifically from Southern Unami (ISO: **unm**), which has also been called Oklahoma Delaware and Lenape. Examples are from the translations of Ira D. Blanchard, done in what is now Kansas between 1834 and 1842 (Goddard 2019, principally Blanchard 1837 [1839]), and from materials obtained by C. F. Voegelin (mostly in 1938; Voegelin 1945, 1946) and myself (1966–70).

Morphology and Terminology

Verb Types

The Unami verb types (1) are those generally found in Algonquian languages. They include AI and TA stems lexically specified as taking a secondary object, which may be of either gender (the AI+O and TA+O).[2] In both these cases the secondary object corresponds to an English direct object; with a double-object TA (TA+O) the primary object is the English indirect object.[3]

(1) *Verb types in Unami*

Animate intransitive (AI)
Inanimate intransitive (II)
Transitive animate (TA)
Transitive inanimate (TI; classes la, lb, 2, and 3)
AI taking a secondary object (transitivized AI; AI+O)
TA taking a secondary object (double-object TA; TA+O)
TI not taking an object (objectless TI; TI-O)

The verb types are lexical categories, but many verbs that take a secondary object are also lexically subcategorized as being used without one, as ordinary AIs and TAs. Similarly, many objectless TIs also have a use as ordinary TIs, with an object.

Syntactic Roles

The syntactic roles of nominals (2) include not only subject and the two kinds of object, but also oblique (of two kinds) and adjunct (which, strictly speaking, has no syntactic role). Transitive verbs in the independent indicative mode have both an objective inflection, indicating that the object (or inverse subject) is a definite third person, and an absolute inflection, indicating that the object (or inverse subject) is an indefinite third person. (If the subject is the indefinite person [X] this contrast of definiteness is not made, and only ostensibly objective inflections exist.) When the definite object (or inverse subject) is a nominal, the inflection functions as agreement. When there is no overt nominal object (or inverse subject), an objective verb makes pronominal reference to the argument, and an absolute verb may be used for an indefinite object ('some, any'). The independent indicative also has an objective inflection for definite secondary objects; an indefinite secondary object is indicated by an ordinary AI or TA inflection on an AI+O or TA+O verb.

(2) Syntactic roles of nominals in Unami

Arguments:

subject

primary object (first object)

definite vs. indefinite (with independent indicative verb)

secondary object (second object)

definite vs. indefinite (with independent indicative verb)

Obliques:

oblique complement of relative root (initial or stem having an oblique valence)

instrumental oblique (complement of a verb subcategorized for an instrumental)

Adjuncts:

not syntactically linked to any word

An oblique complement of a relative root and an instrumental oblique have lexically licensed syntactic links to a verb (except if the relative root is in a free particle), but adjuncts by definition are not verbal complements.

Verbal Orders and Modes

The Unami verbal modes are given in (3) to provide context, but only the two modes of the independent order and the participle will be relevant in what follows. The subordinative mode is an innovation of Eastern Algonquian (Goddard 1974:320, 1983).

(3) Verbal orders and modes in Unami

Independent order

independent indicative (IND)

independent subordinative (SBD)

Conjunct order

plain conjunct; perhaps not distinct from the changed conjunct

changed conjunct

subjunctive

changed subjunctive
participle (PPL): an internally headed relative clause

Imperative order

imperative
negative imperative, or prohibitive
future (or contingent) imperative

Independent Indicative Mode

Independent Indicative Central Ending Sets

There are three central ending sets used with contrastive functions in the independent indicative, each characterized by a different formative element, which comes first in the ending complex (4, 5). These are used with pronominal prefixes: |nə-| 1, |kə-| 2, |wə-| 3. The m-endings have no third person prefix and mark the third person with a suffix $|\text{-w}|_{\text{m}}$, which is not the same as the $|\text{-w}|_{\text{w}}$ that is the formative of the w-endings.[4] The m-endings have taken over the inflection for an indefinite person (X) subject from the n-endings, but the ending sets otherwise remain distinct.

(4) Unami independent indicative central ending sets

	m-endings (w. 2 prefixes)	w-endings (w. 3 prefixes)	n-endings (w. 3 prefixes)
1s	|-(əhm-)|	$|\text{-w}|_{\text{w}}$	|-ən(ē-)|
2s	|-(əhm-)|	$|\text{-w}|_{\text{w}}$	|-ən(ē-)|
3s	(see 3,0)	$|\text{-w}|_{\text{w}}$	|-ən(ē-)|
X	|-ən(ē-)| (= n-ending)	$|\text{-w}|_{\text{w}}$	|-ən(ē-)|
1p	|-əhmənā|	|-wənā(n-)|	|-ənēn(ā(n)-)|
12	|-əhmənā|	|-wənā(n-)|	|-ənēn(ā(n)-)|
2p	|-əhmwā|	|-wəwā(w-)|	|-ənēwā(w-)|
3p	(see 3,0)	|-wəwā(w-)|	|-ənēwā(w-)|
3,0	$|\text{-w}|_{\text{m}}$		

The uses of the n-endings are summarized in (5) and explained in greater detail below, with examples in (6–11). The m-endings are used for intransitives, in TA forms that have no third person (themes 3 and 4),[5] and to furnish the absolute inflection of transitive verbs, which is used if the object (or inverse subject) is indefinite, or if there is no object (with a TI-O). The w-endings are used for TA verbs with definite primary objects (or inverse subjects).[6]

(5) Use of the Unami central ending sets in the independent indicative

m-endings:

AI and II

TA themes 3 and 4

TA themes 1 and 2 absolute (i.e., with indefinite object, or inverse subject)

TI absolute (i.e., with indefinite object)

TI-O (i.e., with no object)

w-endings:

TA themes 1 and 2 objective (i.e., with definite primary object or inverse subject; also, with indefinite person [X] subject)

n-endings:

TI objective (i.e., with definite object; also, with indefinite person [X] subject)

TA inverse objective with definite inanimate subject

AI+O objective (i.e., with definite secondary object)

TA+O objective (i.e., with definite secondary object)

AI, TA, TI with definite oblique, instrumental, or adjunct

Independent Indicative N-Endings

In the independent indicative the n-endings are used in several ways. Their core contrastive function may be taken to be making the TI objective paradigm, marking agreement with (or referring pronominally to) the definite object of a TI (6).[7]

(6) N-ending for the definite object of a TI

a. nəmáxkamən 'I found it' (B, V; |maxk-| TI(1a) 'find', |nə–amən| 1s–$0s_{(1a)}$/IND)

b. nəwe·t·ənəmə́na 'I picked them (inan.) up' (OA; |wētən-| TI(1b) 'pick up, take, receive', |nə–əməna| 1s–$0p_{(1b)}$/IND)

c. no·wá·to·n 'I know it' (B, V, OA, ME; |wəwāht-| TI(2) 'know', |nə–ōn| 1s–$0s_{(2)}$/IND)

d. mwí·č·i·n 'he or she ate it' (B, V, OA, ME; |mīčī-| TI(3) 'eat', |wə–n| 3s–$0s_{(3)}$/IND)

They are also used, in a reciprocal fashion, with a TA stem and an inverse theme sign to indicate a definite (or pronominal) inanimate subject (7):

(7) N-ending for the definite inanimate subject of a TA

a. mɔnt·uwwá·k·an ntap·i·tá·k·o·n 'his spiritual power is in me' (B; |wə-| 3s, |manətōwəwākan| IN power'; |apīhtaw-| TA 'be in', |nət–əkōn| 0s–1s/IND)

b. mwəšhika·k·wəné·ɔ 'they were infected by it' (ME; |məšəhkaw-| TA 'benefit, infect', |wə–əkwənēwā| 0s–3p/IND)

c. mo·šə́š·a kkwi·tələt·əwá·k·an ntəlkó·ne·n 'Moses's law tells us' (B; mo·šə́š·a 'Moses (abs.)'; |wə-| 3s, |kwəhtələtəwākan| 'law'; |əl-| TA 'say {so} to', |nə–əkōnēn| 0s–1p/IND)

N-endings are similarly used for the definite secondary object of a TA+O (8) or an AI+O (9). The use of an n-ending for the subject (or inverse object, as in 8e) specifies the secondary object as definite, or (as in 8a–f) pronominal. As in their core function, n-endings in the additional functions surveyed here (except, apparently, when used for obliques) may be followed by a peripheral (outer) suffix for a plural or obviative (6b, 8b–f, 9b,c, 13a,b). The animate plural suffix with a singular subject was |-āk| for the speakers I heard (8c,d, 9b); Blanchard appears consistently to have |-ak| (9c, 13b). After the plural n-endings the vowel of the peripheral suffixes is |ī| (8e, 13a).

(8) N-ending for the definite secondary object of a TA+O

a. nəmí·la·n 'I gave it to him, them' (B, ME; |mīl-| TA+O 'give O2 to', |nə–ān| 1s–3+0s/IND)

b. nəmi·lá·na 'I gave him (obv.), them (inan.) to him, them' (OA; |nə–āna| 1s–3+3′,0p/IND)

c. kəmi·lí·na·k=á· 'you ought to give them (anim.) to me' (OA; |kə–īnāk| 2s–1s+3p/IND; =á· POT)

d. kəmillə́na·k 'I gave them (anim.) to you (sg.)' (OA; |kə–ələnāk| 1s–2s+3p/IND)

e. nkəmo·t·əmuk·o·ne·ná·ni 'they stole him (obv.) from us (exc.)' (B; |kəmōtəm-| TA+O 'steal O2 from'. |nə–əkōnēnānī| 3p–1p+3′/IND)

f. nəmahəlama·k·é·na 'I sell them (inan.)' (V; *lit.*, 'they (inan.) are bought from me'; |mahlamaw-| TA+O 'buy O2 from', |nə–əkēna| X–1s+0p/IND)

(9) N-ending for the definite secondary object of an AI+O

a. nəwáni·n 'I forgot it' (ME; |wanī-| AI+O 'forget', |nə–n| 1s+0s/IND)

b. nəwaní·na·k 'I forgot them (anim.)' (ME; |wanī-| AI+O 'forget', |nə–nāk| 1s+3p/IND)

c. hákink=č lanihí·nak 'they (anim.) will be thrown down'

(B; hákink 'below'; =č FUT; |əlanihī-| AI+O 'throw to {smwh}', |–nak| X+3p/IND)

d. nəwaní·na 'I forgot them (inan.)' (ME; |wanī-| AI+O 'forget'. |nə–na| 1s+0p/IND)

In an exactly parallel fashion, an n-ending can be used for a definite oblique (10) or an instrumental oblique (11). When an n-ending indicates the oblique complement of a relative root, the inflection is the same as for an inanimate singular secondary object and is likewise glossed with "+0s" (10). In this construction, the ostensible agreement is typically with a demonstrative pronoun (which is often preceded, immediately or discontinuously, by the focus peg *ná* PRES) or with the question word *tá* WH, used in expressions for 'what?', 'when?', 'where?'. 'why?', 'which?', 'how long?', and 'how?'. (In contrast, *awé·n* 'someone' and *kéku* 'something', when used in questions for 'who?' and 'what?' [if not with a relative root], are indefinite, as in their other uses (12). Rarely, *tá* WH is also used this way (10h).) The verbs that can use an n-ending to indicate an instrumental oblique (11) are presumably lexically subcategorized as optionally taking an instrumental. The examples found have verbs of hitting, piercing, or tying.

(10) N-ending for a definite oblique[8]

a. ná=nə ntə́li-kí·spwi·n 'I got full on it'; *lit.*, 'I got full that way' (OA; ná PRES; nə́ 'that (inan.)'; |əlī| PV '{so}'. |kīsəpwī-| AI 'be full', |nət–n| 1s+0s/IND)

b. ná=tá=nə ntəle·ləmúkwsi·n ní·, . . . 'That's how *I* was created to be, . . . ' (ME; ná PRES; =tá FOC; nə́ 'that (inan.)'; |əlēləməkwəsī-| AI 'be divinely created {so}', |nət–n| 1s+0s/IND; ní· 1s/EMPH)

c. ná=nə ntəlí·ha·n 'that's what I did to him' (OA; ná PRES; nə́ 'that (inan.)'; |əlīh-| TA 'do {so} to'. |nət–ān| 1s–3+0s/IND)

d. ná=nə le·lá·i tɔ́hələ·n. 'he set him in the middle there.' (B; ná PRES; nə́ 'that (inan.)'; le·lá·i 'in the middle'; |ahl-| TA 'put {smwh}', |wət–ān| 1s–3+0s/IND)

e. ná=nə tɔ́·n 'that's where he went' (OA; ná PRES; nə́ 'that (inan.)'; |ā-| AI 'go {smwh}', |wət–n| 1s+0s/IND)

f. ná=nə tə́nta-pá·tama·n. 'There he prayed.' (B; ná PRES; nə́ 'that (inan.)'; |talī| ~ |-ənta| PV '{smwh}', |pāhtamā-| AI 'pray', |wət–n| 3s+0s/IND)

g. takó· nə́ni núnči-pá·wən 'I did not come because of that' (B; takó· NEG; nə́ni 'that (inan.)'; |wənči| PV 'from {smwh}', |pā-| AI 'come', |nə–wən| 1s+0s/IND.NEG)

h. tá=háč ktá·n? 'Where are you going? Where did you go?' (ME; tá WH; =háč Q; |ā-| AI 'go {smwh}', |kət–n| 2s+0s/IND)

i. tá=háč ksá·ki-witahpi·məlané·ɔ. 'How long will I be with you (pl.)?'
(B; tá WH; =háč Q;
|sahkī| PV '{so long}', |wītapīm-| TA 'be with', |kə–ələnēwā| 1s–2p+0s/IND)

j. tá=háč kúnči-wwá·hi·n? 'How come you know me?' (B; tá WH; =háč Q;
|wənčī| PV 'from {smwh}', |wəwāh-| TA 'know', |kə–īn| 2s–1s+0s/IND)

(11) N-ending for a definite instrumental oblique

a. pɔ́k·ama·n 'he struck him with it' (B; |pakam-| TA 'hit', |wə–ān| 3s–3′+0s/IND)

(12) M-ending with indefinite question word

a. awé·n=háč kənat·o·naɔ́həmɔ? 'Who are you looking for?' (B; awé·n 'who?'; =háč Q;
|natōnaw-| TA 'look for', |kə–āhmwā| 2p–(3)/IND)

b. kéku kənat·o·namúhəmɔ? 'What are you (pl.) seeking?'
(B; kéku 'what?'; |natōn-| TI(1a) 'look for', |kə–amə́hmwā| 2p–$(0)_{(1a)}$/IND)

c. kéku=č=háč ntəlsíhəna? 'What shall we (exc.) do?' (B; kéku 'what?'; =č FUT;
=háč Q; |əlәsī-| AI 'do {so}, be {so}', |nət–h(mə)nā| 1p/IND)

d. tá=háč ktá? 'Where are you going?' (cf. 10h)
(B; tá WH; =háč Q; |ā-| AI 'go {smwh}', |kət–| 2s/IND)

And finally, an n-ending may also be used for an inflectional link to an adjunct (13).

(13) N-ending for a definite adjunct

a. aləwí·i ktəla·ɔhti·ne·ɔ́·i·k čo·ləntə́t·ak.
'You (pl.) are worth more than the little birds.' (B; aləwí·i P 'more';
|əlāwatī-| AI 'be worth {so}', |kət–nēwāwīk| 2p+3p/IND; čo·ləntə́t·ak 'birds (dim.)'

b. ktaləwa·p·ensí·nak kíči-xkwé·ɔk 'you (sg.) are more blessed than your fellow
women' (B; |aləwāpēnsī-| AI 'be more blessed', |kət–nak| 2s+3p/IND;
|kə-| 2s, -íči PV 'fellow', |axkwēw-| 'woman', |-ak| AN.PL)

In the examples in (13) the verb shows agreement with the adjunct that follows, in both cases a standard of comparison. As adjuncts are not verbal complements like secondary objects and obliques, they must be recognized as nominals that verbs can be inflected for but have no syntactic link to.

Participles

The categories of nominal that can be indicated by the use of n-endings when they are definite are syntactically miscellaneous (6–11, 13), but the set they constitute is not random and is, in fact, encountered elsewhere. These same categories of nominal can be the heads of participles—those of all the types in (2), including adjuncts (14fg), which, again, have no syntactic link to the verb. In addition, the head of a participle may be the possessor of the subject (14h), or one component of a conjoined subject (14i), also categories of nominal with no direct syntactic link to the verb.[9]

(14) Heads of participles

a. subject:
ké·pča·t lə́nu 'foolish man'
(B; |kəpəčā-| AI 'be foolish', |IC–t| 3/PPL(AN.SG); lə́nu 'man')

b. primary object:
mehɔ́·č·i 'the one (obv.) he ate' (ME; |məhw-| TA 'eat', |IC–āčī| 3s–3′/PPL(OBV))

c. secondary object:
mi·lianpáni·k 'the ones (anim.) that you (sg.) gave me'
(B; |mīl-| TA+O 'give O2 to', |IC–əyanəpanīk| 2s–1s/PPL.PRET(AN.PL))

d. oblique complement of relative root:
e·li·t·é·ha·t 'his will' (B; |əlītēhā-| AI 'think {so}', |IC–t| 3s/PPL(OBL))

e. instrumental oblique:
takó· kéku . . anshi·k·é·an 'nothing for you (sg.) to scoop up water with'
(B; takó· NEG; kéku 'anything';
|ansahīkē-| AI 'scoop up (water)', |(IC)–yan| 2s/PPL(IN.SG))

f. adjunct (nominal inside quoted speech):
nál=tá wáni e·ləwe·á·nəp, "no·t·é·ka·kw . . ."
'This is the one of whom I said, "He comes after me . . ."'
(B; nál PRES; =tá FOC; wáni 'this (anim.)';
|ələwē-| AI 'say {so}', |IC–yānəp| 1s/PPL.PRET(AN.SG);
|wətēhkaw-| TA 'follow, come after', |nə–əkw| 3s–1s/IND)

g. adjunct (agent of a passive):
šinka·lké·ankw 'our (inc.) enemy (*lit.,* the one we are hated by)'
(B; |šīnkāl-| TA 'hate', |(IC)–əkēyankw| X–12/PPL(AN.SG))

h. possessor of subject:
ni·š·í·nxke txə́n télən txá·pxki entxí·li·t wsɔ·čəlә́ma 'one who had twenty thousand soldiers' (*lit.*, 'he of whom his soldiers were 20,000')
(B; ni·š·í·nxke '20'. txə́n '{so many} times', télən txá·pxki '1,000';
|(-ən)taxī-| AI 'be {so many}', |IC–līt| 3'/PPL(AN.SG); wsɔ·čəlә́ma 'his soldiers')

i. component of conjoined subject:
mé·li ne·xkuntíhti·t 'Mary, who was engaged to him' (B; mé·li 'Mary';
|naxkōntī-| AI 'agree together; be engaged to marry', |IC–hətīt| 3p/PPL(AN.SG))

Subordinative Mode

In contrast to the complex pattern of distinctions marked by the ending sets in the independent indicative (5), the independent subordinative mode uses only the n-endings for the AI, TA, and TI, and no peripheral suffixes. (The lack of an n-ending in the II is explained by the fact that there is no n-ending for an inanimate subject; see (4).) The subordinative inflections are thus identical to those of indicative verbs with definite oblique complements.

The subordinative most typically makes subordinate clauses that are complements of higher verbs or other ostensible predicates. It has distinct uses with and without the pleonastic preverb *lí* (|əlī|) PV '{so}'. The subordinative without this preverb (15) is used as the complement of, for example, *want* (15a), *be difficult* (15b), and *let,* and also of sentence-initial *ná* '(and) then' (15d) (as if 'and then it was that') and other particles (15e). It also makes nominalizations functioning as secondary objects (15f).

(15) Subordinative without |əlī| PV '{so}' in complements
Complement of a verb:

a. nkat·á·t·amən ko·la·mhitai·né·ɔ 'I want you to believe in me'
(B; |katāt-| TI(1a) 'want', |nə–amən| 1s–0s/IND;
|wəlāməhtaw-| TA 'believe', |kə–īnēwā| 2p–1s/SBD)

b. áhɔt nkɔ·nší·pha·n 'it is hard for me to hide from him'
(ME; |àhwat-| II 'be difficult', |-w| 0s/IND;
|kwānšīpah-| TA 'hide from', |nə–ān| 1s–3/SBD)

c. máta=háč wəli·x·ənó·wi laxə́na·n? 'Is it not right for her to be untied?'
(B; máta NEG; =háč Q; |wəlīxən-| II 'be right', |-ōwī| 0s/IND.NEG; |laxən-| TA 'untie', |–ān| X–3/SBD)[10]

Complement of a particle:

d. ná tɔlə́mska·n 'then he departed'
(B 3x; ná '(and) then'; |alə̀məskā-| AI 'depart', |wət–n| 3s/SBD)

e. kwə́lah=á· nəwi·č·əmə́k·e·n 'I wish I would be helped'
(OA; kwə́la(h) '(I) wish'; =á· POT; |wīčəm-| TA 'help', |nə–əkēn| X–1s/SBD)

Nominalization as a secondary object:

f. nɔxpí·k·i·n kɔk·e·p·ínkɔ·n 'he was born blind'
(B; |naxpīkī-| AI+O 'be born with O2', |wə–n| 3s+0s/IND; |(-k)akēpīnkwā-| AI 'be blind', |wə–n| 3s/SBD)

Much less common is the use of the subordinative as a main-clause verb. This is found in narrative after the mention of earlier acts, perhaps simply with *ná* 'then' understood (16a,b); utterance-initially as a statement of the speaker's immediate intent (16c); and as a request or advice ('let (first or third person) do so'; 16d,e).

(16) Subordinative without |əlī| PV '{so}' in main clause

a. pwéči-né·ma·n '. . . , and he came back seeing.'
(B; péči PV 'come', |nēmā-| AI 'see', |wə–n| 3s/SBD)

b. tɔlə́mska·n[.] 'And he left.'
(Voegelin 1945:115 [whole sentence, punctuated as a separate paragraph]; |alə̀məskā-| AI 'depart', |wət–n| 3s/SBD; cf. 15d)

c. nəmái-no·t·aménsi·n. 'I'm going fishing.' (B; translating KJV "I go a fishing."; |mawī| PV 'go to', |nōtamēnsī-| AI 'fish', |nə–n| 1s/SBD)

d. ke·k·e·p·inkɔ́·č·i·k tɔləmo·x·ɔla·né·ɔ ke·k·e·p·inkɔ·lí·č·i.
'Let the blind lead the blind.'
(B; |(-k)akēpīnkwā-| AI 'be blind', |IC–čīk| 3/PPL(AN.PL); |aləmōxwal-| TA 'lead', |wət–ānēwā| 3p–3'/SBD; |(-k)akēpīnkwā-| AI 'be blind', |IC–līčī| 3'/PPL(OBV))

e. lahápa ní· hítami ntalə́mska·n 'let me first take the time to go'
(B; lahápa P 'taking the time; for a while'; ní· 1s/EMPH; hítami P 'first'; |alə̀məska·-| AI 'depart', |nət–n| 1s/SBD)

When used WITH *lí* (|əlī|) PV '{so}' (17) the subordinative makes the complement of certain other verbs (for example, *know* [17a], also *say, tell, think, see,* and *hear*); in purpose clauses (17 b); and after focus-fronted nominals (17c,d). There is also an idiom that has a subordinative verb with *lí* (|əlī|) PV '{so}' after the presentational particle *ná* PRES (17e; contrast 15d); the meaning is something like 'And with that', 'And so', or 'and proceeded to'.

(17) Subordinative with lí (|əlī|) PV '{so}'

Complement of a verb:

a. no·wá·to·n táli-=č -pá·n 'I know that he will come' (B; |wəwāht-| TI(2) 'know', |nə–ōn| 1s–$0s_{(2)}$/IND; |əlī| PV '{so}', |pā-| 'AI 'come', |wət–n| 3s/SBD; =č FUT)[11]

Purpose clause:

b. məšá·ke· táli-=á· -mí·tsi·n 'he sat down to eat' (B; =á· POT; |məšahkē-| AI 'take a seat', |–w| 3s/IND; |əlī| PV 'so', |mītəsī-| AI 'eat', |wət–n| 3s/SBD)

With focus-fronted nominal:

c. ní· ntáli-ló·s·əmən 'I'M the one who burned it' (Voegelin 1946:150; ní· 1s/EMPH; |əlī| PV '{so}', |lōs-| TI(1b) 'burn', |nət–əmən| 1s–$0_{(1b)}$/SBD)

d. nčí·sas=tá ntáli-ki·k·éhko·n. 'It was Jesus that cured me.' (B; nčí·sas 'Jesus' [WS]; =tá FOC; |əlī| PV '{so}', |kīkēh-| TA 'cure', |nət–əkōn| 3–1s/SBD)

With ná PRES *and* |*əlī*| *PV* '{*so*}':

e. ná táli- palí·i -a·né·ɔ. 'And with that they went away.' (B; ná PRES; |əlī| PV '{so}', |ā-| AI 'go {smwh}', |wət–nēwā| 3p/SBD; palí·i 'away')

Conclusion

The subordinative has the shape of a verb with a definite oblique, instrumental, or adjunct, but it functions as a separate mode of the independent order and is otherwise unlike a verb with an oblique or adjunct. The use of identical morphology does not point to an identity of function but is only an identity of form. A single morphological process (here, a certain inflection) marks multiple grammatical categories. A thread of similarity between these categories might be imagined (perhaps something generic and imprecise like 'additional deixis'), but the functional categories are nevertheless distinct. They cannot be taken to be manifestations of a single, more abstract grammatical category, and they do not need to be.

Such paradoxes of partial similarity pose a fundamental problem for the formal analysis of morphology. There is no way to formally recognize partial similarity as partial identity. But cases of partial similarity, like this one, suggest that it could be useful to recognize looser and more contingent connections between morphological components than may ordinarily seem advisable or even possible.

NOTES

1. I am grateful for the helpful comments of two anonymous referees.
2. The variable terminology that has been used for AI+O and TA+O verbs is summarized in Goddard (1974:319).
3. Grammatical abbreviations: abs. = absentative, AI = animate intransitive, AI+O = animate intransitive taking a secondary object, AN and anim. = animate, dim. = diminutive, EMPH = emphatic, FOC = focus, FUT = future, IC = initial change, (IC) = non-overt initial change, II = inanimate intransitive, IN, inan. = inanimate, IND = independent indicative, KJV = King James Bible, NEG = negative, O2 = secondary object, OBL = oblique, OBV = obviative, p, PL = plural, POT = potential, PPL = participle, PRES = presentational, PRET = preterite, PV = preverb, Q = question, SBD = subordinative, s and SG = singular, TA = transitive animate, TA+O = transitive animate taking a secondary object, TI = transitive inanimate, TI-O = objectless transitive inanimate, WH = question word.

   1 = first person; 1s = first person singular; 1p = first plural exclusive; 12 = first plural inclusive; 2 = second person; 3 = third person animate; 3′ = third person obviative; 0 = third person inanimate; X = indefinite (person).

   Glossing conventions: an en-dash (–) separates the pronominal glosses of the subject and the primary object; parentheses after an en-dash enclose the pronominal gloss of an indefinite primary object (or inverse subject); parentheses after "PPL" or "PPL.PRET" enclose the gloss of the head of the participle; + precedes the pronominal gloss of a definite secondary object, oblique, instrumental oblique, or adjunct; curly braces ({. .}) enclose the conventional abstract gloss of an oblique valence.

   Sources: B = Ira D. Blanchard; ME = Martha Ellis; OA = Ollie Anderson; V = C. F. Voegelin (Willie Longbone); WS = Willie Snake.
4. The third person m-ending suffix $|\text{-w}|_{\text{m}}$ causes umlaut of |ā| to |ē|; the formative $|\text{-w}|_{\text{w}}$ of the w-endings does not.

5. TA verbs have four themes (marked by different theme signs), whose functions in the independent order are as follows: |-ā| theme 1 (direct; non-third person on third, proximate on obviative); |-əkw| theme 2 (inverse; third on non-third, obviative on proximate), with variant |-əkĕ| (indefinite person on non-third); |-ī| theme 3 (second on first); |-əl| theme 4 (first on second).
6. W-endings may also be used, apparently optionally, with indefinite animate inverse subjects and first or second person objects.
7. Examples are given for all three TI classes. The analysis of the verbs of Class 2 and Class 3 as TIs follows Bloomfield (1962:145). Unlike AI+O verbs, these are paired with TAs and take only inanimate objects; they differ from Class 1 TIs only in their theme sign or lack thereof.
8. In Goddard (1979:48–49) the use of n-endings to mark obliques was taken as a use of the subordinative mode, but when this use of these endings is compared to the full range of other uses with verbs that function as independent indicatives (8, 9, 11, 12), it is clear that the use to mark obliques is entirely parallel.
9. More comparative data on the participles in Algonquian languages would be welcome; Meskwaki, at least, has all the same kinds of participles as Unami (Goddard 1987).
10. The verb *wəlí·x·ən* 'it is right or lawful' is also used with |əlī| PV '{so}'.
11. By convention, the hyphen that joins the parts of a compound stem that are separated by the internal word boundary is repeated after the space that follows an enclitic (or other intervening word) that is not part of the compound stem.

REFERENCES

Blanchard, Ira D., [and James Conner]. 1837 [1839]. *The History of our Lord and Saviour Jesus Christ.* Shawanoe Baptist Mission: J. Meeker [and John G. Pratt]. (Reprinted: *The History of our Lord and Savior Jesus Christ.* Bartlesville, I.T., 1906. Online: http://www.kansasmemory.org/item/211693/page/4.)

Bloomfield, Leonard. 1962. *The Menomini Language.* New Haven: Yale University Press.

Goddard, Ives. 1974. Remarks on the Algonquian Independent Indicative. *International Journal of American Linguistics* 40:317–332.

Goddard, Ives. 1979. *Delaware Verbal Morphology: A Descriptive and Comparative Study.* New York: Garland.

Goddard, Ives. 1983. The Eastern Algonquian Subordinative Mode and the Importance of Morphology. *International Journal of American Linguistics* 49(4):351–387.

Goddard, Ives. 1987. Fox Participles. *Native American Languages and Grammatical Typology,* ed. by Paul D. Kroeber and Robert E. Moore, pp. 105–118. Bloomington: Indiana University Linguistics Club.

Goddard, Ives. 2019. The Kansas Unami Writings of Ira D. Blanchard, Pioneering Algonquian Linguist. *Papers of the 48th Algonquian Conference,* ed. by Monica Macaulay and Meg Noodin, pp. 87–106. East Lansing: Michigan State University Press.

Voegelin, Carl F. 1945. Delaware Texts. *International Journal of American Linguistics* 11.2:105–119.

Voegelin, Carl F. 1946. Delaware, an Eastern Algonquian Language. *Linguistic Structures of Native America,* by Harry Hoijer et al., pp. 130–157. Viking Fund Publications in Anthropology 6. New York: Viking Fund.

Numeral Classifiers in Ojibwe

Cherry Meyer

This paper presents ongoing research with the goal of providing a more complete and current description of classifiers in Ojibwe.[1] This description is grounded in the typological literature on noun categorization and recent fieldwork with two Odawa speakers. Classifiers are defined as free or bound morphemes occurring in specifiable morphosyntactic units that denote a property of the referent of a noun and may co-occur with that noun (Aikhenvald 2000:13, Grinevald 2000:64). The current typology of classifiers recognizes multiple types of classifiers throughout the world's languages. The different types are labeled according to the morphosyntactic locus of the classifier, that is, the morpheme to which it is adjacent or attached (Grinevald 2000:62–63). For example, free morphemes that occur adjacent to nouns are called noun classifiers, bound morphemes that occur attached to verbs are verbal classifiers, free or bound morphemes that occur with numerals are numeral classifiers. This typological description was developed to distinguish different types of noun categorization broadly, for example, gender and classifiers, as well as different types of classifiers, both across and within languages (Grinevald 2000:58). A language may have distinct sets of classifiers that occur in distinct morphosyntactic environments. I focus here only on morphemes that meet the typological definition of numeral classifiers, and my conclusions are solely applicable to those morphemes when they occur in that morphosyntactic environment, that is, suffixed to only a numeral.[2]

This fieldwork was conducted with speakers Leonard and Elizabeth Kimewon of the Sault Ste. Marie Tribe of Chippewa Indians. Mr. and Mrs. Kimewon speak the Odawa dialect of Ojibwe, having spent several decades on Manitoulin Island. I have standardized spelling in transcribing the data. Aside from some minor lexical differences, the Odawa forms are different from those in Southwestern Ojibwe due to syncope, a phonological process that deletes unstressed vowels.[3] A few examples in what follows are from a handout composed by Mr. Kimewon (n.d.), titled *Mii-jim-daawegamigong* 'In the Grocery Store'. Unless otherwise noted, the examples in this paper come from fieldwork with Mr. and Mrs. Kimewon. The procedure for the data collection consisted of elicitation and acceptability judgments.

Just as classifiers are divided into different types based on their morphosyntactic loci, numeral classifiers also have subdivisions. The two main categories of numeral classifiers are mensural and sortal. I first define these two kinds of numeral classifiers, before listing the working inventory of their forms in Ojibwe. I then review earlier descriptions of these classifiers and make several clarifications, excluding certain forms from the numeral classifier label, and updating the semantics and availability of certain numeral classifiers. I end with a few notes on the relation between numeral classifiers and another type in Ojibwe, verbal classifiers.

Numeral Classifiers

In Ojibwe, classifiers may be suffixed to numeral roots to create a classifier-specific numeral (Valentine 2001:883).[4] Cross-linguistically, numeral classifiers are divided into two semantic subtypes, sortal and mensural (Grinevald 2000:64, Aikhenvald 2000:114–115). Mensural classifiers specify measurements of the nouns to which they refer. Sortal classifiers denote an inherent property of the noun to which they refer, such as shape, flexibility, or material. The distinction between sortal and mensural classifiers is relevant beyond semantics and into the grammar of some languages (Grinevald 2000:64); this is discussed below for Ojibwe. Numeral classifiers are contextualized within other classifier types in Figure 1.

FIGURE 1. Context of Numeral Classifier Types

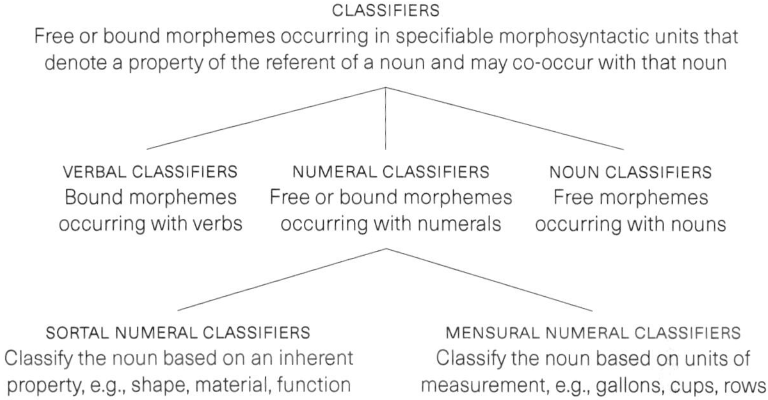

Description of Mensural Classifiers

In many languages, Ojibwe included, nouns are divisible into count and mass categories (Mathieu 2012; Meyer 2018). Mass nouns generally denote a substance and lack clear units, as well as plural forms. Count nouns, on the other hand, have clear units and plural forms. Mensural classifiers may combine with both count and mass nouns, with only a slight difference in the semantics of the classifiers. For mass nouns, classifiers only specify units of measurement, as shown in (1), while for count nouns, they may also specify arrangements, as shown in (2a). The following examples also show that these classifiers occur with nouns of both gender values, inanimate nouns in (1a, 2a) and animate nouns in (1b, 2b).[5]

(1) Mensural Classifiers with Mass Nouns

a. niizho-**kikoons** makade-aaboo
two-can.CL black-liquid.IN
'two cans of coffee'

b. ngo-**dbaabiishkoojgan** giigoonh[6]
one-pound.CL fish.AN
'one pound of fish'

(2) Mensural Classifiers with Count Nouns

a. ngod-**wewaan** mkzin-an
one-pair.CL shoe. IN-IN.PL
'one pair of shoes'

b. ngodo-**gamig** Nishnaabe-g
one-houseful.CL Nishnaabe.AN-AN.PL
'one houseful of Nishnaabeg'

Cross-linguistically, classifiers do not usually bear the feature of number, only their associated nouns do (Aikhenvald 2000:249). Classifiers do not, for example, have singular or plural forms. Ojibwe has number feature values of singular and plural. Count and mass nouns in constructions with mensural classifiers behave as we might expect with regards to the feature of number, that is, count nouns are plural when semantically appropriate, as shown in (3a,b), while mass nouns are never plural, as shown in (4a–c).

(3) Count Nouns Showing Plural Number

a. Ngo-mishkamodens zhigaangwish-**iig** n-wii-giishnan-aag.
one-bag.CL onion.AN-AN.PL 1-FUT-buy.VTA-3.PL
'I will buy one bag of onions.' (Kimewon, n.d.)

b. ngod-makak zaga'igan-**an**
one-box.CL nail.IN-IN.PL
'one box of nails'

(4) Mass Nouns Lacking Plural Number

a. Nswi-mooday minwaagmig n-giishnad-oon.
three-bottle.CL pop.IN 1-buy.VTI2–1>0.SG
'I am buying three bottles of pop.' (Kimewon, n.d.)

b. niizho-dbaabiishkoojgan giigoonh
two-pound.CL fish.AN
'two pounds of fish'

c. *niizho-dbaabiishkoojgan giigoon-**yag**
two-pound.CL fish.AN-AN.PL
int. 'two pounds of fish'

Inventory of Mensural Classifiers

Table 1 is a working inventory of mensural classifiers.[7] For considerations of space, each mensural classifier, shown in bold, is accompanied by the number 'one' and an overt noun.

Description of Sortal Classifiers

Every language has measure terms, for example, English *a head of cattle* or *a pair of shoes,* which may behave similarly to mensural classifiers, but not every language should be labeled a classifier language (Grinevald 2000:58–59; Aikhenvald 2000:115–116). The criterion for a true classifier language is the presence of sortal classifiers, which denote an inherent property of the noun to which they refer, such as shape, flexibility, or material, as shown in (5a,b). Measure terms, in languages with sortal classifiers, act like sortal classifiers, hence the reasoning for labeling them as classifiers, as well. Examples of sortal classifiers in Ojibwe are shown below.[8]

(5) Sortal Classifiers

a. bezhgwa-**mnag** sabaab
   one-round.CL ball.of.yarn.IN
   'one (round) ball of yarn'

b. bezhigw-**aatig** kosmaan
   one-long.narrow.CL squash.IN
   'one (long & narrow) zucchini'

Inventory of Sortal Classifiers

Table 2 is a working inventory of sortal classifiers. There are many more mensural classifiers than sortal ones, which is typologically expected (Grinevald 2000:64). Again for considerations of space, each sortal classifier, shown in bold, is accompanied by the number 'one' and an overt noun.

TABLE 1. Inventory of mensural classifiers

CLASSIFIER EXAMPLE	TRANSLATION
ngo-**dbagan** gdagiigin	one yard of fabric
ngo-**dbagaans** sabaabiis	one inch of string
ngodo-**zid** zenbaanh	one foot of ribbon
ngodi-**nkeawaak** zenbaanh	one armspan of ribbon
ngodo-**kik** nbiish	one pailful/kettleful of water
ngod-**oonag** Nishnaabeg, ngo-**jiimaan** Nishnaabeg	one boatload of Nishnaabeg
ngo-**shkimod** piniig	one bagful of potatoes
ngo-**shkimdenhs** piniig	one small bagful of potatoes
ngod-**ooshkin** piniig	one large bagful of potatoes
ngod-**shkimdes** baakaakwen	one package of chicken
ngod-**wewaan** mkiznan	one pair of shoes
ngod-**wewaan** waanoon	one dozen eggs
ngodo-**naagaans** baasidongaak bkwezhgan	one cup of flour (for bread)
ngo-**mnikwaajgan** zhoomnaaboo	one gallon of wine
ngo-**mnikwaajgaanhs** minwaagmig	one cupful of pop
ngod-**emwkaan** zhiitaagan	one tablespoon of salt
ngod-**emkwaanes** zhiitaagan	one teaspoon salt
ngodi-**ninj** miinan	one handful of blueberries
ngo-**mkaksag** mide	one barrel of oil
ngo-**mkaksagonhs** zhgopwaaboo	one small keg of beer
ngo-**dbaabiishkoojigan** giigoonh	one pound of fish
ngodo-**gamig** Nishnaabeg	one houseful of Nishnaabeg
ngo-**achingan** Nishnaabeg	one roomful of Nishnaabeg
ngo-**doopwin** piniig	one tableful of potatoes
ngo-**daabaan** Nishnaabeg	one carload of Nishnaabeg
ngod-**mkakoons** semaa	one pack/small box of cigarettes
ngod-**mkak** zgaganan	one box of nails
ngo-**chmakak** zgaganan	one large box of nails
ngod-**kikwaakoons** semaa, ngodo-**kikoonhs** semaa	one can of tobacco
ngo-**shkishgagan** zhoomnaaboo	one case of wine (12 bottles)
ngo-**zid-kakadeaa** naakaniigin	one square foot of flooring
ngodo-**mooday** nibi	one bottle of water
ngoding-**nikzat** kosmaan	one piece of pumpkin
ngoding-**nikzat** bkwezhgan	one slice of bread

TABLE 2. Inventory of Sortal Classifiers

CLASSIFIER EXAMPLE	TRANSLATION
bezhigw-**aatig** mtigoonhs	one (long, narrow, rigid) small stick
bezhigw-**eg** waabooyaan	one (sheetlike) blanket
bezhgwa-**minag** sabaab	one (round) ball of yarn

Distinction between Sortal and Mensural Classifiers

In some languages, the distinction between sortal and mensural classifiers goes beyond semantics to being reflected in the grammar, for example by showing distinct linking particles or behavior under anaphoric conditions (Grinevald 2000:59, 64). There is at least one very noticeable distinction between sortal and mensural classifiers in Ojibwe: they are used with different forms of the numeral 'one'. Mensural classifiers are used with /ngodw-/, while sortal classifiers are used with /bezhigw-/. Examples (2a) and (5a) are repeated here as (6a,b) to illustrate the contrast.

(6) Differing Forms of 'One' with Mensural and Sortal Classifiers

a. **ngod**-wewaan mkzin-an
one-pair.CL shoe.IN-IN.PL
'one pair of shoes'

b. **bezhgwa**-mnag sabaab
one-round.CL ball.of.yarn.IN
'one (round) ball of yarn'

c. ***ngo**-minag sabaab
int. 'one (round) ball of yarn'

Both forms for 'one' are traceable to Proto-Algonquian (Rhodes and Costa 2003:181–183). Only a nonindependent form of /ngodw-/ is acknowledged, from Proto-Algonquian *nekwetwi, while only an independent form of *bezhig* is acknowledged, from Proto-Algonquian *peešekwi. However, *bezhig* has both an independent form and a nonindependent form /bezhigw-/ because it shows the same morphological and phonological behavior as /ngodw-/. Namely, classifiers are suffixed to it, causing the glide /w/ and linking vowels to surface. In fact, (6b) above is unacceptable without the glide and linking vowel: **bezhig-minag*. The independent form *bezhig* is used for count nouns, without a classifier, as shown in (7).

(7) Independent Form of 'One' with Count Nouns

Bezhig kosmaan n-wii-giishnad-oon.
one melon.IN 1-FUT-buy.VTI2–1>0.SG
'I will buy one melon.' (Kimewon, n.d.)

Baraga (1878:309) also acknowledges the stem form of /ngodw-/, writing, "Cardinal numbers from one to ten undergo a little change before substantives signifying measure, of time or of other things; and these substantives always remain in the singular." Here, he seems to be referring to mensural classifiers with the term 'substantives', since they have the semantics of measurement, trigger the glide plus linking vowel on numerals (the 'little change'), and lack plural forms. He writes, "instead of *bezhig, niizh, niswi,* etc., we say before those substantives: *ningo, niizho, niswo* . . ." The differing use of /ngodw-/ for mensural classifiers and /bezhigw-/ for sortal classifiers is one concrete distinction between these two types of numeral classifiers, which coincides with typological expectations.

One other minor distinction worth noting concerns the optionality of numeral classifiers. Mensural classifiers are widely used and do not seem to be optional, especially in counting quantities of mass nouns. Sortal classifiers, on the other hand, are much less used. They were only found when elicited, and the numeral without the sortal classifier was often supplied first. Neither speaker found any discernable difference between constructions with or without sortal classifiers. For example, 'one blanket' could be said *bezhigweg waabooyaan* or *bezhig waabooyaan* without a change in meaning. This asymmetry in optionality and frequency of use is also expected from a typological perspective, since all languages have measure terms, but not all have sortal classifiers (Grinevald 2000:58).

Nonclassifier Morphemes of Measurement

Baraga's description of classifiers is early and understandably rudimentary. In the aforementioned quote, he is undoubtedly referring to mensural classifiers and the description is fairly accurate. Several pages later (1878:311), he also gives a description of sortal classifiers, writing, "When the substantive following the Cardinal number, from one to nineteen, signifies objects of wood, stone, metal, etc. or when days are mentioned, the cardinal number is connected with certain syllables alluding to the material, or shape, of the object expressed by the substantive." Instead of referring to the classifier as the substantive, he identifies them as 'certain syllables' and the 'substantive' instead refers to the noun. Baraga mentions measurements of time both in descriptions of mensural classifiers and of sortal classifiers. Valentine (2001:883–887) also includes measurements of time in his description of classifiers.

Measurements of time behave like mensural classifiers in some ways, but crucially, they cannot co-occur with nouns. Classifiers may occur in a clause without an overt noun under certain circumstances, e.g., serving a pronominal function as in (8) where the noun, *logs,* was previously mentioned. However, they are a form of noun categorization and, as such, must at least have the option of co-occurring with nouns. Morphemes that are unable to co-occur with nouns cannot be a type of noun categorization and thus, are not classifiers. A measurement of land is included in the set of nonclassifier morphemes of measurement, as it behaves the same as measurements of time. These forms are given in (9a–f) and (10).

(8) Pronominal Use of Numeral Classifier

Niizhw-aatik	biizh.
two-long.narrow.rigid.CL	bring.VTA.2.SG>3.IMP

'Bring two (logs).'

(9) Measurements of Time

a. /-diba'giiswan/, /-diba'igan/ 'hour'
b. /-diba'igaans/ 'minute'
c. /-giizhig/ 'sky, day'
d. /-anamegiizhig/ 'week'
e. /-giizis/ 'moon, month'
f. /-biboon/, /-boon/ 'winter, year'

(10) Measurement of Land

/-kiins/ 'acre'

These morphemes may be semantically akin to mensural classifiers, and they behave like mensural classifiers in that they attach to the root form of a number. For the number 'one', they attach to /ngo(d)-/, as we would expect for measure terms. Their use with *bezhig* is disallowed, as shown in (11–14), unless a nonmeasurement meaning exists and is intended, as with *bezhik diba'giiswan,* meaning 'one clock' instead of 'one hour'.

(11) a. ngo-diba'giiswan 'one hour' b. *bezhig diba'giiswan (means 'one clock')

(12) a. ngo-diba'igaans 'one minute' b. *bezhigwa-diba'igaans

(13) a. ngo-anamegiizhig 'one week' b. *bezhig-anamegiizhig

(14) a. ngo-kiins 'one acre' b. *bezhig-kiins

Like other mensural classifiers, they also do not have plural forms, as shown below.

(15) a. niso-giizhig 'three days' b. *niso-giizhig-**oog** int. 'three days'

These morphemes are unlike mensural classifiers, however, in that they do not co-occur with nouns, as shown in (16–17).

(16) a. *niizho-biboon nokiiwin int. 'two years of work'
b. niizho-biboon gii-anokii 'he has worked two years' (Baraga 1878:309, accepted by Mr. Kimewon)

(17) a. *ngo-kiins ki, int. 'one acre of land'
b. *ngo-kiins naakaniigin, int. 'one acre of flooring' (e.g., in a giant's mansion)

This inability to co-occur with nouns, as in (16a), may be explained based on the use of verbs in Ojibwe for expressions that English would fulfill with a noun, or on semantic grounds. For example, in (17), the full meaning is contained within the measure term. Thus, the measure term is not highlighting a property of the noun, it is itself supplying all the necessary semantic information. To say **ngo-kiins ki* is repetitive because the meaning 'land' is already contained in the morpheme attached to the numeral. It is not even plausible to say **ngo-kiins naakaniigin* int. 'one acre of flooring' because that is incompatible with the very specific semantics of /-kiins/.

Now that the definitions and inventories of sortal and mensural classifiers are clear, as well as distinctions between them, the next section revisits the semantics and availability of several classifiers to ensure a current description. The earlier descriptions are mostly from Baraga's 1878 grammar, but Valentine (2001:883–885) also provides a brief description of numeral classifiers.

Changes in Semantics

There are not many changes in the semantics of mensural classifiers as compared to those listed in Baraga's grammar. One change, however, concerns the archaic mensural classifier /-sag/. It no longer refers to wooden containers such as barrels, kegs or boxes, as stated by Baraga (1878:311). There are separate classifiers used for a barrel/keg, *mkaksag,* and for a box, *makak,* though it may still be in use as a verbal classifier and content morpheme in nouns with the meaning of '(worked) wood'. Many more changes are observed in sortal classifiers than mensural ones. Semantic changes are observed in the sortal classifiers /-aatig/ and /-eg/.

First, the sortal classifier /-aatig/ may be translated as 'stick-like or wooden', which makes reference to shape, flexibility, and material (Valentine 2001:346, 572).[9] The semantics of this classifier no longer refer to (wooden) material, only the parameters of shape (long and narrow) and consistency (inflexible, rigid). The semantics are then more accurately described as 'long, narrow, rigid'.[10] Nouns with meanings that include wood, but not the correct properties of shape and flexibility, for example, a sheet of wood or a flexible wooden pole, are incompatible with this classifier, as in (18). Nouns with meanings that reflect the shape and flexibility, but not material, for example, a metal or plastic rod, are compatible (19–20).

(18) *bezhigw-aatig mgiskanaak
one-wooden/one-long.narrow.flexible.CL fishing.pole.IN
int. 'one (flexible) fishing pole'

(19) bezhigw-aatig biiwaabik
one-long.narrow.rigid.CL metal.IN
'one metal rod'

(20) a. bezhigw-aatig kiwe'onaatik
one-long.narrow.rigid.CL flagpole.IN
'one (plastic or metal) flagpole'

b. bezhigw-aatig waazkonenjiganaatik
one-long.narrow.rigid.CL light.pole.IN
'one (plastic or metal) light pole'

Second, the classifier /-eg/ has shown a change in semantics concerning flexibility. It is described by Baraga (1878:311) as being used for clothing materials and may be translated as 'sheetlike, cloth' (Valentine 2001:346). However, it is compatible with nouns having referents that are both flexible (21) and rigid (22). The semantics are then more accurately described as 'sheetlike', or simply 'long and wide' with reference only to shape and not to flexibility.

(21) bezhigw-eg pikweshmooniigin
one-long.wide.CL pillowcase.IN
'one (sheetlike) pillowcase'

(22) bezhigw-eg biiwaabik
one-long.wide.CL metal.IN
'one metal sheet'

Changes in Availability

Changes in availability are observed in the sortal classifiers /-aabik/ and /aabiig/. The classifier /-aabik/, translated as 'mineral', has become lexicalized with the meaning 'dollar'. It was previously used as a sortal classifier, denoting that a noun was composed of a mineral material, either metal, stone, or glass. It is used with *bezhig,* like sortal classifiers, and it is incompatible with the root form /ngodw-/ (23a,b). We might expect /ngodw-/ if this classifier were acting as a measure term, for example, for the mass noun *zhooniya* 'money'.

(23) a. bezhigw-aabik
one-dollar.IN
'one dollar'

b. *ngodw-aabik
int. 'one dollar'

Notice that, like measurements of time and land, /-aabik/ is uninflected for number (24).

(24) niizhw-aabik
two-dollar.IN
'two dollars'

Perhaps the best evidence in favor of lexicalization is that dollars are most often made of paper and do not match the 'mineral' semantics of the classifier. While coin dollars are not impossible to come by, they are certainly not the norm in the United States, where Mr. and Mrs. Kimewon have resided for decades. It does not appear to be used as a sortal classifier, i.e., with numerals to highlight the mineral material of the referent of a noun, illustrated by speakers' rejection of (25). More research is needed to confirm this.

(25) *niizhw-aabik naagaan-an
two-mineral.CL dish.IN-IN.PL
int. 'two glass or metal dishes'

Finally, Valentine (2001:883) provides the sortal classifier /-aabiig/, meaning 'stringlike'. I was unable to elicit any examples with this classifier. It is possible that due to a word-final devoicing rule in Odawa (e.g., /-aatig/ is pronounced [-aatik]), that the pronunciation of /-aabiig/ would be /-aabiik/, similar to /-aabik/ 'dollar'. Vowel length alone may not be enough to distinguish these two traditional classifiers, and some current Odawa speakers, including those I work with, do not seem to have this as a sortal classifier in their lexicon. Further fieldwork is needed to say definitively, however.

A Note on Verbal Classifiers

Clarification of the inventory of verbal classifiers versus numeral classifiers is necessary, as there are classifiers that occur in verbs, but not in numerals. This is an area for further research, but I give a few examples here. Compare the disallowed numeral classifiers in (26a–28a) to the accepted verbal classifiers in (26b–28b).

(26) Verbal Classifier /-aakw/

a. *ningow-aak
one-wooden/sticklike.CL
int. 'one sticklike object' ('one hundred')

b. gnw**aakw**izi zhgwaak
be.a.long.wooden.VAI pine.tree.AN
'be a long pine tree'

(27) Verbal Classifier /-aagam/

a. *bezhig-agaam
one-liquid.CL
int. 'one liquid object'

b. dak**aagam**ig mnwaagmik
be.cold.liquid.VII pop.IN
'it is cold pop'

(28) Verbal Classifier /-sag/

a. *ngod-sag
one-wooden.CL
int. 'one (wooden) object' (*ngodsagoons* 'one thousand')

b. gnoo**sag**aa naakaniigin
be.long.wooden.VII floor.IN
'it is a long floor'

Further research is needed to complete the inventory of numeral classifiers and identify those which may be used as both numeral and verbal classifiers, as the two sets of classifiers are not identical.

Conclusion

I have provided a typologically informed and current description of numeral classifiers in the Odawa dialect of Ojibwe, including inventories. I identified a previously unmentioned distinction between the mensural and sortal types of numeral classifiers, that they occur with distinct root forms of the numeral 'one'. It was shown that measurements of time and land are to be excluded from the category of numeral classifiers, for although they share semantic and some morphosyntactic properties with classifiers, they do not co-occur with nouns. Lastly, changes in the semantics and availability of several numeral classifiers were documented.

NOTES

1. Chimiigwech to Mr. and Mrs. Kimewon for sharing the language with me, and to Mrs. Susan Askwith for hosting and mentoring me during my stay in Sault Ste. Marie. I would

also like to thank my advisers, Amy Dahlstrom, Salikoko Mufwene, and Itamar Francez for their feedback on this project. All remaining errors are my own.

2. It should be noted that many of these same morphemes also occur in verbs and in nouns. I set aside a similar description of verbal classifiers for future work, including constructions consisting of numeral + classifier + verb final. Previous work has established that when in nouns, these morphemes function only as content morphemes, and do not meet the typological definition of noun classifiers (Meyer 2019).
3. As an example of syncope, the name for the Ojibwe language in the Southwest dialect is pronounced *Anishinaabemowin.* In the Odawa dialect, the underlined vowels are syncopated and it is pronounced *Nishnaabemwin.*
4. Valentine (2001:883) labels mensural classifiers in numeral + classifier constructions as finals, writing, "A variety of other classifying finals occur which are used with numeral roots." Though he does not refer to them as mensural, they are discussed separately from what are identified here as sortal classifiers, and all examples provided are measurements. Though sortal classifiers are usually taken to be medials, they occur in the same numeral + classifier constructions as mensural classifiers, with no apparent differences in behavior. Further research is needed to confirm, but it seems sortal classifiers may also be considered finals in these constructions.
5. Abbreviations used: AN = animate gender, IN = inanimate gender, CL = classifier, SG = singular, PL = plural, 1 = first person, 2 = second person, 3 = third person, FUT = future, VAI = verb animate intransitive, VII = verb inanimate intransitive, VTA = verb transitive animate, VTI = verb transitive inanimate, IMP = imperative, int. = intended.
6. In some dialects, *giigoonh* 'fish' is a count noun with the plural form *giigoonyag,* but these speakers rejected the plural. A reviewer asked whether this was accurate for Ojibwe or a result of English contact. While contact is a possibility, which nouns are count and which are mass in any given language is a matter of conventionalization. E.g., why are 'corn', 'rice', and 'spinach' all mass nouns in English, but 'peas' are not? Conventionalization causes variation in the application of the count/mass distinction, both across languages and across dialects, and Ojibwe is no different. Mathieu (2012:184), for example, lists *semaa* 'tobacco' as having plural *semaag* based on fieldwork with native speakers at Cape Croker, but no such plural exists in the Southwestern variety or with the speakers in Sault Ste. Marie.
7. Some notes on this table: The classifier /-diba'igan/ seems to have the semantics of any standard measurement, and gains more specific meaning in the context of the noun. For example, *ngo-diba'igan zenbaanh* was supplied for the elicitation 'one mile of ribbon', e.g., for a giant to make a dress.

Jiimaan also occurs as an independent noun meaning 'boat'. Since both /-oonag/ and /-jiimaan/ exist as mensural classifiers for 'boatload, boatful', I tested whether there was any semantic restriction in their use with the noun *jiimaan.* For Mr. Kimewon, the following were acceptable for 'one boatload of boats'/'one boatload of small boats', e.g., a shipment of remote control boats or lifeboats, delivered via boat:

i. *ngod-**oonag** jiimaan/ngod-**oonag** jiimaanhs*

ii. *ngod-**jiimaan** jiimaan/ngod-**jiimaan** jiimaanhs*

Mrs. Kimewon accepted (i), but felt (ii) was not preferable.

The mensural classifier /-wewaan/ has the general semantics of 'a set' and can be used with nouns whose referents typically come in conventionalized numbers, e.g., pairs of shoes or a dozen eggs.

The classifiers /-mnikwaajgaanhs/ and /-naagaans/ both have the meaning of 'one cup', but the former shares its form with the VAI verb *minikwe* 'to drink' and the latter with the independent noun *onaagaans* 'cup'. It seems the former has a more casual use, while the latter may be used for the exact measurement of a cup, e.g., in recipes.

The classifier /-zid-kakade'aa/ contains /-zid/ 'foot' combined with the VII /-gakakaa/ 'be square'.

The classifier /-nikzat/ has the semantics of 'a piece' and has certain restrictions on the nouns with which it can occur. Acceptable noun combinations seem to be those that are those that are nonliquid, and may be of a reasonably sized piece. Mrs. Kimewon did not accept its use with *doodooshaabo* 'milk' or a single piece of coffee grounds, as shown to her on a plate.

8. Valentine (2001:883) refers to numerals with sortal classifiers as 'classificatory numerals'.
9. Valentine (2001:572) remarks that the use of the 'wood' classifier in (i), translated as 'bottle', evokes the past use of wooden containers to store liquor.

   i. bezhgw-aatig   wiishkii
   one-wooden.CL   whiskey.IN
   'one bottle of whiskey'

10. One interesting use of /-aatik/ is found in *bezhigw-aatik bakwezhigan* 'one loaf of bread'. While it is true that loaves of bread are not necessarily inflexible, they are not flexible, either, since it is possible to break them in half. I might describe this as a difference between soft vs. hard instead of flexible vs. inflexible.

REFERENCES

Aikhenvald, Alexandra Y. 2000. *Classifiers: A Typology of Noun Categorization Devices.* Oxford: Oxford University Press.

Baraga, Frederic. 1878. *A Theoretical and Practical Grammar of the Otchipwe Language for the Use of Missionaries and Other Persons Living Among the Indians.* Montreal: Beauchemin & Valois.

Grinevald, Colette. 2000. A Morphosyntactic Typology of Classifiers. *Systems of Nominal Classification,* ed. by Gunter Senft, pp. 50–92. Cambridge: Cambridge University Press.

Kimewon, Leonard. [n.d.] *Miijim-daawegamigong* "In the Grocery Store." Handout.

Mathieu, Eric. 2012. On the Mass/Count Distinction in Ojibwe. *Count and Mass across Languages,* ed. by Diane Massam, pp. 172–198. Oxford: Oxford University Press.

Meyer, Cherry. 2018. Noun Categorization in Ojibwe: Animacy Is Gender and Gender Is Separate from the Count/Mass Distinction. In *Papers of the 47th Algonquian Conference,* ed. by Monica Macaulay and Margaret Noodin, pp. 199–216. East Lansing: Michigan State University Press.

Meyer, Cherry. 2019. The Status of Classifying Morphemes in Ojibwe. In *Papers of the 48th Algonquian Conference,* ed. by Monica Macaulay and Margaret Noodin, pp. 159–172. East Lansing: Michigan State University Press.

Rhodes, Richard A., and David J. Costa. 2003. The History of Algonquian Number Words. *Essays in Algonquian, Catawban, and Siouan Linguistics in Memory of Frank T. Siebert, Jr.,* ed. by Blair Rudes and David J. Costa, pp. 181–215. Algonquian and Iroquoian Linguistics Memoir 16. Winnipeg: Algonquian and Iroquoian Linguistics.

Valentine, J. Randolph. 2001. *Nishnaabemwin Reference Grammar.* Toronto: University of Toronto Press.

Revisiting Prosodic Prominence in Saulteaux Ojibwe

Taylor L. Miller

In this paper, I present and evaluate previous analyses of Ojibwe prosodic prominence, focusing on the Saulteaux Ojibwe dialect spoken in Manitoba (henceforth referred to only as Saulteaux).[1] It is generally accepted that the language demonstrates left-to-right iambic parsing (e.g., Bloomfield 1958; Valentine 1994, 2001), but analyses differ regarding primary stress assignment and the source of word-final prominence. Specifically, there is disagreement regarding whether foot construction is exhaustive in the language (allowing degenerate feet), whether word-final prominence is due to phonological stress or phonetic final lengthening, and how exactly primary stress is assigned.

I find support for word-final prominence in Saulteaux from novel data collected in the field. However, I find no evidence of predicted primary or secondary stress. Instead, I propose iambic foot structure is independent of stress assignment in Saulteaux and reanalyze word-final prominence as final lexical stress. The results in this paper are preliminary and thus necessitate further systematic research. I conclude with a discussion of future research directions, as well as the implications of the proposed analysis for other dialects of Ojibwe and within Algonquian linguistics as a whole.

Phonological Background

I begin by describing the Saulteaux phoneme inventory and the transcription method used in this paper. I then provide a brief explanation of basic metrical theory and foot structure.

Phoneme Inventory

Saulteaux's phoneme inventory is discussed in previous works on the dialect (e.g., Voorhis 1976; Cote 1985; Valentine 1994, 2001). There are multiple approaches to documenting the obstruents in Ojibwe. In some work they are distinguished by voicing only, and in others they are distinguished by a fortis/lenis contrast (e.g., Valentine 2001; Logan 2001). According to Valentine 2001:48, the voiceless obstruents not only differ in voicing but also in duration and muscular intensity. In some work (e.g., Valentine), the fortis obstruents are written as the voiceless counterparts (e.g., /p/), while the lenis obstruents are written as voiced (e.g., /b/). In other work (e.g., Voorhis), the difference is written as fortis /pp/ vs. lenis /p/. Because the fortis consonants may also be accompanied by preaspiration, Logan (2001) transcribes the fortis sound as /hp/ versus lenis /p/. Though there is indeed evidence that fortis obstruents are geminate lenis consonants (see Valentine 2001) and preaspiration does occur (see Logan 2001), the exact nature of the contrast is not germane to the present analysis. A voiced/voiceless distinction in IPA has been adopted for simplicity and easier reading, as presented in Table 1.[2]

TABLE 1. Saulteaux consonants

	LABIAL		ALVEOLAR		ALVEOPALATAL		PALATAL		VELAR		GLOTTAL	
Stops	p	b	t	d					k	g	ʔ	
Fricatives			s	z	ʃ	ʒ						
Affricates					tʃ	dʒ						
Nasals		m		n								
Glides		w						j				

Ojibwe dialects (including Saulteaux) are described as having long and short versions of /i, a, o/ but only a long version of /e:/ (e.g., Valentine 2001; Logan 2001), and this is also adopted here, as shown in Table 2. Piggott (1980) includes an analysis of an abstract /e/ in Odawa. Miller (2016) argues that the short counterpart is an allophone in free variation with other short vowels in Saulteaux, but it is not clear if an abstract phoneme is also active.

TABLE 2. Saulteaux vowels

	FRONT	BACK
High	i/i:	o/o:
Low	e:	a/a:

It is common practice in Ojibwe linguistics to present data using the double-vowel system—an adaptation of Leonard Bloomfield's (1958) work, developed by Charles Fiero and John Nichols (e.g., Nichols and White 1987). This system, as it is largely phonemic, hampers detailed phonetic or phonological analysis. Consider, for example, the stem-final voicing alternation present in the singular and plural forms of 'duck'.[3]

(1)	DV:	zhiishiib	'duck'	zhiishiib-ag	'ducks'
	IPA:	ʃi:ʃi:p	'duck'	ʃi:ʃi:b-ak	'ducks'

While voicing alternations have no bearing on a stress analysis, I have nevertheless opted to use only IPA when presenting Saulteaux data in this paper and in my other work (Miller 2018). My aim in doing so is to make the data more transparent in terms of phonological alternations so as to inform future phonological research and questions.

Metrical Theory

The analysis in this paper crucially relies on basic concepts found in metrical theory (e.g., Hayes 1995). The central claim of metrical theory is that stress is the manifestation of rhythmic structure. Often represented by a metrical grid, varying levels of prominence are associated with different phonological constituents or levels on the grid (syllables or morae, feet, word, phrase, and utterance).

Consider (2), which provides a short example of a metrical grid up to the word level. First, each syllable in the word *Mississippi* is marked with an X. At the next level, pairs of syllables group together to form feet. Disyllabic feet are characterized by one strong (more prominent) syllable and one weak (less prominent) syllable.

The strong syllables (also called foot heads) project an X at the foot layer of the metrical grid. If a foot demonstrates a strong-weak pattern of its components (syllables or morae), it is considered TROCHAIC. If it demonstrates a weak-strong pattern, it is considered IAMBIC. A foot consisting of only a single mora or syllable is called DEGENERATE; some languages ban such feet altogether. In the case of (2), there are two trochaic feet.

(2)					
			X		Word
	X		X		Foot
	X	X	X	X	Syllable
	mɪ	sə	sɪ	pi	

Each level in the metrical grid may only reference the level below it. Therefore, foot heads are the only objects which may be referenced at the word level. According to the property of CULMINATIVITY, one (and only one) foot head projects an X at the word level (the domain for primary stress in English). In (2), the syllable [sɪ] bears primary stress. Secondary stresses are assigned to the other foot heads within the word. Xs may be projected at higher levels, too, yielding phrasal and sentential prominence patterns. In this paper, though, we consider only the syllable, foot, and word levels.

In the remainder of this paper, I have not included metrical grids. Instead, feet are bracketed, and foot heads are bolded. This is only to save space, however, and a grid approach should be assumed for each example.

Stress and Prominence

Previous analyses of stress in Saulteaux have been proposed by Voorhis (1976) and Cote (1984). Logan (2001) summarizes these proposals as follows:

(3) Saulteaux Stress Assignment (Logan 2001:11)

a. Each syllable with a long vowel will be stressed.

b. The last syllable of every word is obligatorily stressed.

c. Every second syllable in a sequence of syllables with short vowels will be stressed. The other short vowels are realized in one of the unstressed allomorphs (often with [ɪ] or [ə]) or are elided—though they are elided far less than in dialects to the east (especially Odawa).

Voorhis (1976) does not overtly mark stress, but there is a brief discussion of vowel deletion (3c), which provides examples of stress assignment. Specifically, different vowels may delete depending on the number of syllables in the word. In (4a), there are four syllables. The long vowel /ó/ is obligatorily stressed because it is both long and it is the final syllable. In a sequence of three short vowels, only the second (/i/ in this case) should be stressed. Therefore, short /a/ may delete. In (4b), however, the person prefix /ki-/ is added to the stem. Long /ó/ is again stressed, but the sequence of short vowels has changed. Short /a/ is now stressed as it is an even numbered syllable, and the preceding /i/ may now delete.

(4) Stress Assignment in Saulteaux (Voorhis 1976, Lesson 15<hy>4)[4]

a. pimip(a)ttón 'Run.'

b. kipim(i)pattó na 'Are you running?'

This analysis is, however, simplified. First, it proposes no distinction between primary and secondary stress. Instead, long vowels, final syllables, and alternating syllables all bear undifferentiated levels of stress. This leads to a potential violation of CULMINATIVITY if each stress is considered to be primary stress. Furthermore, while long vowels typically occupy a strong position in a foot, to claim each long vowel is stressed is misdirected. In fact, it is a persistent problem throughout phonological descriptions to assume that length correlates with stress. A native speaker of English (or another language without contrastive vowel length) may easily mistake length for stress because English stress is marked by length, duration, and amplitude (e.g., de Lacy 2017). This is not the case in every language, however, as the acoustic correlates of stress must not impinge on contrastive features in the language (Vogel et al. 2015, 2016; Athanasopoulou and Vogel 2016). Ojibwe has contrastive vowel length; thus it is expected that length will not play a primary role in marking prominence.

While dialects of Ojibwe differ in terms of how often unstressed vowels are syncopated, there is little cross-dialectal variation proposed in stress assignment, making a larger body of work relevant to the present study of Saulteaux. Previous work on stress in other dialects of Ojibwe has formalized foot construction and differentiated between primary and secondary stress (e.g., Eastern Ojibwe/Odawa in Bloomfield 1956; Kaye 1973; Piggott 1980; Hayes 1995; Valentine 1994, 2001; Piggott and Newell 2006; North Western Ojibwe in Valentine 1994, and Severn Ojibwe in Todd 1972; Valentine 1994).

There is a general consensus in the literature that Ojibwe demonstrates left-to-right iambic parsing (Bloomfield 1958; Todd 1972; Kaye 1973; Voorhis 1976; Piggott

1980; Cote 1984; Hayes 1995; Valentine 1994, 2001; Logan 2001; Piggott and Newell 2006), but previous analyses diverge in other details of the language's stress system. The two main approaches in the literature differ in terms of whether foot construction is exhaustive (allowing degenerate feet), whether word-final prominence is due to phonological stress or phonetic final lengthening, and how exactly primary stress is assigned. As these approaches avoid the aforementioned issues with previous analyses of Saulteaux, and there are no major dialect differences predicted, they are described in the following subsections and subsequently tested in this paper.

The Exhaustive Foot Construction Approach

The Exhaustive Foot Construction Approach (henceforth EFC) builds on the proposal first introduced in Kaye 1973 (Piggott 1980; Valentine 1994, 2001; Piggott and Newell 2006), which requires that foot construction span the entire word, allowing degenerate feet at the right edge of the word.[5] As summarized in (5), long vowels must occur in a strong position, either as the head of an iambic foot or the only syllable in a bimoraic foot.[6] Word-final vowels are perceived as prominent and must also occupy a strong position, regardless of length, even if this yields a degenerate foot. Finally, primary stress is assigned to the foot head (strong position) in the antepenultimate foot of the word.

(5) EFC Stress Assignment in Ojibwe

- a. Parse iambic feet left to right with the following restrictions
    - i. Long vowels must occupy a strong position
    - ii. Word-final vowels must occupy a strong position
- b. Main stress is placed on the strong syllable in the antepenultimate foot

Consider (6–7) from Eastern Ojibwe (Valentine 2001:52) for an example of how stress is assigned under the EFC (5).[7] Iambic feet are parsed left to right. Long vowels necessarily occur in the strong syllable of the foot. If this does not happen, they are forced to form their own foot, and foot parsing begins again immediately to its right, as seen in (7).[8] Degenerate feet are allowed at the right edge, which is also seen in (7). Finally, primary stress is assigned by counting three feet from the end of the word and assigning primary stress to the strong syllable of that foot. If the word is shorter than three syllables, the initial (or only) foot head is assigned primary stress.

(6) [g i **d á**]$_{\Sigma}$ [g o ʃ **i n**]$_{\Sigma}$ 'you arrive'

(7) [**é:**]$_{\Sigma}$ [s i **b a**]$_{\Sigma}$ [n a **g**]$_{\Sigma}$ 'raccoons'

While the EFC addresses the aforementioned issues of differentiated stress levels and vowel length as an indicator of stress for Saulteaux (Voorhis 1976; Cote 1984; Logan 2001), the proposed primary stress rule is typologically unexpected. In fact, it has long been claimed in the literature that primary stress is limited to a maximal three-syllable window at either edge of the word domain (confirmed in Kager 2012). Placing primary stress on the antepenultimate foot-head, on the other hand, requires a noticeably larger five-syllable window.

The Non-exhaustive Construction Approach

The five-syllable window problem is avoided in Hayes's (1995) non-exhaustive construction analysis of Eastern Ojibwe/Odawa stress (henceforth NEC). While iambic feet are still parsed left to right, Hayes proposes a language-wide ban on degenerate feet. He provides support for this proposal with evidence from the third person plural suffix /-wag/ (Hayes 1995:218). When footed, it surfaces as itself (e.g., *dako:zi-wag* 'they are short'). The (final) suffix undergoes an attrition process, though (e.g., *odamino-g* 'they play'), indicating that it is unfooted. Similarly, Hayes claims that the final short syllable [migw] in (8) is left unfooted. Any perceived final prominence, he argues, is phonetic and thus irrelevant at the foot level. Hayes then proposes that primary stress is assigned to the antepenultimate (metrical) syllable.[9]

(8) NEC analysis (Hayes 1995:217; data from Piggott 1980:84)
[o **d a:**]$_{\Sigma}$ [**w é:**]$_{\Sigma}$ [w i **g a**]$_{\Sigma}$ m i g w 'a store'

Hayes proposes that the final foot is extrametrical unless the final foot does not coincide with the word edge (the peripherality condition). Thus, in (9) the final foot is extrametrical. Primary stress is assigned to the antepenultimate metrical syllable, as Hayes predicts.[10]

(9) NEC analysis (Hayes 1995:217; data from Piggott 1980:69)
[n i **n á**]$_{\Sigma}$ [m a **d a**]$_{\Sigma}$ <b i **m i**> 'we (excl.) sit'

To summarize, the EFC and NEC are the best available predictive tests for Saulteaux stress even though each was developed for other dialects of Ojibwe. Both approaches bypass the major theoretical and predictive issues raised for previous Saulteaux analyses (i.e., undifferentiated stress levels, length treated as stress, etc.). The two approaches differ in terms of whether foot construction is exhaustive (allowing degenerate feet), whether word-final prominence is due to phonological stress or phonetic final lengthening, and how exactly primary stress is assigned.

Current Study: Evaluating the EFC and NEC in Saulteaux

In this section, the EFC and NEC are evaluated for Saulteaux. The current analysis is part of a larger dissertation project that was not primarily focused on stress assignment. Thus this analysis is preliminary; systematic analysis requires future research (e.g., controlling for number of syllables, vowels, and eliciting the same words from each speaker). As Saulteaux has contrastive vowel length, length was not considered as a possible correlate for stress. Instead, possible correlates were determined by auditory impressions and then corroborated with visual analysis in Praat. As shown below, the results confirm the presence of a final prominence. Neither the EFC nor NEC is confirmed for Saulteaux, however, as there is no consistent acoustic manifestation of primary or secondary stress.

Data

The Saulteaux data in this paper were elicited during fieldwork in Winnipeg, Manitoba, during summer and fall of 2016. The corpus consists of 24 hours of audio recordings of elicitations with eight (five female, three male) native speakers of Saulteaux between the ages of 45 and 74. Elicitations took place in the speakers' homes, the University of Winnipeg's campus center, or in Winnipeg's Indian and Méti Friendship Centre.

Results

As predicted by both the EFC and NEC approaches, final prominence is confirmed in nouns (10) and verbs (11) both in isolation and within a sentence (12). Impressionistically, this prominence (whether stress or a phonetic phenomenon) is marked by a rise in pitch and intensity. In these examples, this is indicated by underlining the prominent syllable.

(10) Nouns

	a. animoʃ	'dog'
	b. odʒi:bɪk	'root'
	c. wi:pɪt	'tooth'

(11) Verbs

	a. omɪgi:	'to have sores/scabs'
	b. diko:nat	'to cut someone short'
	c. dagobizo	'to drive up among others'

(12)

gi:jose:	-jok	ondʒe	wawaʃke:ʃ	-ən
hunt	-3.PL	for	deer	-OBV

'They hunt for the deer.'

Beyond final prominence, the EFC and NEC sometimes make different predictions regarding primary stress assignment. For example, consider the nouns in (13). In each case, the same iambic foot structure is predicted, though peripheral feet in 'black' and 'hair.PL' are considered extrametrical for the NEC. The main difference arises in the predicted placement of primary stress in the nouns [makəte:wa:] 'black' and [opɪn] 'potato'. The EFC predicts primary stress to fall on the second vowel in both nouns, as that vowel ([ə] and [ɪ]) forms the head of the antepenultimate foot. The NEC predicts it will fall on the initial vowel in both nouns. In 'black', the first vowel is the antepenultimate footed syllable, predicted to attract primary stress. In 'potato', there are not enough syllables to reach an antepenultimate syllable. Therefore, primary stress is predicted to fall on the initial syllable.

(13)

EFC Predictions		NEC Predictions	
[mak**ə́**][te:][wa:]	'black'	[m**á**kə][te:]<wa:>	'black'
[w**í:**][nizɪ][sa:n]	'hair.PL'	[w**í:**][nizɪ]<sa:n>	'hair.PL'
[op**í**n]	'potato'	[**ó**pɪn]	'potato'

In fact, there is no consistent acoustic evidence for either primary or secondary stress in Saulteaux, disallowing confirmation of either approach. Some syllables may sound more prominent, but their location is not predictable from item to item. There are also lexical items that do not demonstrate prominence other than the final prominence mentioned above. First impressions therefore suggest Saulteaux does not mark or differentiate primary and secondary stress.

Proposal

Given the results above, I propose that Saulteaux is a final stress dialect of Ojibwe. Specifically, what has previously been referred to as final prominence (whether a foot head in the EFC or a phonetic boundary phenomenon in the NEC) is in fact lexical stress. With no acoustic manifestation of secondary stress, one might argue there is no evidence for iambic foot structure in the dialect. The phonological process of vowel syncopation suggests this would be an incorrect conclusion, though.

Vowel syncopation is described as a widespread process across Ojibwe dialects in which vowels in the weak positions of iambic feet may delete (see, for example, Valentine 2001). Some dialects (e.g., Eastern Ojibwe) apply vowel syncopation quite freely, often deleting all weak vowels in an utterance. Saulteaux typically retains vowels, but the process does sometimes apply (e.g., in pronominal clitics). Though rare and optional, the fact that the process is active in the dialect at all necessitates the previously proposed iambic foot structure—but not for stress assignment.

An active foot structure without acoustically manifested stress (at least rhythmic secondary stress) is not a novel proposal. Feet and stress are considered intrinsically linked under traditional metrical theory (Hayes 1985, 1995; Hammond 1984; McCarthy and Prince 1996; Kager 1989), but this is not a universally held view. Other researchers have argued for foot structure and stress to be separated, allowing for foot structure to be interpreted outside of stress (e.g., Halle and Vergnaud 1987; Crowhurst 1991; Walker 1997; Idsardi 1992; González 2005, 2007). González (2005) conducts a typological survey of 74 languages and finds strictly stress-sensitive phonology, processes sensitive to both stress and foot structure, and strictly foot-sensitive phonology. Capanahua (Panoan), for example, does not exhibit any acoustic correlates of secondary stress but trochaic foot structure dictates which vowels may reduce (González 2007:63). If the present proposal is confirmed in future studies, the Capanahua situation is analogous to that observed here in Saulteaux.

Summary and Discussion

In this paper, two main approaches to stress and prominence in Ojibwe were evaluated using novel data from Saulteaux Ojibwe. Both the exhaustive foot construction (EFC) and non-exhaustive construction (NEC) approaches predict a word-final prominence, though they differ in the proposed source for the prominence (stress or boundary phenomenon respectively). The approaches make markedly different predictions, though, regarding primary stress assignment. While final prominence is confirmed in Saulteaux, there is no apparent manifestation of the predicted primary or secondary stresses for either approach. Thus, a new proposal that Saulteaux is a final stress dialect was advanced. Subsequently, it was proposed that iambic foot structure is not associated with stress assignment in the dialect. It is still necessary, however, due to vowel syncopation.

A final stress analysis is novel for any dialect of Ojibwe and is therefore equally interesting and suspicious. Barring contradictory results in future research, final prominence is the only clear form of prominence that is active in Saulteaux. The question is then if Saulteaux is unique among other dialects of Ojibwe or if other dialects may also be reanalyzed. If Saulteaux is unique, why is it separate from other dialects? If other dialects may be reanalyzed, is this a newer language change or were the original analyses incorrect? Was the EFC or NEC historically true of Ojibwe, stemming from Proto-Algonquian's alternating rhythmic structure and eventually lost? These questions are left to future research.

Future research must be dual focused. First, as discussed earlier, the next step is a systematic acoustic study of stress in Saulteaux. Acoustic measurements of stress in Ojibwe are lacking, and results may confirm or disconfirm the present preliminary analysis. Such a study should also include native speaker intuitions regarding stress assignment (e.g., the tapping method). Second, other dialects of Ojibwe and neighboring Algonquian languages' stress systems should be analyzed (e.g., nearby Manatoulin Ojibwe or Cheyenne). Results from those studies offer insight into the question of historical or synchronically active stress systems and dialect relationships.

NOTES

1. Many thanks to the Saulteaux community and native speakers who agreed to teach me about their language, to the Jacobs Research Fund for funding the fieldwork in the

community, to Dr. Irene Vogel and the Phonetics and Phonology Lab at University of Delaware for their helpful feedback, to the audience at the 49th Algonquian Conference for a lively discussion, and to the anonymous reviewers who helped make this paper so much better.

2. Abbreviations: 3 = third person, DV = double-vowel system, excl. = exclusive, IPA = International Phonetic Alphabet, OBV = obviative, PL = plural.
3. The noun 'duck' is transcribed here with an initial [ʃ], though the word is spelled with <zh> suggesting a [ʒ]. The voiceless version was consistently produced across Saulteaux speakers, though.
4. The data in (4) is presented in Voorhis's orthography. Long vowels are marked with an acute accent. Fortis obstruents are written as /pp/ and lenis obstruents are written as /p/.
5. It is not immediately clear if "the word" is meant to refer to the phonological word (ω) in previous work, as there is no overt discussion of the exact domain of stress assignment. Piggott and Newell's 2016 analysis of the Odawa dialect's stress adopts a phase-based perspective, thus eliminating the use of prosodic structure entirely.
6. Coda consonants are not moraic. Monosyllabic bimoraic feet will include a long vowel.
7. As mentioned earlier, metrical grids are not provided. Feet are bracketed, while foot heads (strong positions) are bolded. Primary stress is indicated by an acute accent on the stressed syllable's vowel. Bolded syllables (foot heads) without the acute accent (primary stress) bear secondary stress.
8. Note that Valentine (2001:52) uses /e/ to indicate the long vowel in accordance with the Ojibwe standard orthographic practices. I have indicated its length here for easier reading.
9. Hayes also includes a colon or superfoot layer in his analysis. This has been excluded here, as the role of superfeet vs. word domain is not relevant to the basic rules of stress assignment.
10. Piggott and Newell (2006) have criticized the NEC's ban of degenerate feet, specifically arguing that primary stress placement must be assigned to the antepenultimate foot head. They point to the following examples in (i), claiming that in order for any stress to fall on the modifier /bi/ 'toward the speaker' (a word-internal phase) it must form a degenerate foot. Newell (2014) and Piggott and Newell (2014) include additional examples of modifier-final degenerate feet.

(i) a. [b í]$_{\Sigma}$ [i ʒ à:]$_{\Sigma}$ 'he comes'
b. [g í:]$_{\Sigma}$ [b ì]$_{\Sigma}$ [i ʒ à:]$_{\Sigma}$ 'he came'

In the case of (i), primary stress is assigned to the antepenultimate foot word (CP). The modifier appears word-final at spellout, allowing degenerate foot construction. It is through later linearization that this word-finality is obscured. Earlier work on this issue references cyclic phases as nested phonological words (e.g. Piggott and Newell 2006, 2014), but later work argues that phases are all that is necessary (e.g. Newell and Scheer 2017). For this study, the phasal analysis of stress is not important. In a future acoustic study, however, such examples must be included and Piggot, Newell, and Scheer's work must be directly addressed.

REFERENCES

Athanasopoulou, Angeliki, and Irene Vogel. 2016. The Acoustic Manifestation of Prominence in Stressless Languages. Paper presented at the Interspeech conference of the International Speech Communication Association, San Francisco, CA, September 8–12. https://doi.org/10.21437/Interspeech.2016<hy>1424.

Bloomfield, Leonard. 1958. *Eastern Ojibwa: Grammar, Texts, and Word List,* ed. by C. Hockett. Ann Arbor: University of Michigan Press.

Cote, Margaret R. 1985. *Nahkawēwin: Saulteaux (Ojibway Dialect of the Plains).* Regina: Saskatchewan Indian Federated College.

Crowhurst, Megan. 1991. Demorafication in Tübatulabal: Evidence from Initial Reduplication and Stress. In *Proceedings of North East Linguistic Society,* vol. 21. Amherst: GLSA, University of Massachusetts.

Crowhurst, Megan, and Mark S. Hewitt. 1995. Directional Footing, Degeneracy, and Alignment. Unpublished manuscript, University of North Carolina and University of British .Columbia. ROA 65<hy>0000.

de Lacy, Paul. 2017. What We Know about Stress. University of Delaware Linguistics Colloquium, Newark, March 17.

González, Carolina. 2005. Phonologically-Conditioned Allomorphy in Panoan: Towards an Analysis. *Papers in Phonology* 6:39–56.

González, Carolina. 2007. Typological Evidence for the Separation between Stress and Foot Structure. *New Challenges in Typology: Broadening the Horizons and Redefining the Foundations,* ed. by Matti Miestamo and Berhard Wälchli, pp. 55–75. New York: Mouton de Gruyter.

Halle, Morris, and Jean-Roger Vergnaud. 1987. Stress and the Cycle. *Linguistic Inquiry* 18(1):45–84.

Hammond, Michael. 1984. Constraining Metrical Theory: A Modular Theory of Rhythm and Destressing. Indiana University Linguistics Club.

Hayes, Bruce. 1985. Iambic and Trochaic Rhythm in Stress Rules. *Proceedings of the Eleventh*

Annual Meeting of the Berkeley Linguistics Society, ed. by Mary Niepokui et al., pp. 429–446, Berkeley, CA: Berkeley Linguistics Society.

Hayes, Bruce. 1995. *Metrical Stress Theory: Principles and Case Studies.* Chicago: University of Chicago Press.

Idsardi, William. 1992. The Computation of Stress. PhD thesis, Massachusetts Institute of Technology.

Logan, Harold Jeffrey. 2001. A Collection of Saulteaux Texts with Translations and Linguistic Analyses. MA thesis, University of Regina.

McCarthy, John J., and Alan Prince. 1996. Prosodic Morphology 1986. Linguistics Department Faculty Publication Series 13. University of Massachusetts.

Miller, Taylor L. 2016. Re-examining the Front Vowels in Saulteaux Ojibwe: The Role of Short [e]. Paper read at the 48th Algonquian Conference, University of Wisconsin–Milwaukee, October.

Miller, Taylor L. 2018. The Phonology-Syntax Interface and Polysynthesis: A Study of Kiowa and Saulteaux Ojibwe. PhD thesis, University of Delaware.

Kager, René. 1989. A Metrical Theory of Stress and Destressing in English and Dutch. PhD thesis, Utrecht University.

Kager, René. 2012. Stress in Windows: Language Typology and Factorial Typology. *Lingua* 122(13):1454–1493.

Kaye, Jonathan. 1973. Odawa Stress and Related Phenomena. *Odawa Language Project: Second Report,* ed. by G. Piggot and J. Kaye, pp. 42–50. Toronto: Centre for Linguistic Studies, University of Toronto.

Newell, Heather. 2014. Representation and Linearization: Interface Issues. Paper read at Reading Tobias Scheer Workshop, Ecole des Hautes Etudes en Sciences Sociales (EHESS), Paris, February 6–8.

Newell, Heather, and Tobias Scheer. 2017. Prosodic Domains: Overthrowing the Hierarchy. Paper read at the 25th Manchester Phonology Meeting, University of Manchester, May 26.

Nichols, John D., and Lena White. 1987. *Nishnaabebii'gedaa: Exercises in Writing for Speakers of Central Ojibwe and Odawa. Readers and Study Guides.* Winnipeg: Native Languages Programme, Department of Native Studies, University of Manitoba.

Piggott, Glyne L. 1980. *Aspects of Odawa Morphophonemics.* New York: Routledge.

Piggott, Glyne L., and Heather Newell. 2006. Syllabification, Stress and Derivation by Phase in Ojibwa. *McGill Working Papers in Linguistics* 20(2), ed. by R. Mercado and Y. Furukawa, pp. 9–64.

Piggott, Glyne L., and Heather Newell. 2014. Interactions at the Syntax-Phonology Interface:

Evidence from Ojibwe. *Lingua* 150:32–362.

Todd, Evelyn M. 1972. Ojibwa Syllabic Writing and its Implications for a Standard Ojibwa Alphabet. *Anthropological Linguistics* 14(9):357–360.

Valentine, J. Randolph. 1994. Ojibwe Dialect Relationships. PhD thesis, University of Texas at Austin.

Valentine, J. Randolph. 2001. *Nishnaabemwin Reference Grammar.* Toronto: University of Toronto Press.

Vogel, Irene, Angeliki Athanasopoulou, and Nadya Pincus. 2015. Acoustic Properties of Prominence in Hungarian and the Functional Load Hypothesis. *Approaches to Hungarian 14,* ed. by Katalin É. Kiss, Balázs Surányi, and Éva Dékány, pp. 267–292. Amsterdam: John Benjamins.

Vogel, Irene, Angeliki Athanasopoulou, and Nadya Pincus. 2016. Prominence, Contrast and the Functional Load Hypothesis: An Acoustic Investigation. *Dimensions of Phonological Stress,* ed. by Jeffrey Heinz, Rob Goedemans, and Harry van der Hulst, pp. 123–167. Cambridge: Cambridge University Press.

Voorhis, Paul H. 1976. *A Saulteaux (Ojibwe) Phrase Book Based on the Dialects of Manitoba.* Brandon, Manitoba: Department of Native Studies, Brandon University.

Walker, Rachel. 1997. Mongolian Stress, Licensing, and Factorial Typology. Unpublished manuscript, University of California, Santa Cruz.

Blackfoot Pitch Contour

An Instrumental Investigation

Mizuki Miyashita and Natalie Weber

Word prominence in Blackfoot is characterized by high pitch peaks associated with certain syllables of a word.[1] These syllables are expressed at a relatively higher pitch than neighboring syllables. Frantz (2017) calls this type of prominence PITCH ACCENT, and this term has been widely adopted (Kaneko 1999; Miyashita 2011; Van der Mark 2003; Weber 2016; among others).[2] Several articles have been written on the phonetic correlates of pitch accent in Blackfoot (Miyashita 2019; Van Der Mark 2003) and the predictivity of pitch accent location in terms of metrical stress theory (Weber 2016; Kaneko 1999) and morphology (Weber and Allen 2012). (However, see Stacy 2004 for arguments against a metrical account of pitch accent and in favor of a tonal analysis.) The current paper takes a holistic approach and describes pitch movement across words. We claim that prosody in Blackfoot is better characterized by the shape of the pitch contour than by individual accented syllables.

As briefly described in Taylor (1969), there seem to be pitch contour patterns that hold across words, regardless of length. In this paper we augment his observation with acoustic measurements of two major pitch contours. We claim that pitch contours and the variations on contour shape result from an interaction between pitch accent location (a local pitch maximum) and pitch declination toward a final low pitch target (a boundary pitch minimum). We propose an analysis of our observations in an autosegmental-metrical (AM) model of intonational phonology (Pierrehumbert 1980; Ladd 2008; among many others), where pitch contours are phonetically interpolated between the beginning of an utterance, an H* pitch accent, and an L% boundary tone.

The rest of the paper is organized as follows. In the next section we briefly overview previous descriptions in the Blackfoot literature on pitch accent and word prominence. We then describe our methods for collecting and analyzing word forms, before laying out our observations of the data. Following that, we discuss how these observations relate back to Taylor's description of two pitch contours, and how this study could be augmented in the future. The final section concludes.

Pitch Accent and Contours in Blackfoot

Blackfoot pitch accent manifests as a raised F_0 on a syllable (Frantz 2017; Van Der Mark 2003) and is marked in the orthography with an acute accent (Frantz 2017; Frantz and Russell 2017), as in the examples in (1). The acute accent on the vowel of the first syllable in (1a) indicates that the highest pitch of this word falls on the first syllable. In (1b), on the other hand, pitch accent falls on the second syllable, and the pitch of this accented syllable is higher than the preceding and following syllables.[3] These examples show that the location of pitch accent is distinctive in that it can disambiguate word forms.

(1) a. ákaohkiimiwa 'he's married'
b. akáóhkiimiwa 'he has many wives' (Frantz 2017:3)

Note that pitch accent in Blackfoot is privative. While some syllables have a high pitch peak (pitch accent), no syllables are specified for a low pitch. Instead, as we will see, the pitch contour is simply interpolated between pitch accents and other tonal targets. Each word has at least one pitch peak, but may contain more. There are a number of examples with multiple accents in Frantz and Russell (2017) and Taylor (1969), and those examples tend to be highly polymorphemic. However, our discussion is limited to words with only one pitch peak.

According to Frantz (2017), pitch falls steadily across an utterance. This pitch declination affects the pitch of accented syllables such that an accented syllable toward the end of an utterance may have a lower F_0 than an unaccented syllable earlier in the utterance. In contrast, Taylor (1969) describes several different word melodies, depending on where accent generally falls within a word. He categorizes them into two major types: PITCH CONTOUR NUMBER ONE and PITCH CONTOUR NUMBER TWO. In Pitch Contour Number One, the first word prominence is on or before the penultimate syllable. "The highest pitch in this contour is found with the first stressed syllable.... Any syllables... which precede the first stress are lower in pitch than the stressed syllable, but are of higher pitch than any stressless syllables which follow" (Taylor 1969:49). He describes several different pitch decrescendos after the first accented syllable, which depend on the number of pitch accents in the word and where long vowels are located (see Stacy 2004 for a summary). In Pitch Contour Number Two, the first word prominence is on the final syllable and "the entire contour is pronounced with a slow, deliberate, almost solemn cadence, and on a low pitch level" (Taylor 1969:51). The final syllable "is distinguished by its greater relative intensity, but its pitch does not differ from that of any preceding syllable or syllables" (Taylor 1969:51). However, because the Blackfoot word can be extremely long due to its polysynthetic nature, the number of syllables in a word varies significantly, making it difficult to generalize pitch patterns based only on Taylor's description.

For this reason, this study controls for number of syllables and only uses words that have two, three, and four syllables with a single pitch accent. Under this context, our study provides empirical support for Taylor's claim that there are two pitch contours in Blackfoot that are correlated with whether pitch accent falls on the final syllable of the word or elsewhere. We turn now to a discussion of our methods.

Method

The data provided here are taken from recordings made in October 2013 with a male native speaker of Montana Blackfoot who was in his 80s at the time of recording. This speaker is knowledgeable in the tribe's culture and history, and he is an expert storyteller and traditional singer. According to Tsunoda (2005), ability to perform storytelling is a sign of high fluency and proficiency, and thus we expect his speech to reflect traditional Blackfoot prosody. The original study collected words of various lexical classes (including nouns and inflected verbs) in order to study the segmental inventory of Blackfoot.[4] Pitch accent was not one of the original variables, and

TABLE 1. Number of words by accent location

ACCENTED SYLLABLE	FIRST	SECOND	THIRD	TOTAL
Two-syllable word	7	11	n/a	18
Three-syllable word	4	10	5	19
Four-syllable word	3	6	4	13
Aggregate	14	27	9	50

consequently, the data for the present study is not equally balanced in terms of pitch accent location. Even so, the data separate into several clear patterns, as we discuss in our final section, and we believe that these observations will be robust in future studies of Blackfoot pitch contours.

The speaker was asked to pronounce each Blackfoot word in isolation, that is, in citation form, repeating each word three times. The speaker is not literate in Blackfoot, so English translations of the target words were given as prompts. In total, 175 Blackfoot words were recorded as part of the original study. From this total, we excluded words containing syllabic (interconsonantal) fricatives resulting from vowel-consonant coalescence (Miyashita 2018), such as the [x̩] in *omahkinaa* [omx̩kina:] 'old man'. These fricatives are voiceless and cannot therefore carry pitch; we excluded them because the relatively long interval between the vowels on either side of a syllabic fricative could potentially change the pitch contour shape. Most words were spoken with a level high pitch on accented vowels, but a few words (e.g., *mííni* 'berry', *píítaa* 'eagle') were pronounced with a pitch rise toward the end of a long accented vowel and so were excluded. Finally, we excluded words that were longer than four syllables. The number of remaining words with two, three, and four syllables were 18 two-syllable words, 19 three-syllable words, and 13 four-syllable words, as in Table 1. (Note that there were no four-syllable words with fourth syllable accent in our data.)

All of the words in our data set are four syllables or shorter and have only one pitch accent. Because the words were pronounced in isolation, each word is simultaneously an entire utterance or intonational phrase. Therefore, the present study cannot determine whether the domain of pitch contours is properly the word or utterance level, and later studies may show that some of our observations hold of multiword utterances rather than individual words.

We considered only the second of the three repetitions of each word, in order to avoid initial or final pitch effects from list intonation. We extracted the

TABLE 2. Pitch range of unaccented syllables

SYLLABLE COUNT	FIRST	SECOND	THIRD	FOURTH
Two-syllable word	81–98	53–68		
Three-syllable word	79–101	67–91	58–68	
Four-syllable word	80–99	80–98	68–84	51–74

fundamental frequency (F_0) of all vowels in each word using Praat (Boersma and Weenink 2013). The F_0 of each vowel was measured at its highest level pitch point as measured in Praat and determined by our own perception. In the next section we turn to our observations of the changes in F_0 across a word, and the interaction of F_0 with pitch accent.

Observations

We observed three major patterns. First, the pitch measurements of unaccented syllables describe a line of pitch declination throughout the utterance, which corroborates the description in Frantz (2017). Second, the pitch peak of accented syllables is higher than the line of declination. Third, there are two major pitch contours, depending on whether the word-final syllable is accented.

Declination

Pitch declination is the fall of fundamental frequency (F_0) across an utterance (Gussenhoven 2004:97). It is most easily seen across syllables that might be expected to be of equal pitch. For tonal languages, a sentence can be constructed with words that all have the same tone, and pitch declination can be clearly seen across the utterance. Recall that Blackfoot pitch accent is acoustically manifested by a pitch peak on a syllable, but unaccented syllables have no particular pitch target and might be expected to be pronounced with equal pitch. Therefore we plotted the pitch range of only UNACCENTED syllables in order to reveal the line of pitch declination in Blackfoot. Table 2 shows the pitch range of unaccented vowels in two-, three-, and four-syllable words. The pitch falls between successive pairs of syllables throughout the word. Since all of the ranges in Table 2 are from the pitch of unaccented syllables, we can conclude that pitch declines throughout the

TABLE 3. T-tests assuming unequal variances comparing unaccented final syllables in two-, three-, and four-syllable words

TEST	*P*-VALUE	SIGNIFICANT?
2 × 3	0.230121	No (p > 0.1)
3 × 4	0.680275	No (p > 0.1)
2 × 4	0.199935	No (p > 0.1)

utterance, regardless of the location of pitch accent in any particular word (which is not included in Table 2 at all).

Interestingly, the pitch of an unaccented final syllable (bolded in Table 2) falls within a low narrow range from 51Hz to 74Hz, regardless of how many syllables are in the word. We consider this to be a low pitch target at the right edge of the utterance. To show that the pitch range of unaccented syllables in two-, three-, and four-syllable words is not statistically different, we ran three two-sample t-tests assuming unequal variances. The three t-tests compared the mean pitch of unaccented final syllables in (1) two-syllable versus three-syllable words [2 × 3], (2) three-syllable versus four-syllable words [3 × 4], and (3) two-syllable versus four-syllable words [2 × 4]. Table 3 gives the p-values for each of the three tests. None of the tests were significant ($p > 0.1$), which shows that there is no significant difference between pitch ranges of final unstressed vowels in words of any length. We take this as evidence that pitch declines throughout an utterance to this particular pitch target (around 51Hz–74Hz).

The charts in Figure 1 are a graphical representation of pitch declination in two-, three-, and four-syllable words, respectively. The open dots represent the pitch of each unaccented syllable, where the position of the syllable is represented by equal intervals along the *x*-axis, and frequency from 40Hz to 120Hz is along the *y*-axis. The dotted line is the line of best fit through these points, and represents the PITCH DECLINATION throughout the word (Ladd 1984). In all three graphs, the line crosses the final column of pitch points at the same range (51Hz to 74Hz), which is due to the final low pitch target. As shown here, pitch falls quickly in two-syllable words and more slowly in three- and four-syllable words in order to meet the low pitch target.[5]

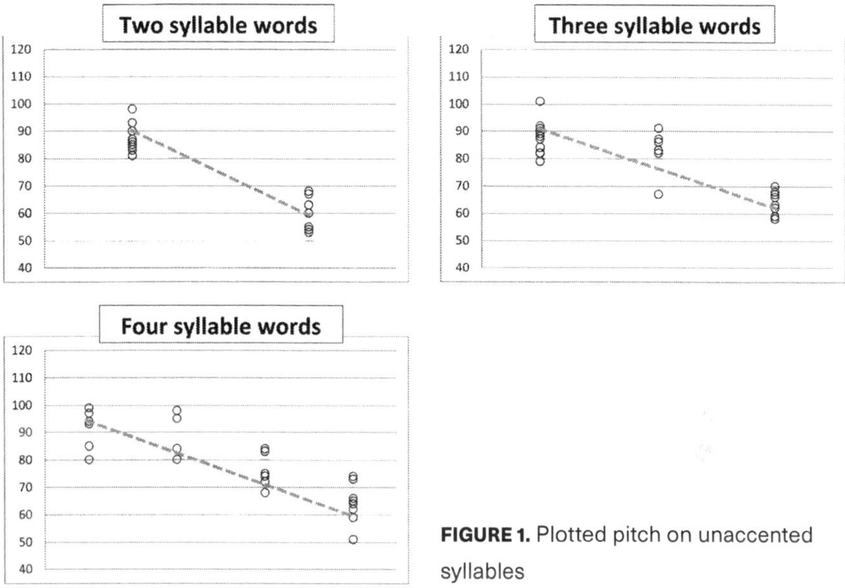

FIGURE 1. Plotted pitch on unaccented syllables

Pitch Peak

The pitch of accented syllables is always higher than the line of declination. Pitch accent is thus a deviation from the neutral pitch declination of the utterance, or a pitch movement toward a high local pitch maximum. Figure 2 illustrates this for two-, three-, and four-syllable words. These graphs include the open dots from Figure 1, representing the pitch of unaccented syllables, and the dotted line of declination, but also include black dots representing the pitch of accented syllables. The average pitch of accented syllables is higher than the line of declination, regardless of the length of the word.

We now turn to a description of two different pitch contour shapes, depending on where pitch accent falls.

Pitch Contour 1: Accent on Nonfinal Syllable

In this section we describe the pitch contour of words with accent on a nonfinal syllable. Figure 3 illustrates the pitch movements throughout the words in two-, three-, and four-syllable words. The *x*-axis shows each successive syllable at equal intervals; the *y*-axis shows the range of F_0 from 40Hz to 120Hz. The values plotted are the average F_0 of each syllable, and we have shown all possible contours for each

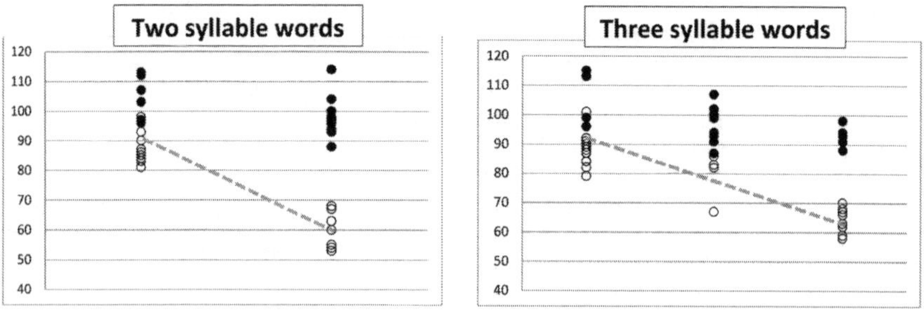

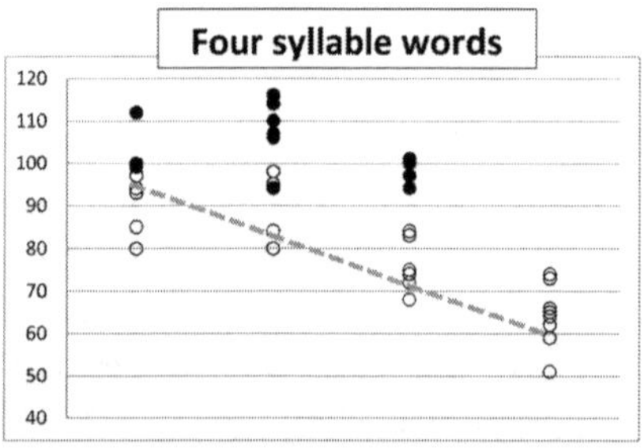

FIGURE 2. Plotted pitch on accented and unaccented syllables

word length in one plot. Disyllabic words have only one possible contour if accent falls on the nonfinal syllable. Three-syllable words have two possible contours with nonfinal accent: accent falls either on the first or second syllable. Similarly, the accent in four-syllable words may fall on the first, second, or third syllable. In these words, pitch rises from the beginning of the utterance to the pitch peak of the accented syllable if those two positions are distinct, and then falls toward the word-final low pitch target. The difference in F_0 between the pitch peak and the word-final target is greatest when accent falls on the initial syllable, and is smallest near the end of the word.

Pitch Contour 2: Accent on Final Syllable

In this section we describe the pitch contour of words with final accent. Figure 4 is a graph of the average pitch of syllables in two- and three-syllable words with accent on the final syllable. (Recall that our sample did not include any four-syllable words with final accent.) From the start of the utterance, pitch rises slightly to the final accented syllable, but the movement is perceptually (to the authors' ears) flat or monotonous. Taylor describes this pitch contour as having a "measured, monotonous quality" (Taylor 1969:51).

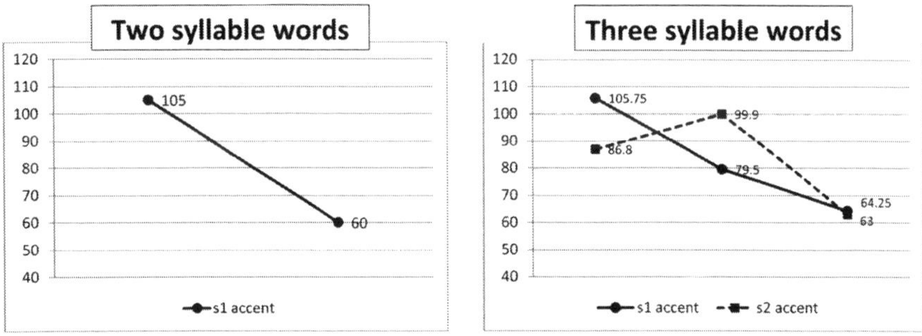

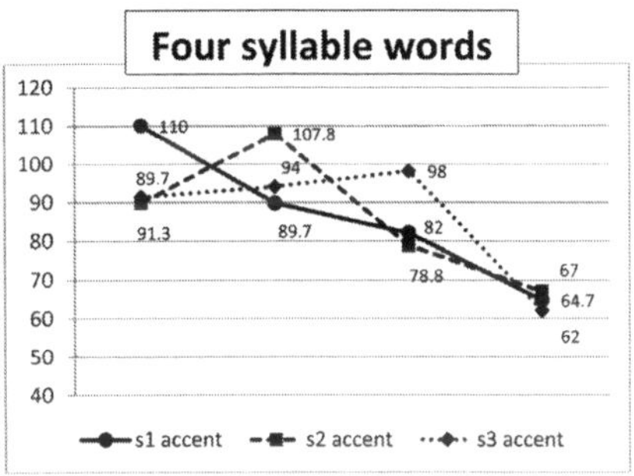

FIGURE 3. Pitch contour of words with non-final accent

The pitch of the final syllable has a higher pitch range (88Hz–114Hz) than the range of the low pitch target found on final unaccented syllables (51Hz–74Hz), discussed above. In this case, there is no evidence that there is a final low pitch target. Because there is no obvious pitch declination, we take this as evidence that when pitch accent and boundary pitch targets conflict, the high pitch target of the pitch accented syllable is preserved over the low pitch target at the right edge

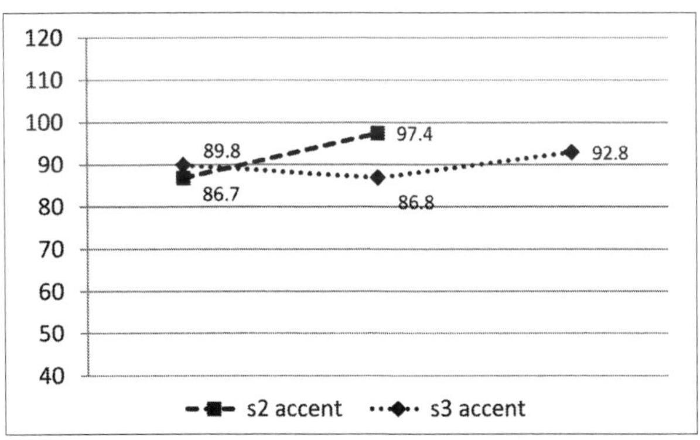

FIGURE 4. Pitch contour of words with non-final accent

of the utterance. However, the pitch range of the accented final syllables is not as high as the pitch of accented syllables that fall closer to the left edge of the word. Thus, the perceptually flat pitch contour of words with final accent results from the interaction between pitch declination and pitch accent (Ladd 1984).

Summary

Our observations can be summarized as follows. (i) There is a pitch declination throughout a word that is revealed by plotting a line of best fit through the pitch of unaccented syllables. (ii) An accented syllable has a high pitch target, which is shown by pitch movement above the line of declination to a pitch peak on an accented syllable. (iii) When a nonfinal syllable is accented, the pitch falls from the pitch peak down to the low target at the right edge of the utterance. (iv) When the final syllable is accented, the pitch contour is perceived as flat, but acoustic measurements show that pitch rises slightly to the final accented syllable.

Discussion

In this section we propose an autosegmental-metrical (AM) analysis of Blackfoot pitch contours and discuss how it explains the observations above. We also discuss our contribution to the field of Blackfoot prosody.

Analysis

In an autosegmental-metrical model of intonational phonology (Pierrehumbert 1980; Ladd 2008, and subsequent work), intonational melodies are represented by a string of H and L tones on an autosegmental tier that associate to syllables in the utterance. The tones are manifested by local pitch maxima or minima and come in two types: pitch accents (T*) associate with stressed syllables, while boundary tones (T%) associate with prosodic domain boundaries. In this system, Blackfoot pitch accent is modeled as an H* tone that associates to particular syllables and creates a pitch maximum in the pitch contour. In words with nonfinal accent, the lowest point of the pitch contour is a targeted pitch range on the final syllable, which can be modeled as a boundary L% tone that associates to the final syllable of a prosodic domain.

In an AM analysis, intonational contours are underspecified phonologically and phonetically. Pitch is simply interpolated between tonal targets, which is one reason why pitch contours take different shapes on words of different lengths. This is exactly what we see in Blackfoot: the pitch contour is interpolated from the start of the utterance to the H* pitch accent, and then down to the L% tone. However, the height of F_0 on a pitch accented syllable is constrained by pitch declination. A pitch accent toward the left edge of the word will have a much higher F_0 than one toward the right. Note that a final accented syllable cannot be analyzed as a downstepped !H*, which is the lowering of subsequent H tones. The reason is that none of the words in our sample included multiple pitch accents. A final accented syllable is therefore a true H*. To explain why the pitch peak is so low, we suggest that F_0 height is determined by an interaction between LEXICAL PITCH ACCENT LOCATION and PITCH DECLINATION toward the final low (L%) boundary tone.

In the following section we demonstrate how this analysis accounts for the pitch contour of four-syllable words.

Case Study: Four-Syllable Words

We use schematic illustrations of pitch movement in this section to show how the pitch contour is formed in four-syllable words with pitch accent on the first, second, or third syllables. In the figures below, the line of declination was calculated from the fundamental frequency of unaccented syllables and is indicated with a dotted line (Figures 5–8). In these illustrations, we have plotted the average pitch of only the initial, final, and accented syllables. An accented syllable creates a pitch movement above the line of declination, which changes the slope of the remainder of the pitch contour (shown with a solid line).

For example, Figure 5 shows a four-syllable word with initial accent, where the pitch of the accented syllable is raised above the line of declination, as indicated by the arrow. The pitch contour is then interpolated from this pitch peak down to the low L% boundary tone realized on syllable four.

Similarly, pitch accent on the second syllable creates a pitch peak that is raised above the line of declination (indicated by the arrow in Figure 6). Pitch rises from the beginning of the utterance to this peak, and then falls to the low boundary tone on the final syllable.

Similarly, a four-syllable word with penultimate accent shows a pitch contour that rises slightly to the pitch peak of the accented syllable and then falls to the

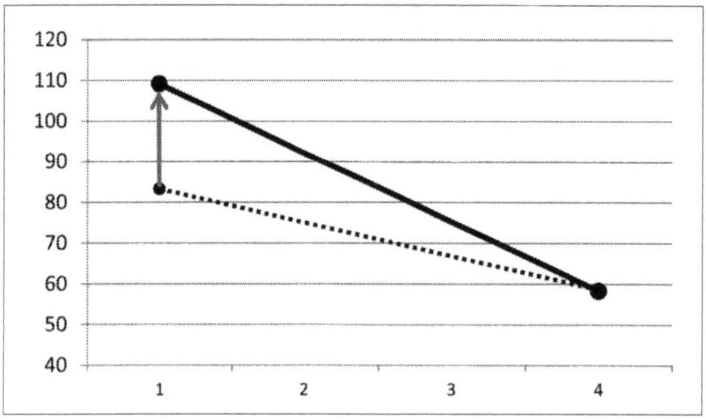

FIGURE 5. Schematic of a pitch contour of a four syllable word with initial accent

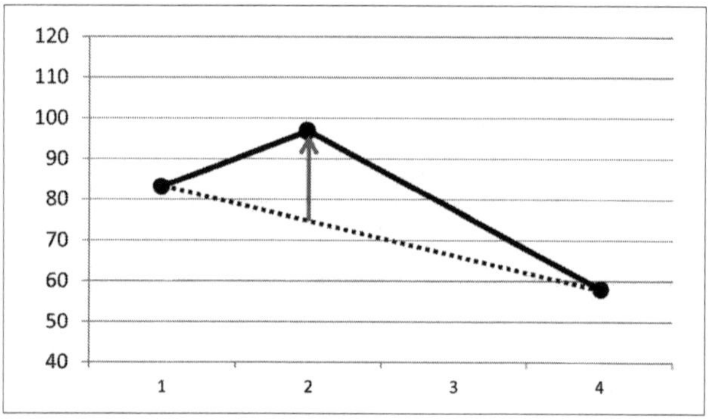

FIGURE 6. Schematic of a pitch contour of a four syllable word with second syllable accent

final low boundary tone. The slope of the pitch contour from the beginning of the utterance to the pitch peak is very slight, and almost flat. Under our account, the pitch peak of the accented syllable still forms a local maximum. However, the pitch has declined so low by this point in the utterance that this pitch peak is no longer necessarily a global pitch maximum. As shown in Figure 7, the pitch of the accented syllable is raised above the line of declination, but is not much higher than the pitch at the start of the utterance.

Finally, although we did not record four-syllable words with a final accent, we can discuss what happens in three- (or two-) syllable words when accent is word-final. In all other cases, the low boundary tone (L%) at the right edge of the domain was realized on the final syllable. In this case, when both pitch accent and the low boundary could potentially be realized on the final syllable, pitch accent supersedes. The resulting pitch is higher than the normal low boundary tone (Figure 8).

In sum, we have treated pitch contours in Blackfoot as an interpolation of

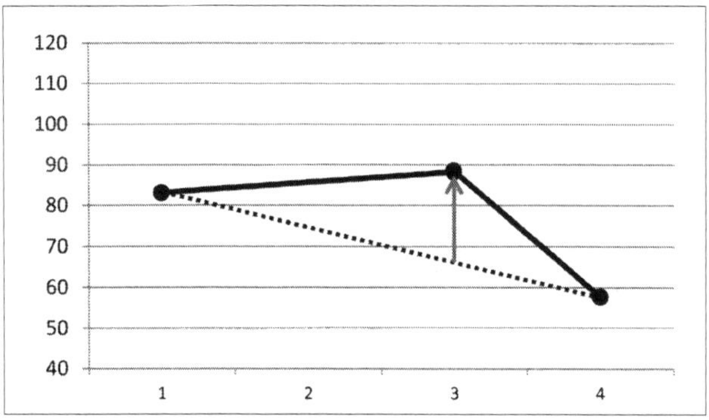

FIGURE 7. Schematic of a pitch contour of a four syllable word with penultimate accent

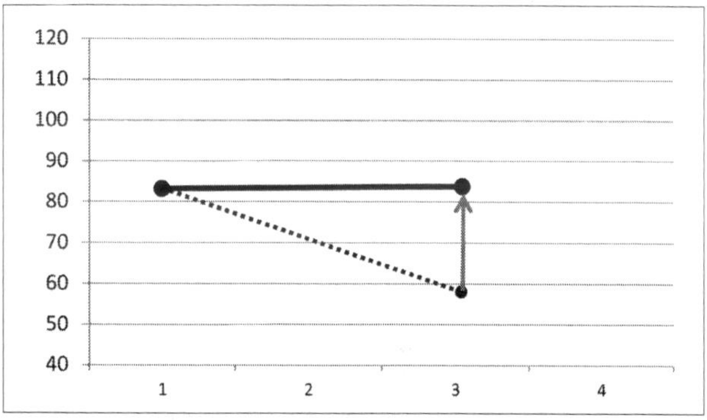

FIGURE 8. Schematic of a pitch contour of a word with final accent

pitch between the start of the utterance, pitch accented syllables, and a final low pitch target, which successfully accounts for all the patterns in our data. In the next section, we briefly compare our account of pitch contours to the description found in Taylor (1969) and note one difference between our findings and those in Van Der Mark (2003).

Reexamining Taylor's Description of Two Pitch Contours

As mentioned earlier, Taylor (1969) provides impressionistic descriptions and categorizes pitch patterns into two: Pitch Contour Number One and Pitch Contour Number Two. There are several distinct subpatterns of each contour, which he claims depend on the number of pitch accents in the word as well as where long and short syllables fall. However, it is not clear how these descriptions can generalize to all word shapes and sizes.

In many ways, our observations largely support Taylor's descriptions. For instance, our words with accent on a nonfinal syllable seem to broadly match Taylor's descriptions of Pitch Counter Number One. Likewise, our words with final accent have a nearly flat and steady pitch contour, which broadly matches Taylor's description of Pitch Contour Number Two. However, our pitch categorization depends solely on where pitch accent falls (final versus nonfinal syllables). Pitch movement across the utterance is predictable once the accent location is determined, because we regard the pitch contour as being the interpolation of pitch between tonal targets. We also controlled for word length (number of syllables), which Taylor did not specifically do. Vowel length was not controlled in this study, but also did not affect our general observations. Thus, this acoustic study verifies the impressionistic description in Taylor (1969) while also providing a more general framework for future research. We believe an AM analysis will extend to other Blackfoot words as well.

Comparison to the Findings in Van Der Mark (2003)

As discussed in our observations above, we found that pitch on an accented syllable was consistently higher than the line of pitch declination. Put another way, the pitch of an accented syllable was consistently higher than the pitch of an unaccented syllable would have been in the same position. This result is difficult to reconcile with Van Der Mark (2003), who found no significant differences between the pitch ranges of accented versus unaccented syllables in four out of five speakers. Our study suggests that the reason is that Van Der Mark did not control for syllable position within the word (e.g., first syllable, second syllable, etc.). We suspect that an analogous study that controls for syllable position will find significant differences between the ranges of accented and unaccented syllables relative to each position in the word.

Further Study

The AM model gives us several possible future lines of inquiry. First, in utterances with multiple pitch accents, we expect there to be multiple local pitch maxima, even if these do not deviate much from the line of declination. Second, because our data were composed of words recorded in isolation, the left and right edges of the word are also phrasal and intonational boundaries. While we have posited a L%

boundary tone at the right edge of a prosodic domain, our data cannot determine which domain this is. Therefore, future research should investigate pitch contours of words in context and of utterances in order to determine if the L% tone falls at the right edge of every word, the right edge of phrases, or the right edge of utterances. Third, pitch accents are known to shift due to focus and other information structure effects, and boundary tones are often determined by speech acts or clause types. Thus, it would be interesting to investigate whether these intonational contours change based on pragmatic function. Fourth, one question that remains is how the locations of pitch accents are determined. Several studies have claimed that Blackfoot pitch accent is determined by metrical structure (Kaneko 1999; Weber 2016) or morphology (Weber and Allen 2012). Currently, this study does not impact these claims; we describe how pitch contours may be predicted by the location of pitch accent, but make no claim as to how pitch accent location is determined.

Application

The study of pitch contours can also contribute to Blackfoot language pedagogy. Though accent location is indicated in samples in the grammar (Frantz 2017) and dictionary (Frantz and Russell 2017), relative pitch and pitch movement are not manifested in writing. Consider that disyllabic words with initial accent (CVCV) and final accent (CVCV) are orthographically mirrored in terms of accent location, but the pitch contours of these words are not mirror images. Fish and Miyashita (2017) suggest the use of visual guides for pitch movement and provide illustrations of pitch movement called PITCH ART. The two examples in Figure 9 are from Fish and Miyashita (2017:205).

While Fish and Miyashita have recognized these patterns and suggested the use of visual guides for teaching purposes, these patterns in Blackfoot pitch contours

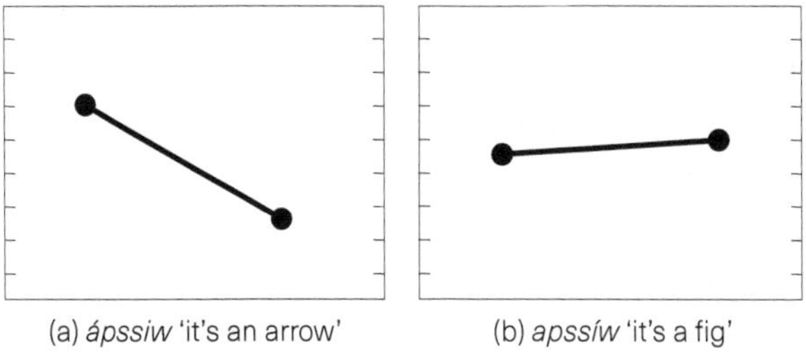

(a) *ápssiw* 'it's an arrow' (b) *apssíw* 'it's a fig'

FIGURE 9. Examples from Fish and Miyashita (2017): Visual representation of pitch

have not been presented in formal research. The current study recognizes that there are patterns in Blackfoot pitch contours, and thus supports their pedagogical activity.

Conclusion

The current study presented an acoustic investigation of Blackfoot pitch movement and a preliminary analysis using an autosegmental-metrical (AM) model. The shape of a pitch contour throughout a word is determined by the location of pitch accent and the line of pitch declination. The remainder of the pitch contour is phonologically unspecified, and is phonetically interpolated from the beginning of the utterance to the H* pitch accent and then down to a L% boundary tone. This results in a variety of shapes that fall into two major categories: (1) when the accent falls on a nonfinal syllable, the pitch contour rises from the beginning of the utterance to the pitch peak and then falls to a low pitch target; (2) when the final syllable is accented, pitch remains perceptually flat across the utterance because the local pitch maximum on the accented syllable is low compared to the start of the utterance. Under our account, the second shape obtains because a low boundary tone at the right edge of the utterance is superseded by the high pitch accent. The acoustic investigation in this study supports the impressionistic description of pitch contours in Taylor (1969) as well as the use of pitch contours for pedagogical activity, as suggested by Fish and Miyashita (2017). Though the current study is based on a limited number and type of words, we have suggested ways that our model can be used as the basis for further studies.

NOTES

1. We would like to thank Mr. Earl Old Person, a native speaker and the chief of the Blackfeet tribe, for sharing his knowledge of the language, and his grandson, Mr. Arlan Edwards, for serving as a liaison. We thank the Piegan Institute and teachers at Cuts Wood School for their encouragement regarding our research. This study is supported by an NSF Documenting Endangered Languages (DEL) grant (BCS-1251684) and a grant from the Phillips Fund of the American Philosophical Society awarded to the first author. We also acknowledge research assistants Naatosi Fish, Bonny Lahey, and Cavan Wagner, who contributed to the initial stage of the data processing. We also thank the audience at

the 49th Algonquian Conference. All errors are ours.

2. The term "pitch accent" is controversial, because so-called pitch accent languages do not behave universally but rather combine various properties from 'tone' and 'stress' prototypes (Hyman 2009). Nevertheless, it persists in the Blackfoot literature. We adopt this term here to emphasize that Blackfoot utilizes pitch to distinguish word forms and to tie our account into the autosegmental-metrical literature on pitch accents in intonational contours. We do not intend to claim that Blackfoot instantiates a "pitch accent" language type that is distinct from languages with tonal or stress properties.
3. Long vowels and diphthongs are represented via digraphs (i.e. two vowel symbols). A level high pitch during the long vowel is represented with acute accents over both symbols, as in this example. If pitch falls over a long vowel, only the first vowel is marked (e.g., *kitáaksipii* 'you will enter').
4. Due to time constraints, no words were included that contain a syllabic (interconsonantal) /s/ (Goad and Shimada 2014).
5. Pierrehumbert (1980) hypothesizes that pitch declination can be reduced to downstep, which is the lowering of pitch at successive pitch accents. (See discussion in Ladd 2008:75ff.) Downstep cannot explain the pitch declination in our sample since all of the words only include one pitch accent.

REFERENCES

Boersma, Paul, and David Weenink. 2013. *Praat: Doing Phonetics by Computer* [Computer program]. Version 5.3.51, retrieved 2 June 2013 from http://www.praat.org.

Fish, Naatosi, and Mizuki Miyashita. 2017. Guiding Pronunciation of Blackfoot Melody. In *Honoring Our Teachers,* ed. by Jon Reyhner, Joseph Martin, Louise Lockard, and Willard Sakiestewa Gilbert, pp. 203–210. Flagstaff, AZ: Northern Arizona University.

Frantz, Donald G. 2017. *Blackfoot Grammar.* 3rd ed. Toronto: University of Toronto Press.

Franz, Donald G. and Norma Jean Russell. 2017. *Blackfoot Dictionary of Stems, Roots, and Affixes.* 3rd ed. Toronto: University of Toronto Press.

Goad, Heather, and Akiko Shimada. 2014. In Some Languages, /s/ is a Vowel. In *Supplemental Proceedings of the 2013 Annual Meeting in Phonology,* ed. by John Kingston, Claire Moore-Cantwell, Joe Pater, Robert Staubs, pp. 1–12. University of Massachusetts Amherst. Retrieved from http://journals.linguisticsociety.org/proceedings/index.php/amphonology/article/view/50

Gussenhoven, Carlos. 2004. *The Phonology of Tone and Intonation.* Cambridge University Press.

Hyman, Larry. M. 2009. How (not) to do Phonological Typology: The Case of Pitch-accent.

Language Sciences 31(2): 213–238.

Kaneko, Ikuyo. 1999. A Metrical Analysis of Blackfoot Nominal Accent in Optimality Theory. MA thesis, University of British Columbia.

Ladd, D. Robert. 1984. Declination.: A Review and Some Hypotheses. *Phonology Yearbook, 1,* 53–74.

Ladd, D. Robert. 2008. *Intonational Phonology.* 2nd edition. Cambridge University Press.

Miyashita, Mizuki. 2011. Five Blackfoot Lullabies. *Proceedings of The APS* 155(3): 276–293.

Miyashita, Mizuki. 2018. Vowel-consonant Coalescence in Blackfoot. In *Papers of the Forty-Seventh Algonquian Conference,* ed. by Monica Macaulay, and Margaret Noodin, pp. 217–235. East Lansing: Michigan State University Press.

Miyashita, Mizuki. 2019. Pitch and Intensity of Lexical Accent in Blackfoot. *Papers of the Forty-Eighth Algonquian Conference,* ed. by Monica Macaulay and Margaret Noodin, pp. 173–189. East Lansing: Michigan State University Press.

Pierrehumbert, Janet. 1980. The Phonology and Phonetics of English Intonation. PhD thesis, Massachusetts Institute of Technology.

Stacy, Elizabeth. 2004. Phonological Aspects of Blackfoot Prominence. MA thesis, University of Calgary.

Taylor, Allan. R. 1969. A Grammar of Blackfoot. PhD thesis, University of California at Berkeley.

Tsunoda, Tasaku. 2005. *Language Endangerment and Language Revitalization: An Introduction.* New York: Mouton de Gruyter.

Van Der Mark, Sheena C. 2003. The Phonetics of Blackfoot Pitch Accent. MA thesis, University of Calgary.

Weber, Natalie. 2016. Accent and Prosody in Blackfoot Verbs. *Papers of the Forty-Fourth Algonquian Conference,* ed. by Monica Macaulay, Margaret Noodin, and J. Randolph Valentine, pp. 348–369. Albany: State University of New York Press.

Weber, Natalie and Blake Allen. 2012. Blackfoot Pitch Accent: Insights from Morpho-phonology. Unpublished manuscript, University of British Columbia, Vancouver. http://hdl.handle.net/2429/43085.

Chronicling the Ungava Naskapis

Lessons in Historiography

Toby Morantz

The Naskapi Nation of Kawawachikamach occupies a village they largely built in the early 1980s.[1] Agreements with the federal government, following from the Northeastern Quebec Agreement (NEQA) of 1977, granted them powers similar to a municipality and a major role in determining their economic development. Thus, the Naskapi Council assumed the responsibility of providing local services such as health, education, housing, and infrastructure. An indication of how some of these institutions are tailored to Naskapi values is their use of sentencing circles to restore good relations in the community. There are also a number of other civic, business, and cultural activities all bearing a distinctive Naskapi character.[2]

Long ago the Naskapis were an autonomous people, even during the early European fur trade era, because their main subsistence economy was the hunting of caribou, much less so of furs for the international market. It was the decline of the Ungava caribou herds and the later involvement of the Canadian government that generated this loss of autonomy or self-government that they now are in the process of regaining, to the degree possible in Canadian society. In this paper, I trace their history on the Quebec-Labrador Peninsula, beginning in the late 1700s, to illustrate some of the major events that shaped their responses to new circumstances. I use this history as one example of the variety of internal and external forces that infringed on First Nations and Inuit societies. It is an attempt to provide a more nuanced or balanced view of the loss of autonomy among Canada's Indigenous peoples.

The following simple outline of the Naskapi past fulfills two objectives. One is to give the Naskapis attention beyond the linguistic work done by Marguerite McKenzie, Sandra Clarke, and their colleagues. The other purpose is to confront the current sociopolitical climate that judges or interprets past actions by applying present-day notions and values. It is what historians call "presentism." Bundled into this myopic view of the past is the tendency to telescope events, that is, view the past as monolithic. As one example, we learned from Prime Minister Justin Trudeau that "the Indigenous peoples have been victims of oppression from the very time when the first explorers celebrated their discovery of a 'new' world" (Globe and Mail, 1 July 2017). It is not an uncommon view. Many Canadians have come to view Canada's relations with the Indigenous peoples in simple black-and-white terms. My perspective is somewhat different in that I see the history of the Naskapis and their relations with the larger society as captured by contemporary views of our colonial past. I was a student in the 1960s in Manitoba and worked or studied with a number of provincial and federal bureaucrats involved in First Nations issues. I would never ascribe to them a malicious intent. Nor would I say this is the sense one derives from reading the correspondence and reports of the Departments of Northern and Indian Affairs of the 1950s and 1960s. Rather, I see the fur traders and bureaucrats molded and constrained by the racist views of their societies that did not privilege Indigenous peoples' needs enough to provide adequate funding to meet the requirements for healthy living nor involve them in the decision-making. Additionally, most of their clients were confined to remote areas and out of sight. Indisputably, this deplorable state of affairs continues today despite all the rhetoric. Additionally, the clergy and bureaucrats subscribed to other widely held views, for example, that people can adapt to new situations within a generation or two. I often was told that immigrants to Canada assimilated rapidly without any understanding of the significant differences in culture, economy, education, religion, motivation, or location that characterized the Indigenous peoples' experience and desire to avoid assimilation.

Accordingly, it is the intent of this article to demonstrate that Naskapi history is a composite of a number of different histories, some of their making, others inflicted on them. It is a history of how the Naskapis lost their autonomy to external agents.

First fur traders, then missionaries, and finally federal bureaucrats of the 1970s imposed solutions—some of which were welcomed by the Naskapi—to resolve dire circumstances. With my limited access to oral history, this outline of selected events is drawn, almost entirely, from Eurocentric documents.

Although the Naskapis are closely related linguistically to the James Bay Crees and the Innus, they have remained identifiable in the records, due to their geographic location and greater reliance on one resource. The barren ground caribou habitat was in the interior of the Quebec-Labrador Peninsula. These animals migrated there, having spent summers on the coast away from flies and wolves, to pass the fall and winter months in the shelter of the forest tundra transition zone. Until the late 1800s, the Naskapis were akin to a monocrop farmer, though they depended on fish, fowl, and smaller animals if need be. Their subsistence priority was always caribou. The hunt, originally by ambush using spears, took place mainly in the fall when the caribou, in herds of thousands, were crossing waterways (Low 1896:319). Some hunts yielded 200 or even as many as 1,000 caribou. The anthropologist William Strong reports that in the early 1900s, Naskapi families on George River had plenty of meat over two years (Leacock and Rothschild 1994:116). Such a bounty of caribou meat enabled large numbers of families to camp together in winter months, enhancing their lifestyle. However, the North American caribou herds, including the Ungava herds, declined significantly in number starting in the late 1800s and into the early 1900s, enormously affecting the northern populations. Biologists in a Quebec government report: "Although hunting by humans can now be eliminated as a possible cause, no one really knows what triggered the most recent decline and several Aboriginal groups have paid dearly for the resulting lack of food." They further explain there are a number of hypotheses for this decline, such as pressure on the habitat and climatic factors, but no commonly held explanation (Couturier et al. 2004:1).

The Naskapis' hunting grounds centered on Indian House Lake on the George River, in the early 1800s when they are first discussed in the Hudson's Bay Company (HBC) journals of the Ungava region. The constant movement of caribou over large areas was mirrored by the Naskapis' occupation of vast areas by small bands of people whose population size was proportional to the size of the herd. In contemporary times, one band of Naskapis, the Natuashish, ended up at Davis Inlet in Labrador, while another band, known today as the Naskapi Nation of Kawawachikamach, ended up in at Schefferville in Quebec. It is by and large the latter's forebears I am tracing. In the records I used they are known as the Ungava Naskapis.

Early History

The Naskapis were first mentioned by Europeans in the HBC journal of 1750 for Richmond Gulf Post. Referring to them as the "Nashcoppees," the postmaster noted that they did not come to trade with the English or French but traded with other Indians (Francis and Morantz 1983:69). This trade was in "deer skins," as caribou were called. The Naskapi fur trapping was of martin, mink, and otter, not beaver, whose range did not extend that far north. Over the decades, the HBC traders continued to despair that the Naskapis were not "annuall visitors." In 1815, Thomas Alder at Great Whale River wrote, "They are little beholden to us; the Deer furnishes them with both food and raiment and if in return for a few deerskins they can procure ammunition, tobacco, etc. with a hearty drink of grog, their wants are wholly supplied." At these times, the company complained they had to close posts because the caribou hunters were not bringing them furs (Morantz 1983:62–63).

In Ungava, the Naskapis first appear in the Fort Chimo [Kuujjuaq] journal in September 1831, a year after the post was established, having traded previously at a post near Bestiamites on the lower north shore of the St. Lawrence and at the Moravian mission at Okak on the Labrador coast. Their appearance was noteworthy for another reason: the seeming cordial relations between the Naskapis and Inuit, two peoples who had a history of hostilities but were destined to frequent Fort Chimo together until the 1950s. In an attempt to make the fur trade more attractive to Naskapis, a post was established at Fort Nascopie in 1838 (until 1873) on Lake Petitsikapau (southeast of Schefferville). The posts inland from Fort Chimo always were difficult to supply, and both Naskapis and HBC men suffered from the shortage of food. If the supplies for the post did not arrive, then the Naskapis were deprived of such "necessities" as guns and ammunition. The HBC men were then deprived of fresh country foods supplied by the Naskapis, subjecting them to scurvy. Although the Naskapis preferred to trade in caribou hides, they were better rewarded for trading fur pelts.

The Fort Chimo post was closed in 1843 due to the cost of transporting supplies overland from Hudson Bay. At the time, it was frequented by 130 individuals, including 24 families of Naskapis and a number of Inuit. The post was reopened 23 years later, in 1866, when oceangoing steamships and the promise of a commercial salmon fishery motivated the HBC to return to the region. One of the benefits of reopening the post, said the HBC governor, George Simpson, was to draw the

Naskapis to Fort Chimo, away from the influence of the Catholic priests and the traders on the St. Lawrence (Tremblay 2007:183–184). By that time, a Protestant missionary, E. A. Watkins, had settled on the northeast James Bay coast, while S. M. Stewart had established a mission at Fort Chimo. From 1905 until 1930 the mission strategically set about converting the leadership of both the Naskapis and the Inuit family groups (Morantz 2016:83).

Some Naskapi and Inuit hunters became attached to the Fort Chimo post and served as fishermen and woodcutters for the HBC. A perpetual feature of the Ungava post was that years of abundance would give way to years of great want when epidemics, bred in the debilitating effects of malnutrition, also took their toll, such as in 1841–1842, 1868–1869, and again in 1880–1881. These were some of the years the caribou hunting failed.

The traders often had harsh words to say about the Naskapis because of their seeming independence, marked by their preference for caribou hunting instead of trapping. For example, trader Crawford in 1876 wrote: "They shoot and spear deer then lie in the lodge and gorge themselves . . . [T]hey make the women dress the skins and then come and pay their accounts" (Morantz 2016:44–45).

Decline in Caribou Herds and Increase in Hardship

It was at Fort Chimo that a new policy unfolded for the Naskapis and eventually for all Indigenous subsistence hunters across Canada. In the fall of 1892, the Ungava caribou herd, whose migration routes were usually predictable, moved north instead of south, which left the Naskapis starving to death in the winter. It was estimated that at least 150 of about 300 Naskapis died. The difference between this cruel winter and those of 1888–1889 or 1880–1881 was the presence of an observer, A. P. Low, the geological surveyor. He was horrified at what he had discovered and attributed the deaths to the HBC's refusal to extend them credit or provisions. He reported the tragedy to the press and Indian Affairs, suggesting help. As a result, the HBC, the following year, provided rations to the Fort Chimo Naskapis and was to be reimbursed by the government. According to Hugh Shewell (1995:228ff.; 2004:78ff.), the government viewed this as a once-only event. But the HBC commissioner used it as an opening to urge the government to be ready for other such tragedies and preauthorize all the posts, saying it was "futile to provide relief after the fact" (Shewell 2004:86). Thus arose a country-wide relief policy, called S&D rations, for sick and destitute, that over the years became more systematic and standardized, though always inadequate.

The early 20th century in Ungava and James Bay was a period of declining animal food resources and declining fur markets. The exception was the period from the end of World War I until the Wall Street Crash of 1929, when the Naskapis and their Cree, Innu, and Inuit neighbors profited from the West's seemingly insatiable desire for fur trim and fur coats, mainly of fox, marten, mink, and raccoon. This boom period quickly ended with the Great Depression. The Naskapis, with no caribou and no fur markets, had again to rely on the meager handouts of the government provided by the fur trade companies. One HBC manager at Nemiscau (in Cree territory) queried whether "we are fur trading here or running a 'bread line' for the Department of Indian Affairs."[3] It is not surprising that in setting out the history of rations to the Indigenous people that Hugh Shewell (2004) chose to title his book *Enough to Keep Them Alive.* Rations, he argues, were generally not provided to able-bodied men, and granting them by the HBC trader could be arbitrary (Shewell 1995:131). Following from the revised Indian Act of 1951, a social welfare system, more in line with such programs to the south, was extended to the reserves and administered directly to the individuals by the Department of Indian Affairs. Able-bodied men were included using more objective criteria. The provision of the existing old-age security and family allowance payments had been granted in the late 1940s. According to John Leslie (1999:301), head of the department's Claims and Historic Research Centre, the Indian social integration policy was sanctioned as the goal of Indian administration. Incidentally, for much of the declining fur trade in the 1900s, the government was subsidizing the HBC, country-wide, in its issuing of rations through the company.

The Ungava Naskapis did not need to make the 320 km journey to Fort Chimo after 1916 because the HBC opened a post deep in the Naskapi territory, at Fort McKenzie. It drew about 100 Naskapis (20–25 families). The rest opted to join those at Indian House Lake, which eventually became the Davis Inlet band, today the community of Natuashish. Even though supplying this outpost upriver was extremely arduous, taking 22 days, the HBC made this decision to separate the Naskapis from their competitors, the Revillon Frères at Fort Chimo. Another reason was the contraction of the George River caribou herd and the growing reluctance of the Naskapis to travel through the tundra devoid of caribou to carry their furs to the post (Anderson 1961:50–51).

The Naskapis were not complacent clients of the HBC, complaining as they did about the high price of the imported goods and threatening to boycott the post, though they did not. They continued trading the small fur animals. In exchange, they received tobacco, arms, ammunition, flour, fat, and cloth. Several years later, they were protesting the quantity of the government rations. The decade of the 1930s was a very difficult one, with the drastic decline of the caribou, the depressed prices of furs, and the spread of tuberculosis and other diseases, complicated by malnutrition. In the early 1940s, the Naskapis along with the Inuit benefited from the American air base at Fort Chimo, where they were offered some employment and handouts. However, it closed the same year as Fort McKenzie, drawing 190 Naskapis to Fort Chimo (Morantz 2016:164–167). It left them dependent on the post in a region they did not know well and was not abundant in furs (Duhaime 2001:82).

Throughout the 1930s and 1940s, the government correspondence expresses a common refrain about the absence of country food and furs, coupled with a concern for the ever-mounting relief costs. The records of May 1950 indicate the degree to which the Naskapis had become dependent on Fort Chimo and on the government. They were issued canvas for tents, canoes and food for the month (which did not last) on the condition they move near various lakes where they could obtain wood, fish, and game. One consequence of this move was a drastic decline in school attendance, from 29 children in 1950 to one in 1952. The Naskapis were caught between a choice of relief and schooling (Morantz 2016:168).

Other dilemmas plagued the Naskapis. The Catholic priest offered schooling and food for those Inuit and Naskapis who remained at the old American base, but the Anglican minister and others protested vigorously, pressuring the Naskapis to move back to the post, away from the influence of Father Cyr (Morantz 2016:169).

Ottawa Bureaucrats Seize Control

With these controversies and increasing economic dependency, the Indian Affairs officials in 1953 began thinking of other solutions. A report at the time summed up their economic situation and state of health as "desperate." The Naskapis were consulted about returning to Fort McKenzie with the promise of rations and supplies, to which most agreed. However, the difficulty in organizing the transport and the expense in maintaining the Naskapis at Fort McKenzie prompted government officials to decide the Naskapis might instead be based at Knob Lake, later named Schefferville, where the Iron Ore Company (IOC) had been established (Cooke 1976:73–76). We learn about this period from an excellent MA thesis by Jean-Sébastien Boutet. The Naskapis were given a choice of moving to Schefferville or to Sept-Iles and chose the latter, where they thought they would receive better medical and educational facilities. It is not known why the government changed its mind about Sept-Iles, but the families agreed to move to Lake Wakuach, about 60 miles north of Knob Lake. In the summer of 1956, most of the 175 Naskapis traveled the 400 miles overland, on foot. On arrival, exhausted and close to starvation, they discovered nothing that had been promised had been prepared for them, not the housing, school, infirmary, and so on, so they continued on to Schefferville (Cooke 1976:76–80; Boutet 2012:107). That the Fort Chimo Naskapis resettled as a group is due to their elders having met with the band leaders and entreated them not to go their separate ways but to retain their solidarity, and so they did (Boutet 2012:138, 117–118).

The relocation of the Naskapis was not easy or simple. They had discovered at Lake Wakuach that the hunting territories, promised by Indian Affairs officials, were held by Innus, leading to tensions between the two groups (Boutet 2012:170–172). The Anglican minister countered Indian Affairs claims that they provided the Naskapis with adequate shelter and food; rather, he said they were living in miserable conditions in shacks and tents, had no government-issued clothing and no medical facilities, while the only school was the IOC's Roman Catholic one. Although the Naskapis were living in roughly built shacks without any amenities, the IOC was busy building fully supplied houses for its white employees (Cooke 1976:80–83; Boutet 2012:127). Settled, as they were, in Schefferville, they were removed from their hunting lands but were further discouraged from pursuing a subsistence economy because of the obligation to send their children to school. Not to do so would mean forfeiting the family allowance payments tied to school attendance (Wills 1984:28).

The wage labor that pulled them away from their hunting and trapping economy was nevertheless sought after because it provided a higher income than fur trapping. However, this move to Schefferville (Knob Lake) was not the last Naskapi relocation. Within a couple of years (1960) they were moved nearby to Lake John to share, somewhat uncomfortably, a reserve with Innus who had moved from Uashat-Maliotenam (Sept-Iles) for economic reasons (Boutet 2012:104). The infrastructure on the reserve was minimal, the water unfit to drink, and housing conditions "dire," so the Naskapis and the Innus were moved once again in 1972. This time there was no consultation. The new reserve, Matimekush on Pearce Lake, provided them with new housing of poor construction that quickly became overcrowded housing. The proximity to the town of Schefferville created social problems (Boutet 2012:127–131). Known as the Fort Chimo Band until 1970, they then became the Schefferville Band and numbered 344 individuals (Boutet 2012:127). When the IOC was finally closed in 1982, the Naskapis, benefiting from the James Bay and Northern Quebec Agreement and the later NEQA, designed, built, and settled into within a few years a new village: Kawawachikamach.

Boutet's (2012:107) research has demonstrated that the transfer to Schefferville was largely voluntary. The people "themselves decided to move in the hope of finding employment, housing, medical assistance, and educational facilities for their children in the booming mining town." However, he does note some Naskapis say they were coerced by the government to make this move. Joe Guanish, longtime leader and chief, expressed his view of the relocation this way: "If we went, we would receive an education and a salary. At this mine there would be work for at least a hundred years. Our children would go to school, there would be money for them, and our elders would have a right to a pension."[4]

Discussion

While the caribou herds were numerous, the Naskapis could remain independent of the fur trade and the Europeans. The HBC post records indicate they chose to do so but into the mid-1800s they were engaging more and more as trappers in the fur trade. This change likely was due to the periodic decrease in caribou, perhaps then occurring more frequently, but also likely due to the Naskapis' growing desire for imported goods: metal tools, firearms, clothing, tea, and tobacco. Some items were labor saving, others pleasurable. Thus, a moderate economic dependency arose while they continued to provide their subsistence needs and function as a hunting society.

Although the Naskapis and the HBC formed an interdependent relationship, the HBC did make decisions in its own interest that significantly affected the Naskapis and to which they had to adapt. Of course, if the Naskapis chose not to trap furs, that too affected the company's interests. The opening and closing of posts by the fur traders and withholding of credit affected the Naskapis' hunting strategies in major ways, usually drawing them away from preferred grounds. The caribou were on the tundra; the fur animals were in the forests. Similarly, the availability of relief rations at the posts undermined their independence and prevented some people from hunting far from the post. Yet the impoverishment of the Naskapis, once the caribou herds contracted, was mitigated by the access to HBC-government rations. They had no choice but to succumb to change directed by these outsiders.

The missionaries, little featured here, did embroil them in tensions at the post, but the Catholics and Anglicans were more instrumental in disabusing them of their own religion by vigorously attacking their beliefs and practices, disturbing their cultural stability. The missionaries were also important advisers to the HBC on questions of welfare. On the plus side, the church drew attention to their impoverishment and, at times, provided them with food and clothing.

The third agents to control the Naskapis were the Ottawa-based Indian Affairs bureaucrats and the Royal Canadian Mounted Police constables posted at Fort Chimo. The federal government was the most instrumental and effective in changing Naskapi life by restructuring their society and expediting their shift from subsistence to dependence. Elsewhere, I have outlined my position on bureaucratic colonialism (Morantz 2002:8–9) and maintain here Ottawa officials were the primary agents of change in the post–World War II period. Frank Tester (2017), Arctic ethnohistorian, speaking of the Inuit in the mines in Rankin Inlet in the 1960s, expressed the belief that to understand the government policies one has to examine the personalities of the individuals in the bureaucracy. I agree, but I also hold more responsible the general position of the government's frugality to which the bureaucrats were bound. I start with the catchphrase "Follow the money." It is an exaggeration, perhaps, reading the Northern Administration correspondence, but it seems saturated with the word "cost." Sally Weaver (1983:67), writing of the 1960s, found in her study of the Department of Indian Affairs that "the system of financing rather than the needs and aspirations of people, has become the driving force in policy formulations." According to John Leslie (2013:23) there was a "never-ending government quest to end the cycle of dependency," which translates as keeping costs down. Surely the expenditure management process of the government controlled the type of programming and stifled any initiative and goodwill by individual civil servants. As Michael Pitfield, Pierre Trudeau's clerk of the Privy Council, remarked, "The role of public servants is surely to maintain stability and order" (Gray 2017). Another thought is that some of the policies may well have been derived from academic interests in anthropology and sociology, for instance, the emphasis on social change in the 1960s.

The literature detailing the policies of the Department of Indian Affairs and Northern Development is vast and segmented into periods, reflecting the government's ever-changing schemes regarding the First Nations. Here I can draw attention only to a few as they entangled the Ungava Naskapis. As known, the long-standing policy within Indian Affairs was assimilation. This objective was to be met via the introduction of enfranchisement, Christianity, schooling, settlement, agriculture, and so forth, all recast as social and political integration in the late 1950s. Although the government dictated change toward centralization of Indigenous communities, it did not equip them financially nor help develop organizational skills to adapt to their new sociopolitical reality.

I need not dwell on the universal recognition that British or Western society viewed itself as technologically, morally, and spiritually superior and believed it could improve the lot of those people who were not Western and Christian. It also resulted in an attitude of "blaming the victim." We might say that in the 1970s, Canadians attempted to start letting go of this conviction. Some multicultural policies began working their way through society, but the social, cultural, and economic damage was already done.

The former minister of Indigenous services, Jane Philpott, referred to the government's earlier policy of "forced mass resettlement," without acknowledging that resettlement was considered the solution for the 1960s.[5] Premier Smallwood of Newfoundland, following confederation, promoted a policy providing healthcare, schools, roads, and other services to all its citizens. He recognized that this objective could be achieved more cheaply and efficiently "if people moved from small, isolated settlements to larger centers." Between 1956 and 1975, over 300 settlements were abandoned and 28,000 people resettled. This is known as "forced mass settlement." Unless everyone in the outport community agreed to the move, no one would receive the monetary compensation offered by the government. This program had a profound and lasting impact.[6]

Researchers indicate that the Naskapis' relocation from Fort Chimo was voluntary, but it was carried out most frugally and, thus, insensitively. They were forced to undergo several relocations into new terrains, among strangers, Innus, and whites. The housing and infrastructure did not meet basic standards, resulting in poor health conditions and demoralization. In other words, it was a vicious cycle. The Naskapis, as other First Nations, were poorly prepared for this radical change to urban life. Furthermore, the Naskapis were settled on their ancestral lands that had been yanked from them and given to mining interests without any consultation or legal redress. Strangers in their own lands. Worse, this act of relocation to towns severed the Naskapis from their core subsistence and cultural practices, as did the provincial game laws. Boutet (2012:127) remarks that despite the botched planning and other obstacles, the federal authorities appeared satisfied that they had achieved the best possible outcome for the Naskapis "in their long and difficult march toward civilization."

As for the drive to turn the hunters into industrial workers (and reduce the welfare rolls), Ottawa officials were so determined to find sources of employment they pleaded with Ungava mine bosses to employ Inuit and Naskapis, setting aside labor regulations to make it attractive (Morantz 2016:182). In Schefferville, they were engaged in labor-intensive, short-term, seasonal work that, according to Helen Buckley (1992:110–112) writing of the prairies, fostered a short-term outlook, no sense of planning, and an expectation that social services would be provided. This latter expectation resulted from the government's having seized control of the community's economy and infrastructure. Furthermore, although the Naskapis were promised in the mid-1950s that "the jobs would last 100 years," by 1975 the IOC was wound down and no Naskapis were hired. It closed in 1982. One can imagine the frustration, again, of the Naskapis (and Innus) at losing what had developed as employment and a way of life.

In Canada, people mean well in blaming the shameful conditions and problems of Indigenous peoples on the colonial masters, specifically the government, but the circumstances and policies that led to injustice and impoverishment cannot be viewed in unequivocal terms. For reasons provided above, the subsistence life was no longer viable. Briefly stated, this is accounted for by the decline in caribou, the loss of the fur trade, epidemics, settlement, and industrial life, and, above all, the false promises of the government. The civil servants reluctantly took charge of peoples in remote areas, I would argue, with generally good intentions. However, these officials lacked understanding of important social dynamics, the equilibrium of a culture and of social change. This insensitivity was greatly compounded by fiscal restraints then, as now.

It is a complex history and is a disservice to the history of the Naskapis to portray them as falling victims to oppression at the outset of the arrival of the Europeans. It ascribes to them powerlessness when they were not powerless. It robs them of their indispensable role in the fur trade as providers of furs for the commercial market and country food for the maintenance of the post. It also denies them making rational choices in their interest and the ability to adapt to new situations.

On the other hand, it is also deceptive to depict the Euro-Canadians as willfully and intentionally destructive of Naskapi society, although grave consequences resulted from their inadequate and penny-pinching policies. The reality is far more layered, as this brief overview of Naskapi history demonstrates.

NOTES

1. The author wishes to thank the two reviewers who helped clarify my thoughts and strengthen the paper.
2. "Our Organizations," Naskapi Nation of Kawawachikamach website, http://www.naskapi.ca/nk/Corporate.
3. HBCA. B.142/a/11, 23 Jan. 1939. D.G. Boyd, Manager.
4. "Portrait of the Naskapi Nation: History," Nametau innu website, video, 10:28, http://www.nametauinnu.ca/en/culture/opening/detail/55/129.
5. Jane Philpott, speech to the public policy forum Partners in Reconciliation: Recognizing and Respecting Indigenous Health, September 26, 2017, National Arts Centre, Ottawa, Ontario, transcript, https://www.canada.ca/en/indigenous-northern-affairs/news/2017/09/reconciliation_andthehealth-relatedcallstoactionthehonourablejan.html.
6. "'No Great Future': Government Sponsored Resettlement in Newfoundland and Labrador since Confederation," Maritime History Archive, 2004, https://www.mun.ca/mha/resettlement/.

REFERENCES

Anderson, William A. 1961. *Angel of Hudson Bay. The True Story of Maud Watt.* Toronto: Clarke, Irwin and Company.

Boutet, Jean-Sébastien. 2012. An Innu-Naskapi Ethnohistorical Geography of Industrial Iron Mining Development at Schefferville, Quebec. MA thesis, Memorial University.

Buckley, Helen. 1992. *From Wooden Ploughs to Welfare: Why Indian Policy Failed in the Prairie Provinces*. Montreal and Kingston: McGill-Queen's University Press.

Cooke, Alan, 1976. A History of the Naskapis of Schefferville. Presented to the Naskapi Band Council of Schefferville, typescript

Couturier, S., D. Jean, R. Otto, and S. Rivard. 2004. Demography of Migratory Tundra Caribou (Rangifer tarandus) of the Nord-du-Québec Region and Labrador. Ministère des Ressources Naturelles, de la Faune et des Parcs. ftp://ftp.mern.gouv.qc.ca/Public/Bibliointer/Mono/2014/06/1153287.pdf

Duhaime, Gérard, ed. 2001. *Atlas historique du Québec. Le nord: Habitants et mutations.* Ste-Foy, QC: Les Presses de l'Université Laval.

Francis, Daniel, and Toby Morantz. 1983. *Partners in Furs: A History of the Fur Trade in Eastern James Bay, 1600–1870.* Montreal: McGill-Queen's University Press

Gray, John. 2017. Pierre Trudeau Ally Michael Pitfield Was Canada's Top Bureaucrat. *The Globe and Mail,* October 20. https://www.theglobeandmail.com/news/national/trudeau-ally-michael-pitfield-was-canadas-top-bureaucrat/article36680434/

Hudson's Bay Company Archives. [n.d.] Series B.142/a/11. Nemiscau Post Journal 1938–39. Provincial Archives of Manitoba.

Leacock, Eleanor, and Nan Rothschild (eds.). 1994. *Labrador Winter: The Ethnographic Journals of William Duncan Strong, 1927–1928.* Washington, DC: Smithsonian Institution.

Leslie, John F. 1999. Assimilation, Integration or Termination? The Development of Canadian Indian Policy, 1943–1963. PhD thesis. Carleton University.

Leslie, John F. 2013. The Policy Agenda of Native Peoples from World War II to the 1969 White Paper. *Aboriginal Policy Research: Setting the Agenda for Change,* vol. 1, ed. by Peter White, P. Maxim, & D. Beavon, pp. 15–28. Thompson Educational Publishing. https://ir.lib.uwo.ca/cgi/viewcontent.cgi?article=1284&context=aprci.

Low, A. P. 1896. *Report on Explorations in the Labrador Peninsula among the East Main, Koksoak, Hamilton, Manicouagan and Portions of Other Rivers in 1892–93–94–95.* Ottawa: Dawson.

Morantz, Toby. 1983. "Not Annuall Visitors": The Drawing in to Trade of Northern Algonquian Caribou Hunters. *Actes du 14e Congrès des Algonquinistes,* ed. by William Cowan, pp. 57–71. Ottawa: Carleton University.

Morantz, Toby. 2002. *The White Man's Gonna Getcha: The Colonial Challenge to the Crees in Quebec.* Montreal: McGill-Queen's University Press.

Morantz, Toby. 2012. Reflections on the Annual Manitoba Indian and Metis Conferences of the Early 1960s. *Papers of the 40th Algonquian Conference, 2008,* ed. by Karl Hele and J. Randolph Valentine, pp. 310–325. Albany: SUNY Press.

Morantz, Toby. 2016. *Relations on Ungava Bay: An Illustrated History of Inuit, Naskapi and Eurocanadian Interaction, 1800–1970.* Montreal: Avataq Cultural Institute.

Shewell, Hugh. 1995. Origins of Contemporary Indian Social Welfare in the Canadian Liberal State: An Historical Case Study in Social Policy, 1873–1965. PhD thesis, University of Toronto.

Shewell, Hugh. 2004. *"Enough to Keep Them Alive": Indian Welfare in Canada, 1873–1965.* Toronto: University of Toronto Press.

Tester, Frank. 2017. The Rankin File: Inuit Health and the Canadian Liberal Welfare State.

Paper read at the American Society for Ethnohistory, Winnipeg.

Tremblay, Sigfrid. 2007. La subsistance des Naskapis et les intêrets de la compagnie: Une perspective territoriale sur le commerce des fourrures (1830–1870). MA thesis, University of Quebec at Montreal.

Weaver, Sally. 1983. *Making Canadian Indian Policy. The Hidden Agenda, 1968–1970.* Toronto: University of Toronto Press.

Wherry, Aaron. 2017. From Borden to Pearson to Trudeau: How Canada Day Has Defined a Nation. *CBC Radio Canada,* July 1. https://www.cbc.ca/news/politics/trudeau-speech-canada-day-analysis-wherry-1.4184264.

Wills, Richard H. 1984. *Conflicting Perceptions: Western Economics and the Great Whale Cree.* Chicago: Tutorial Press.

Ezhi-enendamang Anishinaabebiigeng

Theories of Anishinaabe Rhetoric and Composition

Margaret Noodin

The title of this essay, "*Ezhi-enendamang Anishinaabebiigeng:* Theories of Anishinaabe Rhetoric and Composition," illustrates the gap, and a proposed link, between Anishinaabemowin and the field of writing instruction. In Anishinaabemowin the title uses verbs to question "the way we think about writing in Anishinaabemowin." In English, the subtitle uses three nouns, "theories," "rhetoric," and "composition," to focus on ideas about narrative construction. Rhetoric can include all the ways linguistic expression can be analyzed, while composition focuses on writing praxis. The instructional model proposed here is based on the belief that all languages have practices related to narrative construction that are worthy of analysis by both learners and experts.

Anishinaabemowin is not a language with an extensive corpus of written stories. Most stories stem from oral tradition, and few speakers today are focused on creative writing. However, there is a growing number of learners who need to be challenged, which is why I have attempted to respectfully and humbly combine my desire to preserve and honor oral narrative traditions while at the same time positioning Anishinaabemowin as a living modern language deserving of critical attention. This desire should be fully disclosed as rooted in my position as a speaker who became literate as an adult, after 1990, with the patient support of fluent teachers who represent at least seven different dialects. Conversations between generations, involving more than two speakers, regularly occur in my home and workplace, often on a daily basis, certainly several times a week. I have been to 40 of the 48 nations on the coastline of the Great Lakes and over 30 different inland Anishinaabe nations. Many times I have encountered a spectrum of dialects within a single nation due to migration, intermarriage, and relocation. I have come to see my own usage, as well as that of my peers, my two daughters, and my students, as reflective of cumulative cognitive linguistic experience that varies greatly from one individual to another. Some are more grounded in a single speech community, while others participate in a growing diaspora of speakers. Some are skilled at lexicon and grammar, while others have memorized the narratives needed to preserve ceremonies. I firmly believe that our remaining first speakers are the experts, and we must continue to seek their counsel. Yet if we wish to speak of everything around us, we frequently are forced to rely on shared neologisms that may or may not gain traction. Today's young speakers need to accurately imitate the past while creating the future. As a teacher, with strengths and weaknesses of my own, I believe both teachers and students need to apply their skills and think deeply about what they are doing when they speak and write Anishinaabemowin. For these reasons I propose that together we all begin to document the ways in which we think about speaking, composing narratives and defining Anishinaabe rhetoric and composition.

If first-year language courses are producing sufficient comprehension and speaking skills, second-year students should progress to create their own texts and discourse. In the case of endangered languages, this requires the development of indigenous pedagogical frameworks aligned with best practices in rhetoric and composition. It is important that developing speakers learn not only the structure, but also the style, of the language they are acquiring. This essay centers on the example of Anishinaabemowin, an Algonquian language of the Great Lakes region, and draws from several dialects. It begins with a review of earlier work focused on pedagogy in the Anishinaabemowin classroom, then offers a model for defining rhetoric and composition as parts of a continuum of learning grounded in grammar and progressing to the construction and performance of stories. The essay then presents sample texts for teaching beginners the concepts of wordplay and narrative construction, which are the building blocks of more complex ideologies. Finally, the essay includes samples of contemporary writing by students and their teacher, leading to conclusions about the sustainable future of Anishinaabe literature.

Ezhi-Gikinoo'amawagwaa: How They Are Taught

Often, the presumed precipice of language loss leads to an assumption of solitude and alienation. Because fluent teachers and students are frequently the only speaker in many settings, it is easy for the sense of *nazhikewizing,* being alone, to take over. However, there is a growing body of work on language revitalization that is relevant for anyone working with endangered indigenous languages (Harrison 2007; Hinton 2013; McCarty and Lee 2014; Reyhner 2017). It is also important to reframe and revise the dangerous metaphors of language death and extinction (Perley 2011). Several authors have shared best practices for Anishinaabemowin revitalization specifically (Hermes 2012; McInnes 2014; Noodin 2013), and the network of teachers grows wider as more in-person and virtual means of communicating and learning are available (Noodin and Sheldon 2017). Specific to Anishinaabemowin, several dissertations and articles have explored the relevance of culturally based language instruction (Brown 2008; Chacaby 2011; Hermes and King 2014; Pitawanakwat 2009), while others have examined the success of second-language speakers and language instruction programs (Gresczyk 2011; Mead 2014). This leads directly to the topic of this essay, which is the need for Anishinaabe pedagogical frameworks (Chartrand 2012; Gross 2010; Hermes 2005; Noodin 2013; Treuer 1996 and 2001). Although all of the authors cited here make a clear case for linguistically specific practices, only a few provide pedagogical terms in Anishinaabemowin (Fuhst 2012; Matthews, Roulette, and Valentine 2010; Naokwegijig-Corbiere 2008; Ningewance 2004). As we look to continually improve *ezhi-gikinoo'amawandwaa gikinoo'amaaganag,* the way students are taught, we need to link the many strands of research and understanding.

Several professional organizations, focused on similar work, offer models for teaching that can be blended with Anishinaabe practices. Although the number of tribal nations where children learn their indigenous heritage language is limited, the National Association for Bilingual Education (NABE), with its focus on the importance of learning multiple languages, is an excellent source of research supporting the case for the preservation of linguistic diversity to develop intercultural understanding and bilingual proficiency. As has been noted in previous articles on Anishinaabemowin instruction (Hermes 2007; Noodin 2012), despite its unfortunate and problematic use of the adjective "foreign," the American Council on the Teaching of Foreign Languages (ACTFL) provides an objective definition of proficiency and fluency based on the ability to listen, speak, read, and write that can be adapted to many different languages. The definition of "writing" or "composition" can include the act of recording complex narratives both on and off the page, which aligns with the opinions of many other scholars in the field. The fact that "writing" has come to mean "writing in English" in many schools is unfortunate for those students who wish to compose in other languages. Despite this difference of interpretation, the National Council for Teachers of English (NCTE) has many valuable models that support the idea that polished discourse has many purposes. This organization of teachers supports the belief that formal, edited discourse is embedded in many complex social relationships and serves as a tool for thinking and connecting people to one another. The same ideas are reflected at the Conference on College Composition and Communication (CCCC), where teachers exchange ideas about how language fluency and the construction of narratives require critical thinking, practice, and feedback. These are not new ideas, and they easily translate across many cultures, but too often in language instruction we separate the arduous task of learning and practicing the rules of language to the point of proficiency without remembering to help the next generation reflect on the power of stories.

Aawechiganan: Comparisons

Teaching beyond proficiency to recover traditions of discourse and storytelling begins with the basic ideas related to the task. Moving from the notion of *ozhibii'ig-eng,* which means 'it is written' without indicating who has written what, to the notion of *aadizookawind,* meaning 'telling someone a living story', we find a range of terminology rooted in the structure of Anishinaabemowin itself. This notion that literary theories cannot be imported from one language to another is important for students to understand. Rather than seeking equivalents for literary terms, students and scholars should look at the alternate paradigms for understanding presented by indigenous languages.

All Anishinaabemowin verbs fall into one of four types that can be thought of as dimensions of action. They are mutually exclusive groups based on action and relationships. These verb types can also be considered a model of progressive complexity spanning from action that happens in the universe without an actor in control of it, to action initiated by someone or a group happening with no object or with an object in one of two classes. Table 1 illustrates the ways the Anishinaabe and

TABLE 1. Comparison of English and Anishinaabemowin composition actions

ENGLISH	ANISHINAABEMOWIN			
	ACTION ALONE	ACTION WITHOUT OBJECT	ACTION WITH INANIMATE OBJECT	ACTION WITH ANIMATE OBJECT
Composition	Ozhibii'igaade	Ozhibii'ige	Ozhibii'an	Ozhibii'am(aw)
Rhetoric		Wiikwazonge		Wiikwazom
Literary Arts		Dibaajimo	Dibaadodan	Dibaajimo(taw)
Living Stories		Aadizooke	Aadodan	Aadizookaw

English literary terms can be compared to help students understand the differences between the languages.

In English there are only four terms. It is fairly common to differentiate between composition, rhetoric, and literature, but the table illustrates the difficulty of trying to translate the two forms of literature found in Anishinaabemowin. "Literary Arts" and "Living Stories" are not exactly parallel to the six terms contained in the same rows, but they are attempts to make visible the difference. By comparison, the Anishinaabemowin terms, divided by categories based on verb types, acknowledge the larger range of possible actions and output related to writing. The stem *ozhibii-* meaning 'to write' has four variants, all related to the shaping of lines, marks, meanings, and traces of presence. But etymology has limitations when attempts are made to apply it uniformly. For example, *bii* is not a morpheme but so often ripples through words related to water, presence, and directional movement that it is impossible for a poet to ignore some of the metaphors that occur consciously or subconsciously. The idea for making a mark, composing thoughts, or writing is at the center of what students must do to move beyond simple statements and responses. Students need to practice composing and planning the flow of ideas. What to do with these ideas involves considering the audience, the listener or reader. In English this is considered "rhetoric," the skilled use of language to communicate efficiently or persuade. The Anishinaabemowin term used to approximate the English idea of rhetoric is limited and would not currently be considered comprehensible in many dialect regions. It does imply an attempt to convince someone to do something, but is not a common term, and may never need to be used in this way. However, in this table, it does help students focus on the way persuasion has two forms in Anishinaabemowin: the first, *wiikwazonge,* is used when one persuades; while *wiikwazom* is used to clarify the relationship between the persuader and the persuadee. When teaching with an Anishinaabemowin framework there is always the option for action to radiate in numerous directions. Stories can be created by and for individuals or communities. They can be intended to communicate inclusive and exclusive positionality and embed the ambiguity of a third person that is not male or female specific. Finally, and perhaps most importantly, both *dibaajimong* and *aadizookeng* must be considered. Both translate to 'telling a story' and both have transitive and intransitive variations. However, the fundamental difference is clear when each of the words becomes a noun. As a noun, *dibaajimowin* means 'text, news, report, or narrative' and is considered an inanimate noun. By contrast, *aadizookaan* is often translated as a 'myth or teaching story' and is an animate noun. At times, instructors place too much emphasis on animacy versus inanimacy, but reading it only as a level of complexity, *aadizookaanag* have the potential to direct action. *Indagindaamin dibaajimowinan.* 'We can read stories'. *Indozhibii'aamin dibaajimowinan.* 'We can compose stories'. *Aadizookaanag giwiidookaagonaanig.* 'Stories can help us'.

To ensure the future of both *dibaajimowinan* and *aadizookaanag* we need to move beyond linguistics to composition. As we teach students to pay attention to more than accurate grammar and efficient vocabulary, phonology becomes rhyme and meter; syntax and semantics become form; and variation of dialect and formality become a personal storytelling voice, *ezhi-dibaajimowaad, ezhi-aadizookewaad.* After situating the act of composition and rhetoric as *ozhibiige* or *wiikwazonge* and storytelling or literature-making as *dibaajimo* or *aadizooke,* it is important to consider the cultural protocols that guide Anishinaabe literary style, or *ezhi-dibaajimoyang.*

Table 2 summarizes story protocols that have been useful with students who already have a basic proficiency. These are questions students are directed to ask themselves before they tell a story, following the example of respected elders, who often share some of this information before addressing an audience. They are not intended to be answered in a rote or didactic way, nor would anyone ever demand these answers from a storyteller.

For students familiar with managing content by documenting sources and avoiding plagiarism, this set of questions redirects them to a definition of story as performance in community context. Asking students to situate themselves in relation to the story reminds them of the ways stories are shared. This can be compared to notes and bibliographies appearing as prose in the beginning of a narrative, but it can also be a reminder that stories travel across time. Elements emphasized by

TABLE 2. *Ezhi-dibaajimo* (Story protocols)

Awenen ayaawiyan?	Who are you?
Awenen enawemad?	Who do you sound like? Who are you related to?
Awenen gaa-gikinoo'amaag?	Who taught you?
Awenen nitam gaa-dibaajimod?	What is the story of the story?
Aaniin dash gaa-onji-dibaajimod gemaa gaa-onji-aadizooked?	Why was it being told?
Gego wiikaa wiindamawaakegon ge-izhi-naagadawendang.	Don't be didactic. (Never dictate the moral.)

one culture are sometimes valued differently by another. In contrast to rationality, realism, and intellectualism, Anishinaabe literature often emphasizes ambiguity and existentialism, allowing readers to apply highly personal interpretations within shared cultural boundaries. New words are invented as needed and conversations occur between humans and nonhumans with the emphasis on clear descriptions of action to be interpreted as needed by the listener or reader depending on their personal circumstance and prior experiences.

Like the protocols, the process for composing new Anishinaabe stories should also reflect the language and culture. Summarized in Figure 1, to reflect the continuing evolution of stories, the process includes listening and observing before shaping a story. There are of course many models that could be applied, but this one evokes a nonlinear process that begins with *bizaan-ayaang* 'being quiet', as is needed to *bizindan* ('listen to something') or *bizindaw* ('listen to someone'). Reminded of multiple relationships, students are asked to *maaminonendan* ('contemplate something from all angles') or *maaminonenim* ('contemplate someone from all angles'), which reinforces the need to manage pathways of communication and conjugation. The verbs and description selected need to align as a student begins to *dibaajimo, aadizooke* 'tell a story'.

With a focus on performance, whether that be within a circle of listeners or on a page, the final product mixes intentionality with audience interaction in ways that are more dynamic and less didactic than the final product of a composition course in English. Always, students are reminded, *ntam Anishinaabeyendamag, mii dash bijiinag da-ozhibii'igeyeg* ('think as Anishinaabeg do, and only then, write').

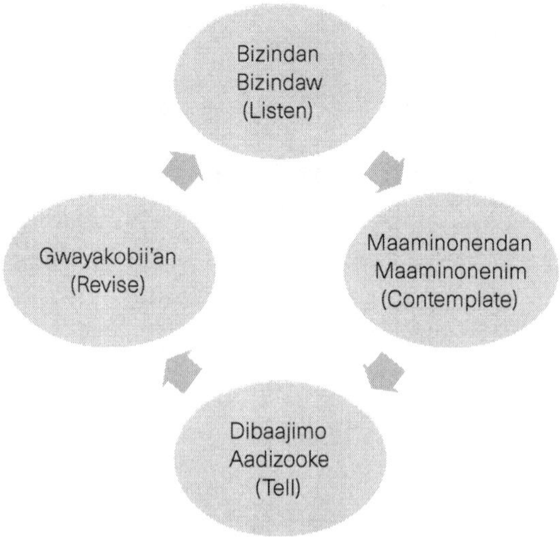

FIGURE 1. *Ezhichigeyaang* (Process)

Anishinaabewibii'igaadewinan: Anishinaabe Texts

Aaniin da agindamang wenji-nitaa-anishinaabebii'igeyaang? 'What material is useful in a second-year composition course?' *Aaniin ezhi-dibaajimowaad miidash aadizo-okewaad oshkianishinaabemowaad?* 'How do new speakers begin to tell stories?' For successful Anishinaabe composition, rhetoric, or story construction, there must be old and new examples that illustrate the full diversity of Anishinaabe genres. Students need to hear or read as many examples of fluent speakers modeling the process as possible. Both *getebiigewinan* ('old compositions') and *oshkibii'igewinan* ('new compositions') are important to expose students to models and inspiration. As it turns out, this can be an excellent use for linguistic fieldwork archives if they contain more than elicitation. Over time many samples were saved and have been used to create lexicons and grammars. Linguists and students can return to these archives now as resources for the composition classroom. The following examples of *Anishinaabeyaajimong* and *Anishinaabeyaadizookeng* encompass a range of genres sometimes labeled science fiction, adventure, mystery, mythology, tragedy, comedy, romance, satire, or fantasy in English.

The story "Nanabushu Slays Toad Woman" by Midaasoganzh (1905) from

Baadwewedamojig *Ojibwe Texts,* collected by William Jones in 1903 and retranscribed by Alan Corbiere and Alana Johns in 2012, offers rich examples of discourse markers, repetition, and moving from prose to lyric as Obiigomakakikwe comes singing with the sound of her rattles. It is a classic epic adventure tale that contains elements of fantasy and drama. Corbiere's contemporary orthography is extremely useful. However, because the English translation originally provided by Jones often contains more or less meaning than the Anishinaabemowin, I have included my own literal translation between the Anishinaabemowin and English in the excerpt below.

> *"Nookomis! Aaniin dash wiin i'iw i'iwe gibiminagamoyan?"*
> My grandmother! Why (3rd person) (discourse marker) that here singing are you?
> "O my grandmother! Pray, what was that you were singing about?"
>
> *"Kaa, gaawiin-ash wiin niinanaandawi'aanaan a'aw ogimaa,*
> No, not at all (3rd person) we are healing this chief,
> "Oh, why, we are ministering to the chief,
>
> *mii dash iw ena'amaan i'iwe nanaandawi'ag:*
> so then this I sing it as I heal him:
> and this is what I sing when I am attending him:
>
> *'Aki ekwaag nimbishinawashin. Aki ekwaag nimbishinawashin.*
> Earth a measure I am rattling. Earth a measure I am rattling.
> 'From the ends of the earth do I come with the sound of my rattles.
>
> *Mii sa iw aapiji giniin niminotaagoo.'"*
> So (emphasis) that much me I nicely sing.
> It is so much pleasure I impart when I sing.'"

Obiigomakakikwe is a vivid character whose voice is made more memorable by her language. Students find in her statements examples of complex healing relationships and a song that transcends everyday speech.

The story *"Bajaaganish miinawaa Makizinish"* by Thomas Stillday (2009) offers an example of animacy turned upside down as a body part and a foot covering debate their feelings and their relationship with their owner. Their exchange offers readers an example of narrative discourse as well as creative use of transitive animate verbs. The passage below is a sample of the way patterns of repetition and the use of discourse markers appear in stories and add emphasis and dimension to a story. Additionally, the playful, teasing humor between two characters highlights the breadth and diversity of Anishinaabe literary style. This excerpt is from the first of two versions published in the *Oshkaabewis Journal.* The transcription and translation by Anton Treuer, with editorial assistance from the author, are quite literal, so I do not provide a line between the Anishinaabemowin and English. I do tell students to watch for certain specific elements: the repetition of *ingoding iidog,* the pejorative ending *-ish,* and articles that appear in English but are not present in Anisinaabemowin. I also point out that *giikademo, wendademowan,* and *mawi* are all translated as "crying."

> *Hay' ingoding iidog, ingoding iidog aya'aa Bajaaganish miinawaa Makizinish gaa-izhi-nakweshkodaadiwaad ayi'ii, mii iwidi maazhendamowaad.*
>
> It's so sad. One time the Bajaagan and the Makizin made an acquaintance of one another, feeling melancholy.
>
> *Aanish naa gaa-izhi-nakweshkodaadiwaad, mii aw Bajaaganish miinawaa Makizinish.*
>
> Well, this is how they met one another, the Bajaagan and the Makizin.
>
> *Miish iidog, mii go iw ezhi-bimoodemod iw aya'aa Bajaaganish. Mii iw ge wiin gaa-giikademo aya'aa Makizinish.*
>
> It must have been that the Bajaagan was crawling by, crying. And the old shoe was crying out loud to himself.
>
> *"Aaniin niijii," odinaan iidog a'aw, mii awe, mii awe, awe sa Makizinish iniw Bajaaganishan. "Aaniish igonaa wendademowan," ezhi-gagwejimaad iniw Bajaaganish.*
>
> "Hello my friend," he must have told him, that old Makizin to the Bajaagan. "Why are you crying?" he asked the Bajaagan.
>
> *"Aaniin. Geget sa ingichi-maazhidoodaag anishinaabe. Mii wenji-mawiyaan," ikidodog Bajaaganish.*
>
> "Hello. I am truly mistreated by the Indian. That's why I am crying," the Bajaagan must have said.

As an example of satire and pathos combined, this is a contribution to the global existential genre no less absurd than *Ubu Roi* or *Waiting for Godot.* In just a small excerpt, Stillday's use of *mii* and *awe* sets up a steady rhythm and most memorably evokes the senses, leading the reader along the inescapable path of exploring the human, and inhuman, condition of existence. Stillday, born in 1934, not only exemplifies fluency marked by a range of vocabulary and command of grammar, he clearly has a storyteller's skill and demonstrates for rule-bound learners the ways the language can be flexible, allowing concepts of animacy to vary as a body part and a moccasin hold a conversation.

Slightly more contemporary texts are also important. *"Nigigoons Zhazhiibitang Gakina Awiya,"* from the book *Awesiinyensag* by Jones et al. (2010) is an example of blended storytelling with a community of authors who came together to create monolingual stories based on traditional activities for young readers in immersion settings. What they achieve, besides age-appropriate challenging texts, are excellent models for dialogue, complex verb construction, and the use of verb phrases where English would favor noun phrases. For example, the characters do not "go to school," they "seek to learn."

> *Migiziins miinawaa Makoons gii pimaazhagaamewag ando-gikinoo'amawindwaa.*
> Little Eagle and Little Bear went traveling in search of learning.
> *"He, giwaabamaa ina giin iwedi," izhi-gagwedwe Migiziins.*
> "Hey, do you see him/her over there?" asked Little Eagle,
> *"Enya. Mii na aya'aa Nigigoons zhooshkojiishkiwebizod," Makoons izhi-nakwetam.*
> "Yes. So there is Little Otter sliding around," Little Bear replied.
> *"Daga sa naa ganoonaadaa!"*
> "Please let's talk to him/her!"

The story also models useful, short vernacular speech sprinkled with the discourse markers that give it the flavor or fluency so often lost when only grammar is learned.

The story "*Babaamosedaa:* Let's Go for a Walk," written and translated by Patricia Ningewance (2013) and the Manitoba Indigenous Cultural Education Centre, is similarly useful as a contemporary text but in this case illustrates how Anishinaabemowin fits into an urban landscape and is as modern as any other language. Like the other examples, it includes rich dialogue and complex grammar in context, in this case obviatives with transitive animate verbs. As Ben tells his cousin about the city, it is clear that he is eager to share his connection with the landscape. Because Ningewance is an excellent storyteller in both languages and her phrasing and syntax varies from one language to another, I have included my own literal translation between the Anishinaabemowin and English to illustrate some of the differences students discuss in class. While the middle line may appear to be inelegant English, students are often delighted by the flexible syntax of Anishinaabemowin.

Gii-dayaa wiin oodenaang Ben.
Did live he in town, Ben.
Ben is an Anishinaabe who lives in town.

Aabiding ogii-bi-mawadisigoon odi-nawemaaganan Jenii-wan.
Once, she did here visit his relative Jenii.
One day, his relative Jenii, comes to visit him.

Maagizhaa nindaa-babaamosemin oodenaang ayinendam Ben. Maagizhaa odaa-jiikendaan iwe.
Perhaps we should walk in town thinks Ben. Perhaps she would like that.
Ben was thinking they should go for a walk in town. She might like that.

. . .

Giga-izhaamin wedi ziibing. Aapiji onizhishin imaa jiigibiig.
We should go there to the river. So much it is beautiful by the shore.
Let's go down to the river. It's beautiful by the river.

Onizhishin na gaye omaa oodenaang jiigibiig?
Beautiful is it, also here in town by the shore?
Is the riverside here in town beautiful as well?

Miinange. Gaawiin eta bagwadakamig gaa-onizhishing.
Of course. Not only in the country is it beautiful.
Of course! We have beautiful rivers here too.

Students experience these texts in many ways; some are more purely linguistic while others are more grounded in culture. Both Native and non-Native students learn more than the language as they read original texts that represent the art of Anishinaabe storytelling in Anishinaabemowin.

The ideal way for second-year students to study these texts is through reading, retelling, and discussing the details of each sample. Depending on the fluency level of the instructor and students, the class might engage in qualitative analysis of optional vocabulary, discourse markers, and idioms. In all instances students should use a close reading approach to confirm comprehension and discuss the cultural context of the story. Students should read narratives aloud and discuss the stories in the target language to practice pronouncing and conjugating new words and writing new phrases while also increasing conversational skill. All of this should culminate in students beginning to creatively use what they have learned. Shifting classes to writing workshops combines traditional models of apprenticeship and storytelling, which further stretches the limits of language use. The poems below were written in a second-year course. They are creative examples of language use not intended to be discourse or story. They do not conform to standard phrasing, and in some cases, the authors intentionally use language in new ways. Both students and teachers need to find their own voices and use the language in new and modern ways that respectfully reflect standard patterns of grammar and can be understood by the previous generation without resorting to mimicry. As long as basic rules of grammar are followed, the individual phrasing of creative writing is never changed. The following unpublished examples are used with the authors' permission. Cynthia Bergloff wrote about the cold, allowing phonemes and internal rhyme to echo across her image of river.

> *Niwii-biingeji bangii*
> I will be a bit cold
> *gii-ikidoyaan, gaawiin mawisiiyaan*
> I said, I am not crying
> *waabandamaan ziibi.*
> I am looking at the river.

In a similarly playful way Angela Uitz uses comparison and descriptive animate intransitive verbs to craft a timeless image:

> *Bimaadiziwin dibishkoo gaawaa oginii-waabigwan,*
> Life is like a thorny rose,
> *gaawiin gwayakonaagaasiinoo,*
> not perfect,
> *mii sa miikawaadad apane.*
> but always beautiful.

As the instructor, I contributed a slightly longer poem to the class conversation. Having spent years teaching students about the agglutinative qualities of Anishinaabemowin, I tried to examine the way homophones are also part of Anishinaabe tradition. Many times I have heard elders take words apart for reasons of style and emphasis. With the title, "Bi Boonig," I wanted to remind listeners or readers of the way /bi/ can be a directional preverb (meaning toward the speaker) or the first syllable of an inanimate intransitive verb (as with *bimadinaa* 'it is a ridge', *bimaadad* 'it is alive', *biboon* 'winter', and others). Those who listen carefully for the /bi/ might enjoy the similarity of the plural command form for 'leave them alone', which in Anishinaabemowin is *bi boonig,* and the phrase 'in winter', which in Anishinaabemowin is *biboong.* The *boo* echoing throughout the poem emphasizes the difference between /boo/ as a syllable and as a part of the morpheme *boon-*, which implies cessation. The poem was written for class in Anishinaabemowin only. It is intended to be an artifact of sound and imagery and not an example of discourse. The English translation below was written by me so that when I read the poem for a non-Anishinaabemowin-speaking audience I can evoke nearly the same sentiment in both languages.

Bi Boonig—Let Them Be Here

Boonipon apii biboong miidash dakaanimad odishiwe daashkikwaading
When it stops snowing in winter and deep cold arrives to crack the ice
Boonitamaang madwezigoshkaag miinawaa bizindaamangidwaa wewenjiganoo zhiinhyag
We stop hearing the freezing then listen for the great horned owls
Boonigidetaadiwag mii maajii'aamiwaad epichii makwamiiwaagamig
They forgive one another and begin to mate while the world is frozen
Booniiwag enaazhi-zhingobiiwaadikwanan nanegaaj waaboozwaagonagaag
Landing on pine branches as snow falls gently in large flakes
Boonam gegapii miidash boonendang aki biinish bookoshkaag.
Eventually she lays an egg then ignores the world until it breaks.

Ultimately, I found that I was able to use a poem to teach students the same lessons I had attempted to present on worksheets in the past. In fact, because it was a more difficult exercise and required a knowledge of my subject along with a bit of creativity, this may have been a more memorable experience for my students.

Noongom da Enendamang: Conclusion

While the speakers of some languages still need to create lexicons, grammars, and multiformat files to document and preserve corpus data, the speakers of other languages, including Anishinaabemowin, should be challenging themselves to contribute to language vitality in new and more complex ways. Instructors should take time to review the literature focused on indigenous language pedagogies, composition, and rhetoric to develop a framework that highlights the differences between languages. This not only enriches the Anishinaabemowin classroom and improves student outcomes for language acquisition and application, it enriches the discipline of second-language instruction, rhetoric, composition, and literary theory by offering Anishinaabe frameworks and methodologies grounded specifically in Anishinaabemowin. A view of contemporary Anishinaabemowin will emerge as students are exposed to the widest possible range of dialects and challenged to view Anishinaabemowin as a living modern language. In practice, this should not threaten or diminish regional variation, but instead it should support a diasporic lingua franca against which regional preferences can be highlighted, celebrated, and preserved. Speaking the language of a specific sovereign nation does not dilute the unifying power of American Indian / Native American / First Nations / Indigenous identity but instead ensures that decolonization continues and the "re" is removed from "revitalization," so languages are grounded in the present and connected to sovereign national histories, as they have been inherited and are evolving.

REFERENCES

Brown, Timothy. 2008. Work Hard, Eat Lots: Lessons Learned from a Case Study of an Ojibwe Educator's Pedagogy. EdD thesis, University of St. Thomas.

Chacaby, Maya. 2011. Kipimoojikewin: Articulating Anishinaabe Pedagogy through Anishinaabemowin (Ojibwe Language) Revitalization. MA thesis, University of Toronto.

Chartrand, Rebecca. 2012. Anishinaabe Pedagogy. *Canadian Journal of Native Education* 35(1):144–162.

Fuhst, Helen C. 2012. *Introduction to the Sound Based Method of Understanding Anishinaabemowin.* Canton, MI: Niish Ishkoden Productions.

Gresczyk, Richard A. 2011. Language Warriors: Leaders in the Ojibwe Language Revitalization Movement. PhD thesis, University of Minnesota.

Gross, Lawrence W. 2010. Some Elements of American Indian Pedagogy from an Anishinaabe

Perspective. *American Indian Culture and Research Journal* 34(2):11–26.

Harrison, K. David. 2007. *When Languages Die: The Extinction of the World's Languages and the Erosion of Human Knowledge.* Oxford: Oxford University Press.

Hermes, Mary. 2005. Ma'iingan Is Just a Misspelling of the Word Wolf: A Case for Teaching Culture through Language. *Anthropology & Education Quarterly* 36(1):43–56.

Hermes, Mary. 2007. Moving toward the Language: Reflections on Teaching in an Indigenous-Immersion School. *Journal of American Indian Education* 46(3):54–71.

Hermes, Mary. 2012. Designing Indigenous Language Revitalization. *Harvard Educational Review* 82(3):381–402.

Hermes, Mary, and Kendall King. 2014. Why Is This So Hard? Ideologies of Endangerment, Passive Language Learning Approaches and Ojibwe in the United States. *Journal of Language, Identity, and Education* 13(4):268–282.

Hinton, Leanne. 2013. *Bringing Our Languages Home: Language Revitalization for Families.* Berkeley, CA: Heyday Books.

Jones, Nancy, Eugene Stillday, Rose Tainter, Anna Gibbs, Marlene Stately, Anton Treuer, Keller Paap, Lisa LaRonge, Michael Sullivan, John Nichols, Lucia Bonacci, and Heather Fairbanks. 2010. *Awesiinyensag: Dibaajimowinan ji-gikinoo'amaageng.* Minneapolis: Wiigwaas Press.

Matthews, Maureen, Roger Roulette, and Rand Valentine. 2010. Anishinaabemowin: The Language of Pimachiowin Aki. Discussion paper for the Pimachiowin Aki UNESCO World Heritage site proposal.

McCarty, Teresa, and Tiffany Lee. 2014. Critical Culturally Sustaining/Revitalizing Pedagogy and Indigenous Education Sovereignty. *Harvard Educational Review* 84(1):101–124.

McInnes, Brian. 2014. Teaching and Learning Ojibwe as a Second Language: Considerations for a Sustainable Future. *Journal of Language Teaching and Research* 5(4):751–758.

Mead, Chelsea. 2014. *Zeziikizit Kchinchinaabe:* A Relational Understanding of Anishinaabemowin History. PhD thesis, Arizona State University.

Midaasoganzh. 1905. Nanabushu Slays Toad Woman. *Ojibwe Texts,* vol. 1, collected by William Jones and retranscribed by Alan Corbiere. Baadwewedamojig. http://ojibweproject.weebly.com/.

Naokwegijig-Corbiere, Mary Ann. 2008. Flying Blind over Strange Terrain, or *Ezhi-Mkoshnang Kweji-Aan'kinoosjigeng:* Issues in English-Nishnaabemwin Translation. *Papers of the 39th Algonquian Conference,* ed. by Karl S. Hele and Regna Darnell, pp. 518–530. London: University of Western Ontario.

Ningewance, Patricia M. 2013. *Babaamosedaa:* Let's Go For a Walk. Winnipeg: Manitoba Indigenous Cultural Education Centre.

Ningewance, Patricia M. 2004. *Talking Gookom's Language: Learning Ojibwe.* Lac Seul, Ontario: Mazinaate Press.

Noodin, Margaret. 2012. *Weweni Nd'nisidotami Ezhi-Anishinaabebiigeyaang:* Carefully We Understand How We Write Anishinaabemowin. *Papers of the 40th Algonquian Conference,* ed. by Karl S. Hele and J. Randolph Valentine, pp. 346–357. Albany: State University of New York Press.

Noodin, Margaret. 2013. *Ezhi-waanimazinbiiganankewag:* The Way They Write Circular Images. *Papers of the 41st Algonquian Conference,* ed. by Karl S. Hele and J. Randolph Valentine, pp. 195–207. Albany: State University of New York Press.

Noodin, Margaret, and Stacie Sheldon. 2017. *Waasamodibaajibiigemaazoying:* Bright Lines of Story in Song. *Studies in American Indian Literatures* 29(1):88–99.

Perley, Bernard C. 2011. *Defying Maliseet Language Death: Emergent Vitalities of Language, Culture, & Identity in Eastern Canada.* Lincoln: University of Nebraska Press.

Pitawanakwat, Brock. 2009. *Anishinaabemodaa Pane Oodenang:* A Qualitative Study of Anishinaabe Language Revitalization as Self-Determination in Manitoba and Ontario. PhD thesis, University of Victoria.

Reyhner, Jon. 2017. Affirming Identity: The Role of Language and Culture in American Indian Education. *Cogent Education* 4:1340081.

Stillday, Thomas. 2009. *Bajaaganish miinawaa Makizinish. Oshkaabewis* (version 1). *Native Journal* 7(1):32–35.

Treuer, Anton. 1996. Building a Foundation for the Next Generation: A Path for Revival of the Ojibwe Language. *Oshkaabewis Native Journal* 3(1):3–7.

Treuer, Anton. 2001. *Living Our Language: Ojibwe Tales and Oral Histories.* St. Paul: Minnesota Historical Society Press.

When Direct and Inverse Are Asymmetrical

Will Oxford

Direct and inverse verb forms are typically morphologically symmetrical, differing only in the theme sign (direct **-a:,* inverse **-ekw*).[1] But there are many exceptions to this generalization. This paper shows that the exceptions, while varying in their details, display a consistent pattern: when direct and inverse forms are morphologically asymmetrical, it is usually the case that the direct form indexes only the higher-ranked argument on the person hierarchy, while the corresponding inverse form indexes both arguments. This asymmetry suggests that the lower-ranked argument in an inverse form (the actor) is more accessible to agreement than the lower-ranked argument in a direct form (the goal)—a conclusion that contributes to our understanding of the inverse construction.

After some background on Algonquian verb inflection, the paper describes four ways in which direct and inverse forms may be asymmetrical: (1) mixed forms may have an objective inverse but an absolute direct, (2) mixed forms may have an objective inverse but a PARTIALLY absolute direct, (3) mixed forms may show a blend of objective and absolute properties that varies between the direct and the inverse, and (4) nonlocal forms may have an objective inverse but an absolute direct. A discussion of these patterns follows.

Background

This section provides background on the inflectional template, the direct-inverse contrast, the absolute-objective contrast, and a particular pattern of number neutralization.

Inflectional Template

In most Algonquian languages, the agreement inflection of the independent order follows the template in (1a). The slot names in this template (e.g., "central suffix") follow Goddard 1969 and Nichols 1980. The template is exemplified by the Proto-Algonquian (PA) 3→1 form in (1b) (Goddard 2007:231, 2015:391).[2]

(1) a. Prefix—Verb stem—Theme sign—Central suffix—Peripheral suffix

b. *newa:pamekona:naki

ne-	wa:pam	-ekw	-wena:n	-aki
1-	see	-INV	-1p	-3p

'They see us.'

The content of the agreement slots is as follows. The THEME SIGN, on a TA verb, is either an inverse marker (PA **-ekw* 'INV') or an object marker (PA **-i* '1OBJ,' **eθ* '2OBJ,' **-a:* '3OBJ' or 'direct'); the analysis of TI theme signs is controversial (Goddard 2007:239–240). The PREFIX and CENTRAL SUFFIX function together as a single "central-participant marker" (Goddard 1969:104) that indexes the argument that ranks highest on the person hierarchy SAP > X > 3 > 3′ > 0, where SAP is a speech-act participant (first or second person), X is an impersonal actor, 3 is an animate proximate third person, 3′ is an animate obviative third person, and 0 is an inanimate third person. In (1b) the highest-ranked argument is the first-person goal, which is indexed by the prefix-suffix combination **ne . . . wena:n* '1p.' The PERIPHERAL SUFFIX functions separately from the prefix and central suffix and always indexes a third person (**-aki* '3p' in (1b)). In many languages the singular peripheral suffixes (PA **-a* '3s,' **-i* '0s') have become null due to the loss of final vowels; for simplicity of presentation, such null suffixes will not be shown in the glosses in this paper.

Proto-Algonquian had three sets of central suffixes, shown in Table 1. The sets share the same pluralizers (*-Ø 'singular,' **-ena:n* '1p,' **-enaw* '21,' **-wa:w* '2p, 3p') but

TABLE 1. Three parallel sets of central suffixes in Proto-Algonquian (Goddard 2007)

M-SUFFIXES		W-SUFFIXES		N-SUFFIXES	
1s, 2s	-e	1s, 2s, 3s	-w	1s, 2s, 3s	-en
1p	-ehmena:	1p	-wena:n	1p	-ene:na:n
21	-ehmena	21	-wenaw	21	-ene:naw
2p	-ehmwa:	2p, 3p	-wa:w	2p, 3p	-ene:wa:w

are distinguished by the FORMATIVE ELEMENT (Goddard 2007) that precedes the pluralizer: the "m-suffixes" begin with a formative **-ehm-* (except in the singular, where the *-hm-* portion was lost), the "w-suffixes" begin with a formative *-w-*, and the "n-suffixes" begin with a formative **-en(e:)-*. Each set of central suffixes was used in a different morphosyntactic context (Goddard 2007:264).

Although the historical origins of the formative elements of the central suffixes are clear (Goddard 2007:259–263), it is less clear whether a synchronic morpheme boundary remains between the formative and the pluralizer. Is a w-suffix such as **-wena:n* '1p' synchronically segmentable as a meaningful unit **-w* plus a pluralizer **-ena:n* '1p'? Pentland (1999) and Goddard (2007) give opposite answers; in this paper I follow Goddard in regarding the central suffix as a single functional unit characterized formally by a distinct formative element.

It should also be noted that the **-w-* formative element of the w-suffixes is sometimes absent from the surface form due to regular phonological coalescence, as in (1b) above, where underlying **-ekw-wena:n-* surfaces as **-ekona:n-*. Even where a surface **-w-* is absent, the w-suffixes remain distinct from the m-suffixes and n-suffixes due to the lack of an **-hm-* or **-en-* formative element.

Direct and Inverse Forms

The term INVERSE is sometimes used to label any form in which the goal outranks the actor on a 2>1>X>3>3′>0 hierarchy. In this paper I adopt a more restrictive empirical definition: a form is inverse only if it contains the inverse theme sign (PA **-ekw*) or one of its variants (e.g., impersonal **-eko:*, Meskwaki inanimate *-ekwi*). The term DIRECT cannot be similarly defined, as the so-called direct theme sign **-a:* is in fact just one of several object-marking theme signs: **i* 1OBJ, **-eθ* 2OBJ, **-a:* 3OBJ, *-am* 0OBJ (Rhodes 1976). In this paper I label as "direct" any form that stands in minimal contrast to an inverse form. The Cree 3→1 inverse form in (2a) thus has as its direct counterpart the 1→3 form in (2b) (Wolfart 1973). I will refer to forms such as those in (2), which involve a speech act participant (SAP) and an animate third person, as MIXED ANIMATE forms.

(2) a. INVERSE (3→1)

niwa:pamikona:n			
ni-	wa:pam	**-ikw**	-ina:n
1-	see	**-INV**	-1p

'S/he sees us.'

b. DIRECT (1→3)

niwa:pama:na:n			
ni-	wa:pam	-a:	-ina:n
1-	see	-3OBJ	-1p

'We see him/her.'

In the same way, the Cree 0→1 inverse form in (3a), with inanimate actor, has as its direct counterpart the 1→0 TI form in (3b). Labeling TI forms as "direct" is nonstandard—though see Todd 1970:135 for a precedent—but it captures the fact that the inflections in (3a–b) stand in exactly the same relation to each other as do those in (2a–b), even though the lexical verb stem differs (TA *wa:pam-* in (3a), TI *wa:paht-* in (3b)).

(3) a. INVERSE (0→1)

niwa:pamikon			
ni-	wa:pam	**-ikw**	-in
1-	see	**-INV**	-1s

'It sees me.'

b. DIRECT (1→0)

niwa:pahte:n			
ni-	wa:paht	-e:	-in
1-	see.TI	-TI1	-1s

'I see it.'

I will refer to forms such as those in (3), which involve an SAP and an inanimate third person, as MIXED INANIMATE forms. Most of the patterns discussed in this paper involve either mixed animate or mixed inanimate forms.

The restrictive definitions that I have adopted mean that not all transitive forms can be characterized as direct or inverse. For example, the Cree 3→1 conjunct form in (4a) does not qualify as inverse because its theme sign is not inverse *-ikw* (but rather *-i* 1OBJ). The corresponding 1→3 form in (4b) thus does not qualify as direct, as it does not stand in minimal contrast to an inverse form. These forms simply stand outside of the direct-inverse system.[3]

(4) a. e:-wa:pamit

e:-	wa:pam	**-i**	-t
SUB-	see	**-1OBJ**	-3

'(that) s/he sees me' (3→1)

b. e:-wa:pamak

e:-	wa:pam	-Ø	-ak
SUB-	see	-3OBJ	1s:3

'(that) I see him/her' (1→3)

TABLE 2. Unami mixed inanimate, direct

	OBJECTIVE (SAP→0DEF)	ABSOLUTE (SAP→0INDEF)
1s→0s 1s→0p	n- . . . -am-ən n- . . . -am-ən-**al**	n- . . . -am
2s→0s 2s→0p	k- . . . -am-ən k- . . . -am-ən-**al**	k- . . . -am
1p→0s 1p→0p	n- . . . -am-əne:n n- . . . -am-əne:na:n-**i:l**	n- . . . -am-əhməna:
21→0s 21→0p	k- . . . -am-əne:n k- . . . -am-əne:na:n-**i:l**	k- . . . -am-əhməna:
2p→0s 2p→0p	k- . . . -am-əne:wa: k- . . . -am-əne:wa:w-**i:l**	k- . . . -am-əhmwa:

MORPHEMES: prefixes *n-* '1', *k-* '2'; theme sign *-am* 'TI1'; central n-suffixes *-ən* '1s, 2s', *-əne:n(a:n)* '1p, 21', *-əne:wa:(w)* '2p'; central m-suffixes *-əhməna:* '1p, 21', *-əhmwa:* '2p'; peripheral suffix *-al* ~ *-i:l* '0p'.

Since the forms in (4) are neither direct nor inverse, they are not relevant to this paper, as our focus is only on inflectional asymmetries in direct-inverse forms. This is an important point, because the forms in (4) certainly do show an inflectional asymmetry: the central suffix is *-t* '3' in (4a) but *-ak* '1s:3' in (4b). Such asymmetries are easy to find, but their existence is unsurprising: since these forms stand outside the direct-inverse system, there is no reason to expect them to be symmetrical in the first place. Our interest lies in forms that meet the more restrictive direct-inverse definitions, like those in (2) and (3) above, and yet still display asymmetrical inflection—a much rarer occurrence.

Absolute and Objective Inflections

The independent order in some Eastern Algonquian languages shows a contrast between ABSOLUTE and OBJECTIVE inflections (Goddard 1967; 1974; 2007). An objective form agrees for number and animacy with a third-person argument that is unindexed in the corresponding absolute form. For example, in the Unami Delaware mixed inanimate direct paradigm in Table 2 (Goddard 1969:179), the objective forms in the first column show central agreement for the SAP actor (e.g., *n- . . . -əne:n* '1p') and peripheral agreement for the third-person goal (e.g., *-i:l* '0p') while the absolute forms in the second column show only central agreement for the SAP actor (e.g., *n- . . .* -əhməna: '1p'); peripheral agreement is absent. The lack of a peripheral suffix in the absolute forms makes them number-neutral with respect to the goal: in contrast to the distinction between 1p→0s and 1p→0p objective forms,

TABLE 3. Unami mixed inanimate, inverse

	OBJECTIVE (0DEF→SAP)	ABSOLUTE (0INDEF→SAP)
0s→1s 0p→1s	n- . . . -əkw-ən n- . . . -əkw-ən-**al**	n- . . . -əkw
0s→2s 0p→2s	k- . . . -əkw-ən k- . . . -əkw-ən-**al**	k- . . . -əkw
0s→1p 0p→1p	n- . . . -əkw-əne:n n- . . . -əkw-əne:na:n-**i:l**	n- . . . -əkw-əhməna:
0s→21 0p→21	k- . . . -əkw-əne:n k- . . . -əkw-əne:na:n-**i:l**	k- . . . -əkw-əhməna:
0s→2p 0p→2p	k- . . . -əkw-əne:wa: k- . . . -əkw-əne:wa:w-**i:l**	k- . . . -əkw-əhmwa:

MORPHEMES: as in Table 2, plus theme sign *-əkw* 'INV'. ALLOMORPHY: *-əkw-əne:n* → *-əko:ne:n*.

there is just a single 1p→0 absolute form. In Unami the absolute-objective contrast marks definiteness: the objective inflections in Table 2 are used with definite goals, while the absolute inflections are used with indefinite goals.

In addition to their differential treatment of the inanimate goal, the objective and absolute inflections also show different forms of the central suffix that indexes the SAP actor. The objective inflections in Table 2 show an "n-suffix" that includes the formative element *-ən-* (1s/2s *-ən,* 1p/21 *-əne:n(a:n),* 2p *-əne:wa:(w)*) while the absolute inflections show an "m-suffix" that includes the formative element *-əhm-* (1s/2s -Ø, 1p/21 *-əhməna:,* 2p *-əhmwa:*). The *-hm-* formative in the plural m-suffixes, a telltale marker of an absolute form, has become *-m-* or *-p-* in most other languages due to regular sound change.

Alongside the mixed inanimate direct forms in Table 2 (SAP→0), the corresponding mixed inanimate inverse forms (0→SAP) display the absolute-objective contrast as well, as shown in Table 3 (Goddard 1969:174–176). In the inverse, as in the direct, the contrast is conditioned by the definiteness of the third-person argument, but in an inverse form, this argument is the actor rather than the goal: objective inflections are used with definite actors, while absolute inflections are used with indefinite actors. Note that the inverse inflections in Table 3 show full morphological symmetry with the direct inflections in Table 2: corresponding direct and inverse inflections differ only in the theme sign (*-am* 'TI1' in direct, *-əkw* 'INV' in inverse).

TABLE 4. Munsee mixed inanimate, objective

DIRECT (SAP→0DEF)		INVERSE (0DEF→SAP)	
1s→0s	n- . . . -am-ən	0s→1s	n- . . . -əkw-ən
1s→0p	n- . . . -am-ən-al	0p→1s	n- . . . -əkw-ən-al
2s→0s	k- . . . -am-ən	0s→2s	k- . . . -əkw-ən
2s→0p	k- . . . -am-ən-al	0p→2s	k- . . . -əkw-ən-al
1p→0	**n- . . . -am-əne:n**	0→1p	**n- . . . -əkw-əne:n**
21→0	**k- . . . -am-əne:n**	0→21	**k- . . . -əkw-əne:n**
2p→0	**k- . . . -am-əne:wa:**	0→2p	**k- . . . -əkw-əne:wa:**

MORPHEMES: prefixes *n-* '1', *k-* '2'; theme signs *-am* 'TI1', *-əkw* 'INV'; central n-suffixes *-ən* '1s, 2s', *-əne:n* '1p, 21', *-əne:wa:* '2p', peripheral suffix *-al* '0p'.

Number Neutralization with Plural SAPs

The Unami forms in Tables 2–3 show a uniform pattern of third-person number marking: all objective forms mark third-person number, while all absolute forms neutralize it. In some languages, however, the patterns are less uniform. In particular, there is a recurring tendency to neutralize third-person number WHEN THE SAP ARGUMENT IS PLURAL. This is the case for mixed inanimate objective forms in modern Munsee Delaware (Goddard 1969:176, 180), shown in Table 4. Forms involving a singular SAP mark the number of the definite third person, but forms involving a plural SAP (shown in bold) do not. A similar but more restricted pattern of neutralization occurs in mixed inanimate forms in Southwestern Ojibwe (Nichols 1980:282, 292), where number marking for the third-person argument is neutralized when the SAP is FIRST-PERSON plural. Such number neutralizations are interesting in their own right (see Cenerini 2017 for a pan-Algonquian survey and analysis), but they are not relevant to the topic of this paper because they apply equally to direct and inverse forms. The patterns are worth mentioning here for contrastive purposes, however, because we will see below that in other languages, similar neutralizations have applied only to direct forms.

Mixed Forms with Objective Inverse but Absolute Direct

Tables 2, 3, and 4 illustrated the patterning of mixed INANIMATE forms in the Delaware languages. We saw that objective inflections occur when the inanimate third person is definite and absolute inflections occur when the inanimate third

TABLE 5. Munsee mixed animate, definite third person

INVERSE (3DEF→SAP)		DIRECT (SAP→3DEF)	
3s→1s 3p→1s	n- . . . -əkw-w n- . . . -əkw-w-**ak**	1s→3s 1s→3p	n- . . . -a:-w n- . . . -a:-w-**ak**
3s→2s 3p→2s	k- . . . -əkw-w k- . . . -əkw-w-**ak**	2s→3s 2s→3p	k- . . . -a:-w k- . . . -a:-w-**ak**
3s→1p 3p→1p	n- . . . -əkw-wəna: n- . . . -əkw-wəna:n-**ak**	1p→3s 1p→3p	n- . . . -a:-wəna: n- . . . -a:-wəna:n-**ak**
3s→21 3p→21	k- . . . -əkw-wəna: k- . . . -əkw-wəna:n-**ak**	21→3s 21→3p	k- . . . -a:-wəna: k- . . . -a:-wəna:n-**ak**
3s→2p 3p→2p	k- . . . -əkw-wa: k- . . . -əkw-wa:w-**ak**	2p→3s 2p→3p	k- . . . -a:-wa: k- . . . -a:-wa:w-**ak**

MORPHEMES: prefixes *n-* '1', *k-* '2'; theme signs *-əkw* 'INV', *-a:* '3OBJ'; central w-suffixes *-w* '1s, 2s', *-wəna:(n)* '1p, 21', *-wa:(w)* '2p', peripheral suffix *-ak* '3p'. ALLOMORPHY: *-w-w* → *-w*, *-əkw-ak* → *-əko:k*, *-əkw-wəna:* → *-əko:na:*, *-əkw-wa:* → *-əko:wa:*.

TABLE 6. Munsee mixed animate, indefinite third person

INVERSE (3INDEF→SAP)		DIRECT (SAP→3INDEF)	
3s→1s 3p→1s	n- . . . -əkw-w n- . . . -əkw-w-**ak**	1s→3	n- . . . -a:
3s→2s 3p→2s	k- . . . -əkw-w k- . . . -əkw-w-**ak**	2s→3	k- . . . -a:
3s→1p 3p→1p	n- . . . -əkw-wəna: n- . . . -əkw-wəna:n-**ak**	1p→3	n- . . . -a:-hməna:
3s→21 3p→21	k- . . . -əkw-wəna: k- . . . -əkw-wəna:n-**ak**	21→3	k- . . . -a:-hməna:
3s→2p 3p→2p	k- . . . -əkw-wa: k- . . . -əkw-wa:w-**ak**	2p→3	k- . . . -a:-hmwa:

MORPHEMES: as in Table 5, plus central m-suffixes *-hməna:* '1p, 21', *-hmwa:* '2p'. ALLOMORPHY: as in Table 5.

person is indefinite. In mixed ANIMATE forms, the story begins in a similar way. When the animate third person is definite, objective inflections are used throughout both the inverse and the direct, as shown for Munsee in Table 5 (Goddard 1969:171, 174). As above, the inflections in Table 5 show perfect direct-inverse symmetry.

Things change, however, when the animate third person is indefinite. Going by the above, we would expect indefinite third persons to trigger absolute inflection. This expectation is upheld in direct forms, where the indefinite third person is the goal. As shown for Munsee in Table 6 (Goddard 1969:171, 174), direct forms leave the number of the indefinite goal unmarked and show the characteristic absolute m-suffixes. The pattern differs, however, in the inverse forms, where the indefinite third person is the actor. The inflections that appear here are objective: they mark the number of the third person and they lack the characteristic absolute m-suffixes. In fact, these are exactly the same objective inflections that we saw for *definite* third-person actors in Table 5.

Delaware mixed animate indefinite forms are thus our first example of a direct-inverse inflectional asymmetry: direct forms (SAP→3INDEF) are absolute, but inverse forms (3INDEF→SAP) are objective. This asymmetry can be described in terms of the treatment of the third-person argument. If we compare Tables 5 and 6, we see that animate third-person *goals* can appear with either objective inflection (when definite) or absolute inflection (when indefinite), but animate third-person *actors* can appear only with objective inflection regardless of their definiteness (Goddard 1969:174). This asymmetry is also found in Massachusett (Goddard and Bragdon 1988:519) and has been reconstructed for PA by Goddard (1974:322, 2007:267).[4] The asymmetrical treatment of animate third persons in these languages is our first indication that the third-person actor in an inverse form has a structural status different from the third-person goal in a direct form, despite the morphological symmetry that such forms often display.

All of the Central Algonquian languages have lost the absolute-objective contrast; transitive inflections in these languages show a mixture of originally absolute and originally objective forms, but without the functional link to definiteness that these forms carry in conservative Eastern languages. While the resulting paradigms are often symmetrical, some languages show direct-inverse asymmetries that are formally identical to the Delaware pattern discussed above. Consider, for example, the Meskwaki mixed animate dubitative paradigm in Table 7 (Goddard 1994:194–195). The inverse inflections are formally objective: third-person number is marked and m-suffixes are not used. The direct inflections, on the other hand, are formally absolute: third-person number is unmarked and the characteristic absolute m-suffixes appear (with Meskwaki *p* from PA **hm*). The same type of asymmetry arises in the mixed inanimate paradigm in Kickapoo, shown in Table 8 (Voorhis 1974:63, 66–67); again, inverse forms are objective while direct forms are absolute.

TABLE 7. Meskwaki mixed animate, dubitative

	INVERSE (3→SAP)		DIRECT (SAP→3)
3s→1s 3p→1s	ne- . . . -ekw-etoke ne- . . . -ekw-etoke:h-**iki**	1s→3	ne- . . . -a:-p-etoke
3s→2s 3p→2s	ke- . . . -ekw-etoke ke- . . . -ekw-etoke:h-**iki**	2s→3	ke- . . . -a:-p-etoke
3s→1p 3p→1p	ne- . . . -ekw-ena:-toke ne- . . . -ekw-ena:-toke:h-**iki**	1p→3	ne- . . . -a:-pena:-toke
3s→21 3p→21	ke- . . . -ekw-ena:-toke ke- . . . -ekw-ena:-toke:h-**iki**	21→3	ke- . . . -a:-pena:-toke
3s→2p 3p→2p	ke- . . . -ekw-wa:-toke ke- . . . -ekw-wa:-toke:h-**iki**	2p→3	ke- . . . -a:-pwa:-toke

MORPHEMES: prefixes *ne-* '1', *ke-* '2'; theme signs *-ekw* 'INV', *-a:* '3OBJ'; central w-suffixes *-ena:(n)* '1p, 21', *-wa:(w)* '2p'; central m-suffixes *-p* '1s, 2s', *-pena(:)* '1p, 21', *-pwa(:)* '2p'; mode sign *-(e)toke(:h)* 'DUB'; peripheral suffix *-iki* '3p'. ALLOMORPHY: *-ekw-etoke → -eko:toke, -ekw-ena: → -ekona:, -ekw-wa: → -ekowa:*

TABLE 8. Kickapoo mixed inanimate

	INVERSE (0→SAP)		DIRECT (SAP→0)
0s→1s 0p→1s	ne- . . . -ekw-i ne- . . . -ekw-**ani**	1s→0	ne- . . . -a
0s→2s 0p→2s	ke- . . . -ekw-i ke- . . . -ekw-**ani**	2s→0	ke- . . . -a
0s→1p 0p→1p	ne- . . . -ekw-ena:n-i ne- . . . -ekw-ena:n-**ani**	1p→0	ne- . . . -a:-pena
0s→21 0p→21	ke- . . . -ekw-ena:n-i ke- . . . -ekw-ena:n-**ani**	21→0	ke- . . . -a:-pena
0s→2p 0p→2p	ke- . . . -ekw-wa:w-i ke- . . . -ekw-wa:w-**ani**	2p→0	ke- . . . -a:-pwa

MORPHEMES: prefixes *ne-* '1', *ke-* '2'; theme signs *-ekw* 'INV', *-a(:)* '3OBJ'; central w-suffixes *-ena:n* '1p, 21', *-wa:w* '2p'; central m-suffixes *-pena* '1p, 21', *-pwa* '2p'; peripheral suffixes *-i* '0s', *-ani* '0p'. ALLOMORPHY: *-ekw-ani → -eko:ni, -ekw-ena:n → -ekona:n, -ekw-wa:w → -ekoa:w*

Mixed Forms with Objective Inverse but Partially Absolute Direct

The direct-inverse asymmetries in the preceding section affect all mixed forms in the relevant paradigms. There are also cases in which the asymmetry affects only a subset of mixed forms. Consider the Meskwaki mixed animate indicative paradigm in Table 9 (Goddard 1994:190–191). Forms involving a singular SAP are symmetrically objective: in both the inverse (e.g., 3s→1s) and the direct (e.g., 1s→3s), the verb agrees

TABLE 9. Meskwaki mixed animate, indicative

INVERSE (3→SAP)		DIRECT (SAP→3)	
3s→1s 3p→1s	ne- . . . -ekw-a ne- . . . -ekw-**aki**	1s→3s 1s→3p	ne- . . . -a:-w-a ne- . . . -a:-w-**aki**
3s→2s 3p→2s	ke- . . . -ekw-a ke- . . . -ekw-**aki**	2s→3s 2s→3p	ke- . . . -a:-w-a ke- . . . -a:-w-**aki**
3s→1p 3p→1p	ne- . . . -ekw-ena:n-a ne- . . . -ekw-ena:n-**aki**	1p→3	**ne- . . . -a:-pena**
3s→21 3p→21	ke- . . . -ekw-ena:n-a ke- . . . -ekw-ena:n-**aki**	21→3	**ke- . . . -a:-pena**
3s→2p 3p→2p	ke- . . . -ekw-wa:w-a ke- . . . -ekw-wa:w-**aki**	2p→3	ke- . . . -a:-pwa

MORPHEMES: as in Table 7, plus central w-suffix *-w* '1s, 2s'; peripheral suffixes *-a* '3s', *-aki* '3p'. ALLOMORPHY: *-ekw-aki* → *-eko:ki, -ekw-ena:n* → *-ekona:n, -ekw-wa:w* → *-ekowa:w*

TABLE 10. Potawatomi mixed animate, indicative

INVERSE (3→SAP)		DIRECT (SAP→3)	
3s→1s 3p→1s	n- . . . -ək n- . . . -əkw-**ək**	1s→3s 1s→3p	n- . . . -a n- . . . -a-**k**
3s→2s 3p→2s	k- . . . -ək k- . . . -əkw-**ək**	2s→3s 2s→3p	k- . . . -a k- . . . -a-**k**
3s→1p 3p→1p	n- . . . -ək-nan n- . . . -ək-nan-**ək**	1p→3	**n- . . . -a-mən**
3s→21 3p→21	k- . . . -ək-nan k- . . . -ək-nan-**ək**	21→3	**k- . . . -a-mən**
3s→2p 3p→2p	k- . . . -ək-wa k- . . . -ək-wa-**k**	2p→3s 2p→3p	k- . . . -a-wa k- . . . -a-wa-**k**

MORPHEMES: prefixes *n-* '1', *k-* '2'; theme signs *-ək(w)* 'INV', *-a* '3OBJ'; central w-suffixes *-nan* '1p, 21', *-wa* '2p'; central m-suffix *-mən(a)* '1p, 21'; peripheral suffix *-(ə)k* '3p'. ALLOMORPHY: *-əkw-ək* → *-əkok*

with both arguments. Forms involving a plural SAP, however, display the now-familiar asymmetry in which inverse inflections are objective, showing peripheral agreement for the third-person actor, while direct inflections are absolute, lacking peripheral agreement with the third-person goal. The same pattern occurs in the Shawnee mixed inanimate forms in Voegelin (1936:396).

A similar but even more restricted pattern of partial asymmetry is displayed by the Potawatomi mixed animate paradigm in Table 10 (Hockett 1966:65–66). Here, all forms are inflectionally symmetrical except for those that involve a *first-person* plural (1p, 21). The 1p and 21 forms are asymmetrical, as usual, in that the inverse inflections are objective, showing third-person peripheral agreement, while the direct inflections are absolute, lacking peripheral agreement. The Shawnee mixed animate forms in Voegelin 1936:396 show this more restricted pattern as well.

The Meskwaki and Potawatomi patterns are the asymmetrical counterparts of the symmetrical number neutralization patterns that were described for Munsee and Southwestern Ojibwe in the background section above. Whereas Munsee plural-SAP forms show neutralization of third-person number in both the direct and the inverse, Meskwaki plural-SAP forms show neutralization of third-person number in the direct (SAP.PL→3), where the third person is the goal, but not in the inverse (3→SAP.PL), where the third person is the actor. Similarly, whereas Southwestern Ojibwe first-person plural forms show neutralization of third-person number in both the direct and the inverse, Potawatomi first-person plural forms show neutralization of third-person number in the direct (1p/21→3) but not in the inverse (3→1p/21).

Mixed Forms That Blend Objective and Absolute Properties

The direct-inverse asymmetries that we have seen thus far are summarized in Table 11. Each asymmetry can be described in the same way: the inverse forms show objective inflection, while the direct forms show absolute inflection.

This section considers three further paradigms that display a similar asymmetry. The patterns are messier, however, in that the absolute and objective inflections show some degree of morphological blending, as indicated in Table 12.

The Potawatomi mixed animate preterit paradigm is shown in Table 13. Like the Potawatomi indicative paradigm in Table 10, the preterit paradigm is asymmetrical in first-person plural forms. The direct first-person plural forms (1p/21→3) are absolute: they lack a peripheral suffix and show the m-allomorph of the central suffix (*-mən(a)* '1p'). The inverse first-person plural forms (3→1p/21) are an objective-absolute blend: they are objective in that they mark the third person with a peripheral suffix, but their central agreement appears to be absolute, as it shows the m-suffix allomorph that normally occurs in absolute forms (*-mən(a)* '1p') rather than the w-suffix that normally occurs in objective forms (*-nan* '1p,' as in the objective forms in Table 10).

TABLE 11. Inflection in asymmetrical mixed forms

MIXED FORMS WITH ASYMMETRY	INVERSE	DIRECT
Munsee inanimate (Table 6)	objective	absolute
Meskwaki animate dubitative (Table 7)	objective	absolute
Kickapoo inanimate (Table 8)	objective	absolute
Meskwaki animate indicative 1p/21/2p (Table 9)	objective	absolute
Potawatomi animate indicative 1p/21 (Table 10)	objective	absolute

TABLE 12. Inflection in asymmetrical mixed forms with blending

MIXED FORMS WITH ASYMMETRY	INVERSE	DIRECT
Potawatomi animate preterit 1p/21 (Table 13)	**blended**	absolute
Miami-Illinois animate 1p (Table 14)	objective	**blended**
Shawnee animate 1p/21 (Table 15)	objective	**blended**

TABLE 13. Potawatomi mixed animate, preterit

INVERSE (3→SAP)		DIRECT (SAP→3)	
3s→1s 3p→1s	n- . . . -ək-pən n- . . . -ək-pənin-ək	1s→3s 1s→3p	n- . . . -a-pən n- . . . -a-pənin-ək
3s→2s 3p→2s	k- . . . -ək-pən k- . . . -ək-pənin-ək	2s→3s 2s→3p	k- . . . -a-pən k- . . . -a-pənin-ək
3s→1p 3p→1p	n- . . . -ək-məna-pən n- . . . -ək-məna-pənin-ək	1p→3	**n- . . . -a-məna-pən**
3s→21 3p→21	k- . . . -ək-məna-pən k- . . . -ək-məna-pənin-ək	21→3	**k- . . . -a-məna-pən**
3s→2p 3p→2p	k- . . . -ək-wa-pən k- . . . -ək-wa-pənin-ək	2p→3s 2p→3p	k- . . . -a-mwa-pən k- . . . -a-mwa-pənin-ək

MORPHEMES: as in Table 10, plus central m-suffix *-mwa* '2p'; mode sign *-pən(in)* 'PRET'.

We can understand the Potawatomi first-person plural preterit forms as showing the same direct-absolute/inverse-objective asymmetry that we have seen elsewhere, but with neutralization of the contrast between the absolute and objective forms of the 1p central suffix (m-suffix *-mən(a)* '1p absolute,' w-suffix *-nan* '1p objective') in favor of the absolute form *-mən(a)*. Halle and Marantz (1993:157) develop an analysis along these lines, positing an impoverishment rule that deletes the case features of the central suffix in the context of the preterit.

The next blended asymmetry involves the Miami-Illinois mixed animate forms in Table 14 (Costa 2003:278–281). In this paradigm, the inverse forms are uniformly objective: they mark the third person with a peripheral suffix, and they never show the m-allomorphs of the central suffix. The direct forms include both objective and absolute inflections: the forms with a singular third-person goal are absolute, while the forms with a plural third-person goal are objective—except for the 1p→3p form, which blends an absolute m-suffix (*-mina:n* '1p') with an objective peripheral suffix (*-aki* '3p').

The Shawnee mixed animate forms in Table 15, collected by Bruce Pearson (cited in Andrews 1994:190), are similar to those of Miami-Illinois: the inverse forms are uniformly objective, while the direct forms include both objective and absolute inflections. Of interest here are the direct 1p→3p and 21→3p forms, which blend an absolute m-suffix (*-pen* '1p') with an objective peripheral suffix (*-iki* '3p'). In the older Shawnee data in Voegelin (1936:396), the peripheral suffix was absent from these forms, so their blended status in the Pearson data may be a recent analogical development in which peripheral agreement was added to an originally absolute form.

These blended patterns can all be understood as instances of analogical leveling serving to reduce, though not eliminate, the morphological asymmetry of the mixed direct and inverse forms. In Potawatomi, certain objective inverse forms have become more like the corresponding absolute direct forms through the extension of the absolute m-suffix *-mən(a)* to the inverse forms, but an asymmetry remains in that the affected inverse forms show peripheral agreement, while the corresponding direct forms do not. In Miami-Illinois and Shawnee, certain absolute direct forms have become more like the corresponding objective inverse forms through the addition of a peripheral suffix to the direct forms, but an asymmetry remains in that the central agreement in the affected direct forms continues to show the originally absolute m-suffix allomorph instead of the objective w-suffix that appears in the corresponding inverse forms.

Nonlocal Forms with Objective Inverse but Absolute Direct

Nonlocal forms are more robustly symmetrical than mixed forms. I am aware of only two instances of direct-inverse asymmetry in nonlocal forms. One is in the Southern East Cree conjunct, where the 3′→3s inverse inflection is *-iko-t-h*

TABLE 14. Miami-Illinois mixed animate

INVERSE (3→SAP)		DIRECT (SAP→3)	
3s→1s	ni- . . . -ekw-a	1s→3s	ni- . . . -a:
3p→1s	ni- . . . -ekw-**aki**	1s→3p	ni- . . . -a:-**ki**
3s→2s	ki- . . . -ekw-a	2s→3s	ki- . . . -a:
3p→2s	ki- . . . -ekw-**aki**	2s→3p	ki- . . . -a:-**ki**
3s→1p	ni- . . . -ekw-ina(:n)	1p→3s	ni- . . . -a:-mina
3p→1p	ni- . . . -ekw-ina:n-**aki**	1p→3p	ni- . . . -a:-mina:n-**aki**
3s→21	ki- . . . -ekw-ina(:n)	21→3s	ki- . . . -a:-mina
3p→21	ki- . . . -ekw-ina:n-**aki**	21→3p	(unattested)
3s→2p	ki- . . . -ekw-wa	2p→3s	ki- . . . -a:-mwa
3p→2p	ki- . . . -ekw-wa:-**ki**	2p→3p	ki- . . . -a:-wa:-**ki**

MORPHEMES: prefixes *ni-* '1', *ki-* '2'; theme signs *-ekw* 'INV', *-a:* '3OBJ'; central w-suffixes *-ina(:n)* '1p, 21', *-wa(:)* '2p'; central m-suffixes *-mina(:n)* '1p, 21', *-mwa* '2p'; peripheral suffixes *-a* '3s', *-(a)ki* '3p'. ALLOMORPHY: *-ekw-aki* → *-eko:ki*, *-ekw-ina* → *-ekona*, *-ekw-wa* → *-ekowa*.

TABLE 15. Shawnee mixed animate (Pearson data)

INVERSE (3→SAP)		DIRECT (SAP→3)	
3s→1s	ni- . . . -ekw-a	1s→3s	ni- . . . -a
3p→1s	ni- . . . -ekw-**ki**	1s→3p	ni- . . . -a:-**ki**
3s→2s	ki- . . . -ekw-a	2s→3s	ki- . . . -a
3p→2s	ki- . . . -ekw-**ki**	2s→3p	ki- . . . -a:-**ki**
3s→1p	ni- . . . -ekw-na	1p→3s	ni- . . . -a:-pe
3p→1p	ni- . . . -ekw-na:-**ki**	1p→3p	ni- . . . -a:-pen-**iki**
3s→21	ki- . . . -ekw-na	21→3s	ki- . . . -a:-pe
3p→21	ki- . . . -ekw-na:-**ki**	21→3p	ki- . . . -a:-pen-**iki**
3s→2p	ki- . . . -ekw-wa	2p→3s	ki- . . . -a:-wa
3p→2p	ki- . . . -ekw-wa:-**ki**	2p→3p	ki- . . . -a:-wa:-**ki**

MORPHEMES: prefixes *ni-* '1', *ki-* '2'; theme signs *-ekw* 'INV', *-a(:)* '3OBJ'; central w-suffixes *-na(:)* '1p, 21', *-wa(:)* '2p'; central m-suffix *-pe(n)* '1p, 21'; peripheral suffixes *-a* '3s', *-(a)ki* ~ *-iki* '3p'.

(-INV-3s-3′), while the 3s→3′ direct form is *-a:-t* (-3OBJ-3s) (Junker and MacKenzie 2011–14). The forms both show a central suffix indexing the proximate argument (*-t* '3s'), but they differ in that an obviative peripheral suffix (3′ *-h*) appears in the inverse, where the obviative argument is the actor, but not in the direct, where the obviative argument is the goal. Although the inflectional structure of the conjunct differs from that of the independent, this is effectively the same pattern that we observed in independent mixed forms: the direct form is "absolute," indexing only the actor, while the inverse form is "objective," indexing both the actor and the goal.

TABLE 16. Blackfoot independent

	INVERSE (3′→3)		DIRECT (3→3′)
3′→3s	ot- . . . -ok-a	3s→3′	. . . -yi:-wa
3′→3p	ot- . . . -ok-oa:-yi	3p→3′	. . . -yi:-yi

MORPHEMES: prefix *ot-* '3'; theme signs *-ok* 'INV', *-yi:* '3OBJ'; central w-suffix *-oa:* '3p'; peripheral suffixes *-(w)a* '3s', *-yi* '3p'.

The other example of a direct-inverse asymmetry in nonlocal forms involves the Blackfoot independent, shown in Table 16 (Frantz 2009:151). The direct and inverse forms both show a peripheral suffix indexing the proximate argument (*-(w)a* '3s,' *-yi* '3p'). The inverse forms additionally show a layer of central agreement that also indexes the proximate argument (*ot-* '3s,' *ot- . . . -oa:* '3p').

The Blackfoot asymmetry differs from the others that we have seen in that the extra layer of morphology in the inverse does not serve to index the actor in addition to the goal, but rather to double-mark the goal. To appreciate this point, compare the Blackfoot forms in Table 16 with the East Cree forms given above. The two languages are alike in that the proximate argument is agreed with regardless of whether it is the actor (in the direct) or the goal (in the inverse). The languages are also alike in that the inverse form shows an extra layer of agreement inflection. In East Cree, the two layers of agreement are used to index different arguments (the proximate goal and the obviative actor), but in Blackfoot both layers of agreement are used to index the same argument (the proximate goal; the obviative actor remains unindexed). Despite this difference, however, there remains a point of commonality between the Blackfoot asymmetry and the asymmetries found in all other languages: the form of the Blackfoot inverse resembles the PA objective (e.g., 3′s→3p **we- . . . -ekw-wa:w-ari*), while the form of the direct resembles the PA absolute (e.g., 3s→3′ **-e:-w-a*). Thus, even though the function of the asymmetry in Blackfoot does not perfectly align with that of the other languages, Blackfoot still conforms to the overall generalization that direct-inverse asymmetries involve objective inverse forms and absolute direct forms.

Discussion

Most direct-inverse asymmetries fit the same description: an inverse mixed form (3/0→SAP) shows peripheral agreement for its third-person actor even when the corresponding direct form (SAP→3/0) lacks peripheral agreement for its third-person goal. This generalization has implications for our understanding of the status of the inverse construction with respect to grammatical relations. Rhodes (1976; 1994:444) has proposed a symmetrical account of grammatical relations in Ojibwe, shown in (5): in both the direct and the inverse, the argument that ranks higher on the person hierarchy is the structural subject (direct actor, inverse goal) and the argument that ranks lower on the person hierarchy is the structural object (direct goal, inverse actor).

(5) a. Direct (e.g., 1.actor→3.goal): [$_{\text{SUBJ}}$ 1.actor] [$_{\text{OBJ}}$ 3.goal]
b. Inverse (e.g., 3.actor→1.goal): [$_{\text{SUBJ}}$ 1.goal] [$_{\text{OBJ}}$ 3.actor]

Since the goal in a direct form (SAP→**3**) and the actor in an inverse form (**3**→SAP) have the same grammatical function, they are predicted to show the same morphosyntactic treatment. This prediction is upheld when direct and inverse forms are symmetrical, as they usually are, but it is falsified by the direct-inverse asymmetries that we have seen in this paper, in which inverse actors are treated differently from direct goals.

A variation on Rhodes's analysis is implicit in generative proposals that inverse forms differ from direct forms in that the inverse goal moves to a position above the actor, while the direct goal does not (Bruening 2001; Bliss 2005; Quinn 2006). This proposal is equivalent to saying that in the inverse, it is the goal that moves out of its thematic position within the verb phrase to become the structural subject of the clause, as in (6b), while in the direct, it is the actor that does the same, as in (6a)—or, more generally, that in both the direct and the inverse, the higher-ranked argument is mapped to the structural subject position, while the lower-ranked argument remains in its thematic position.

(6) a. Direct (e.g., 1.actor→3.goal): [$_{\text{SUBJ}}$ 1.actor$_{i}$] [$_{\text{VP}}$ ~~1.actor~~$_{i}$ V **3.goal**]
b. Inverse (e.g., 3.actor→1.goal): [$_{\text{SUBJ}}$ 1.goal$_{i}$] [$_{\text{VP}}$ **3.actor** V ~~1.goal~~$_{i}$]

As far as the subject position is concerned, this analysis matches that of Rhodes in (5) above: in a direct form, the actor is the subject, while in an inverse form, the goal is the subject. Unlike in Rhodes's analysis, however, the lower-ranked nonsubject arguments in (6) are not mapped to the same core grammatical function. The direct goal in (6a) and the inverse actor in (6b) occupy different positions in the structure: the direct goal is the complement of the verb, while the inverse actor is its specifier.

An analysis along these lines has the potential to capture both the typical direct-inverse symmetry as well as the asymmetrical treatment of direct goals and inverse actors in some paradigms. Morphosyntactic patterns that show direct-inverse symmetry can be understood as distinguishing *subjects* (direct actor, inverse goal) from *nonsubjects* (direct goal, inverse actor). However, because the two types of nonsubjects occupy different structural positions—the inverse actor is higher than the direct goal—it is also possible for the morphosyntax to distinguish them. This, I propose, is the source of the canonical direct-inverse asymmetries that we have seen, in which inverse actors are indexed by agreement, while direct goals are not. We can take the relevant agreement processes to be constrained to look no deeper in the structure than the specifier of VP, which makes it possible to index an inverse actor (which is the specifier of VP) but not a direct goal (which is the complement of V, too low to be accessed by agreement). This account explains why direct-inverse asymmetries show a systematic preference for fuller agreement in inverse forms: when agreement cannot search beyond the specifier of VP, inverse forms contain two accessible agreement triggers (goal in subject position, actor in specifier of VP), while direct forms contain only one (actor in subject position).

This analysis can be extended to account for the more nuanced Delaware direct-inverse asymmetry (Table 6), in which definiteness plays a crucial role. We saw that in Delaware mixed animate forms, the third-person goal of a direct form (SAP→3) is indexed by peripheral agreement if it is definite but not if it is indefinite. In a corresponding inverse form (3→SAP), however, the third-person actor is always indexed by peripheral agreement, regardless of its definiteness. We can understand this pattern if we assume, following Diesing (1992), that definite goals move out of the VP, while indefinite goals remain in situ as the complement of V. Thus, if the relevant agreement process is constrained to look no deeper in the structure than the specifier of VP, it will be able to target a direct goal when the goal is definite, since the goal will have raised out of VP and will thus be accessible to the agreement process, but it will not be able to target a direct goal when the goal is indefinite, since the goal will remain too low in the structure to be accessed by the agreement process. No similar contrast is predicted in inverse forms, since the third-person actor in an inverse form is base-generated in the specifier of VP (see (6b) above) and is thus high enough to be accessible to the agreement process regardless of its definiteness. This difference explains why, in typological terms, Delaware mixed animate direct forms show differential object marking but their inverse counterparts do not show differential subject marking.

The structures in (6) cannot be the whole story, however, as nearly all languages that show a direct-inverse asymmetry show it only in mixed forms. That is, asymmetries in the treatment of a third-person argument normally arise only when the other argument is an SAP. In some cases the number features of the SAP argument also play a conditioning role, with asymmetries in the treatment of the third-person argument appearing only when the SAP argument is plural. The features of the third-person argument itself may also be relevant: some languages show an asymmetry in mixed *animate* forms but not in mixed *inanimate* forms, or vice versa. And, finally, the patterning of direct-inverse asymmetries is often unique to particular paradigms: the dubitative and indicative paradigms in Meskwaki, for example, show different patterns of direct-inverse asymmetry (compare Tables 7 and 9 above), as do the indicative and preterit paradigms in Potawatomi (Tables 10 and 13). A complete analysis of direct-inverse asymmetries across Algonquian will likely have to take into account not only the syntax of the clause, as in (6), but also the features that condition the agreement operation as well as shallower morphological factors such as allomorphy and neutralization.

Conclusion

Contrary to typical descriptions, direct and inverse forms need not be morphologically symmetrical: asymmetrical patterns are attested across the family. The asymmetries involve a strikingly uniform tendency to mark agreement with inverse actors even in contexts that fail to show agreement with direct goals. The grammatical functions of the arguments that rank lower on the person hierarchy—that is, inverse actors and direct goals—thus cannot be equated, even though the two kinds of arguments often share the same patterning. The ultimate conclusion is that, while the person hierarchy plays a prominent role in the morphosyntactic alignment system in Algonquian, it is not, in itself, the entire system. When we look closely, we find that in addition to the well-known inflectional asymmetries that exist between higher-ranked and lower-ranked arguments, there are also inflectional asymmetries between actor arguments and goal arguments, as found so commonly in nominative-accusative languages such as English.

NOTES

1. I am grateful for helpful feedback from the audience at the 49th Algonquian Conference and from two anonymous reviewers. This work was supported by SSHRC (IDG 430-2016-00680).
2. In data cited in this paper, I have standardized the representation of long vowels (using the IPA length mark) in order to facilitate comparison across languages. The following abbreviations occur: 0 = inanimate third person, 3 = animate third person, 3′ = animate obviative third person, DEF = definite, DUB = dubitative, INDEF = indefinite, INV = inverse, OBJ = object, p = plural, PRET = preterit, s = singular, SAP = speech-act participant (first or second person), SUB = subordinator, SUBJ = subject, TI = transitive inanimate, TI1 = class 1 TI theme sign; X→Y = X acts on Y.
3. Describing particular TA forms as neither direct nor inverse is consistent with a Bloomfieldian model of Algonquian inflection. With regard to the independent order, Bloomfield (1962:141) lists seven kinds of TA forms, only two of which are direct and inverse: direct forms, inverse forms, thou-me forms, I-thee forms, third-person passive forms, first- and second-person passive forms, and inanimate actor forms. Bloomfield's list does not apply to the conjunct forms in (4), but it establishes the possibility of analyzing a particular TA form as neither direct nor inverse.
4. Goddard and Bragdon (1988:519) note one exception to this generalization in Massachusett: while ordinary 3→SAP forms are uniformly objective regardless of the definiteness of the third-person actor, absolute inflection does appear when the third-person actor is an interrogative pronoun.

REFERENCES

Andrews, Kenneth. 1994. Shawnee Grammar. PhD thesis, University of South Carolina.

Bliss, Heather. 2005. Formalizing Point-of-view: The Role of Sentience in Blackfoot's Direct/Inverse System. Master's thesis, University of Calgary.

Bloomfield, Leonard. 1962. *The Menomini Language.* New Haven: Yale University Press.

Bruening, Benjamin. 2001. Syntax at the Edge: Cross-clausal Phenomena and the Syntax of Passamaquoddy. PhD thesis, MIT.

Cenerini, Chantale. 2017. The Prominence of Speech-Act Participants: A Study of Diachronic Change in Algonquian Person Agreement. PhD generals paper, University of Manitoba.

Costa, David J. 2003. *The Miami-Illinois Language.* Lincoln: University of Nebraska Press.

Diesing, Molly. 1992. *Indefinites.* Cambridge, MA: MIT Press.

Frantz, Donald G. 2009. *Blackfoot Grammar.* Toronto: University of Toronto Press.

Goddard, Ives. 1967. The Algonquian Independent Indicative. *Contributions to Anthropology, Linguistics I (Algonquian),* ed. by A. D. DeBlois, pp. 66–106. National Museum of Canada Bulletin 214. Ottawa: National Museum of Canada.

Goddard, Ives. 1969. Delaware Verbal Morphology: A Descriptive and Comparative *Study.* PhD thesis, Harvard University.

Goddard, Ives. 1974. Remarks on the Algonquian Independent Indicative. *International Journal of American Linguistics* 40:317–327.

Goddard, Ives. 1994. *Leonard Bloomfield's Fox Lexicon: Critical Edition.* Algonquian and Iroquoian Linguistics Memoir 12. Winnipeg: Algonquian and Iroquoian Linguistics.

Goddard, Ives. 2007. Reconstruction and History of the Independent Indicative. *Papers of the 38th Algonquian Conference,* ed. by H. C. Wolfart, pp. 207–271. Winnipeg: University of Manitoba.

Goddard, Ives, and Kathleen J. Bragdon. 1988. *Native Writings in Massachusett.* American Philosophical Society Memoir 185. Philadelphia: American Philosophical Society.

Halle, Morris, and Alec Marantz. 1993. Distributed Morphology and the Pieces of Inflection. *The View from Building 20,* ed. by Kenneth Hale and Samuel Jay Keyser, pp. 111–176. Cambridge, MA: MIT Press.

Hockett, Charles F. 1966. What Algonquian Is Really Like. *International Journal of American Linguistics* 32:59–73.

Junker, Marie-Odile, and Marguerite MacKenzie. 2011–14. East Cree (Southern Dialect) Verb Conjugation. http://verbs.eastcree.org/.

Nichols, John D. 1980. Ojibwe Morphology. PhD thesis, Harvard University.

Quinn, Conor. 2006. Referential-Access Dependency in Penobscot. PhD thesis, Harvard University.

Pentland, David H. 1999. The Morphology of the Algonquian Independent Order. *Papers of the 30th Algonquian Conference,* ed. by David H. Pentland, pp. 222–266. Winnipeg: University of Manitoba.

Rhodes, Richard A. 1976. The Morphosyntax of the Central Ojibwa Verb. PhD thesis, University of Michigan.

Rhodes, Richard A. 1994. Agency, Inversion, and Thematic Alignment in Ojibwe. *Berkeley Linguistics Society* 20:431–446.

Voegelin, C. F. 1936. Productive Paradigms in Shawnee. *Essays in Anthropology Presented to A. L. Kroeber in Celebration of his Sixtieth Birthday,* ed. by Robert H. Lowie, pp. 391–403. Berkeley: University of California Press.

Voorhis, Paul H. 1974. *Introduction to the Kickapoo Language.* Bloomington: Indiana University.

Wolfart, H. Christoph. 1973. *Plains Cree: A Grammatical Study.* Transactions of the American Philosophical Society, n.s., vol. 63, pt. 5. Philadelphia: American Philosophical Society.

Exploring an Arapaho Classifier

Prototypes, Markedness, and Double Lexical Selection

Allison Sanders and Andrew Cowell

Algonquian languages have inherited classificatory medials from Proto-Algonquian (Bloomfield 1946), including medials for rock-like, sheet-like, stick-like, and string-like objects. The latter classifier is the focus of this paper. These medials can be considered verb classifiers (Grinevald 2000, 2002), with elements of nominal incorporation (Mithun 1999; Valentine 2001; Cowell and Moss 2008). Using Mithun's terminology, these are part of the "classificatory noun incorporation" subtype of verb classifiers (Mithun 1999; Aikhenvald 2000). The range of semantics of these classifiers is not well described for most Algonquian languages (but see Drapeau 2014). They are typically described as referring to "rope-like" or "string-like objects," to use our focus example, but what exactly "string-like" means to speakers of Cheyenne, Arapaho, or Cree is rarely discussed, nor is it well understood how much speakers of the different languages share the same judgments. It is notable that whiskey, in Nishnaabemwin, takes the 'wooden object' classifier (Valentine 2001). This is due to the fact that whiskey was shipped in barrels when the speakers of Nishnaabemwin first encountered it. Clearly, the classifier taken by a given noun in an Algonquian language is not completely predictable, and can be affected by historical and sociocultural factors. Especially in the context of language loss and efforts at language revitalization, it is easy to see the danger of simply transferring English-language concepts of rope-like or string-like onto an Algonquian language, and thus linguistically colonizing the semantics of the language. Here we investigate in depth the string-like classifier in Arapaho, which takes the general form *-oocei-* (also *-ook(ee)-*), the former derived from PA *-aapy(ee)(k)-. This classifier occurs in other Algonquian languages, such as Nishnaabemwin *-aabiig-* (Valentine 2001:331), Cree *-a:pe:k-* (Wolfart 1996:427) and Innu -âpêk- (Drapeau and Lambert-Brétière 2011:300).

Preliminarily, we note that the medial is extremely flexible in usage in Arapaho, as in other Algonquian languages (Valentine 2001; Wolfart 1996): it can be used in reference to intransitive subjects, transitive and ditransitive objects, and instruments, and in relation to both states and modes of action.[1]

(1) *Intransitive subject:*
heeyooceihit
heey-oocei-eihi-t
IC.long-string.like-AI-3S
'it is a long string-like object'

(2) *Intransitive subject, mode of action:*
kooxo'oocei'oot
kooxo'-oocei-o'oo-t
IC.slowly-string.like-go.VAI-3S
'it is slowly moving along in a string-like, snake-like manner'

(3) *Transitive object:*
hee3owooceino'
hee3ew-oocei-n-o'
IC.to.there-string.like-TI-3S
's/he is laying or stretching the rope out over to there'

(4) *Ditransitive object:*
honoonokootooceinowuunoot
honoon-okoot-oocei-n-owuun-oot
IC.REDUP-change-string.like-GLIDE-TA.BENEF-3S/4
'the doctor is performing a heart bypass operation on him/her'
(lit. 'changing his/her veins/arteries around for him/her')

(5) *Instrument:*
honoowoooceinoot
honoow-oocei-n-oot
IC.down-string.like-TA-3S/4
'she/he is lowering him/her/them down by rope'

The oldest speakers of Arapaho today report that classifiers were once used in counting verbs (*yeneinooceihi3i'* 'they are four string-like objects'), but no speakers currently do this, nor did Salzmann record examples in the 1950s. We also note that all nouns in Arapaho or other Algonquian languages are not required to take a classifier. There is no default classifier—unlike in languages such as Chinese—and only a subset of objects take classifiers, so classification in these cases involves lexical selection. This is a point noted cross-linguistically for verb classifier systems (Aikhenvald 2000:149).

Prototype Meaning

Our main focus here however is the classifier's semantic range, and also its extensions to modern objects. Of crucial importance is the fact that the string-like classifier continues to be widely productive in Arapaho, as (4) illustrates. The prototypical (Geeraerts 1989) understanding of this classifier is

1. continuous, single, long, and flexible objects, round in cross-section

However there are a number of radial extensions (Brugman and Lakoff 1988) of this category, several of which violate one or more elements of the prototype. Some of these radial extensions are a direct result of the continued productivity of the classifier, and its use in neologisms, so this paper examines both original "Algonquian" semantics and the process of semantic extension.

Examples (1–3) and (5) illustrate the prototypical uses of the classifier, for ropes, strings, snakes, worms, and so forth. In field research, our first approach was to take the verb in (1), and similar verbs, and ask if they could be used to describe various objects. This allowed us to determine which objects were considered part of the string-like category and which were not. This work was reinforced by examination of natural discourse as well as the range of recorded Arapaho lexical items that include the classifier. Objects that fit the prototype include rope, string, thread, yarn, laces and ties, fishing line, vines, fringes of clothing, electrical cords and extension cords, electric cables, individual roots of a plant used as thread, sinew used as thread, thongs, and bowstrings.

Basic Prototype Extensions

There are several extensions of the prototype that violate one criterion. These include

2a. flat objects, not round in cross-section, but otherwise fitting the prototype: tape measures, suspenders, reins, ribbons, magnetic tape for recording—cassettes, VCR, and so on, flat shoelaces

(6) nihkoxooceinoo'oo'
nih-kox-oocei-n-oo'oo-'
PAST-break-string.like-GLIDE-INCHOAT.VII -0S
'the cassette tape snapped in two'
[Note that the root *kox-* is used specifically for string-like objects.]

(7) tekooceiyoo
tek-oocei-n-yoo
measure-string.like-VTI-INSTR.NI
'tape measure'

2b. stiffer objects, not especially flexible, but otherwise fitting the prototype: wires, fencing wire (but not fences as a whole, which use a different classifier, *-oxoe-*, also used with willow huts and shelters, sweat lodges, and other objects assembled by braiding or interweaving), outdoor telephone lines, outdoor electric lines, stems of plants

(8) bo'ooceibiis
be'-oocei-biis
red-string.like-bush
'red osier dogwood' (lit. 'red stemmed bush')

(9) siikooceiikuu3oo
siik-oocei-kuu-t-yoo
stretch-string.like-CAUS-VTI-INSTR.NI
'wire stretcher' (used for tightening wires on fences)

(10) coowooceise'
ceew-oocei-se-'
IC.along-string.like-lie.VII-0s
'wire'

2c. hollow objects that otherwise fit the prototype: water hoses, arteries, veins, flexible tubing

(11) (same as 4 above) honoonokootooceinowuunoot
'the doctor is performing a heart bypass operation on him/her'
(lit. 'changing his/her veins/arteries around for him/her')

2d. animals: snakes, worms, caterpillars (but not dragonflies, damselflies, or other long, stiff insects)

(12) neesiinoocei'oot
nii-esii-n-oocei-o'oo-t
HABIT-fast-GLIDE-string.like-go.AI-3s
'it crawls/slithers fast'

(13) woo'teenooceihit siisiiyei
woo'oteen-oocei-eihi-t siisiiyei
IC.black-string.like-VAI-3s snake
'a black snake'

2e. stretchy objects that otherwise fit the prototype: rubber bands

(14) seneesiikooceino'
senee-siik-oocei-n-o'
IC.REDUP-stretch-string.like-VTI-3s
's/he is stretching out the rubber band'

(15) niih'ooceini'
niih'-oocei-n-i-'
IC.tight-string.like-VTI-VII.PASSIM-0S
'rubber band' (lit. 'it is stretched tight')

More Distant Extensions

All of the preceding examples are relatively straightforward extensions of the prototype. However, there are other objects in the category that represent increasing distance from the prototype. These include

3a. webs: nets, the internet (but not spiderwebs)

(16) wonoohonooceihit
wonoohon-oocei-eihi-t
IC.united-string.like-VAI-3S
'net'

(17) woohnooceise'
woohn-oocei-se-'
IC.rows/ranks-string.like-lie.VII-0S
'internet' (lit. 'web')

The objects must be made of threads, rope, yarn, and so on, loosely woven so that the individual "stringiness" is still evident (i.e., not cloth-like), and flexible (not stiff, fence-like or willow-lodge-like). These objects are obviously not single, continuous, or even especially long. This extension is likely best considered a part-whole metonymy.

3b. composite objects, which are string-like as a whole: chains, trains, lines of cars

(18) honoowoocei'oo3i' hotiiwo'
honoow-oocei-o'oo-3i' hotiiw-o'
IC.down-string.like-go.VAI-3P car-PL
'the line of cars is winding/snaking down the curvy road'

(19) heeyooceihit heso'oonotii

heey-oocei-eihi-t hes-o'oo-n-otii

IC.long-string.like-VAI-3S fast-going-GLIDE-car

'a long train'

These are clearly not continuous, narrowly speaking, and also may not be round in cross-section, or especially flexible. These are "metaphorical" radial extensions, the first most likely based on ropes (one Arapaho word for 'chain' glosses as 'metal rope'), the next two most likely on snakes (perhaps reinforced by the English usage of describing cars as 'snaking down a winding road').

3c. pipes: water pipes, plumbing.

(20) niiyooceise3eit niiciineno' neciini niiyooceiyoono

nii-(y)oocei-se-t-yei-t nii-ciinen-o'

HABIT-string.like-lie-VTI-VAI.O-3S HABIT-put.down.VTI-3S

neci-ini nii-(y)oocei-n-yoon-o

water-DETACH HABIT-string.like-GLIDE-INSTR.NI-PL

'the plumber puts in the water pipes.'

These are rigid, inflexible objects, and approach the domain of a completely different Arapaho classifier, *-oo'-* (from PA *-aaxkw-), which is used to refer to long, thin, inflexible objects such as sticks, rods, guns, long tools, wagons, and similar objects (in fact, this is the classifier used for pipes in Innu [Drapeau and Lambert-Brétière 2011:303]). Here, however, the category of hollow string-like objects has been radially extended, with the long and hollow quality—and analogy to flexible tubing—leading to the use of the *-oocei-* classifier rather than *-oo'-*.

Objects outside the Category

We find that *masses* of string-like objects do not fall under this category: hair, noodles, or bundles of roots attached to a plant. Note that in Innu, hair and roots do take this classifier (Drapeau and Lambert-Brétière 2011:300).

Analogical, Optional Extensions to Other Classes

Finally, the classifier can be used for objects much longer than prototypical objects of another class, objects that would otherwise take either another classifier entirely, or no classifier at all. These include dachshunds, very tall people, and very long cars (e.g., older-model Oldsmobiles). In almost all cases, it is the verb *heyooceihi-* 'long string-like' that is used. This usage usually includes a joking component (typical of extreme or semicontradictory extensions of categories [Mithun 1999]). Of note in this regard is that the string-like category is often used in Arapaho to describe someone who is lying stretched out drunk. Use of the classifier medial is optional in these types of situations, whereas for central members of the category, it is obligatory. In other words, speakers reject forms such as **heeneihit seenook* 'a long/tall rope', and insist that one must say *heeyooceihit seenook* with the classifier. They also reject descriptions of snakes as **coowokuseet* 'crawling' (lit. 'walking sitting'), saying that this describes people, and insist on *coowoocei'oot,* again with the classifier. On the other hand, one normally says *heeneihit* 's/he is tall', to describe a person, while saying *heeyooceihit* (with the classifier) is a highly marked usage. This optionality is apparent in some cases for the uses described earlier as well. For example, one is not required to describe a line of cars as moving in a string-like fashion (*-oocei'oo-*, (18)). This usage occurs when the objects are especially numerous and close together, on an especially winding path, and still is optional.

Limitations of Classifier Usage in Relation to Prototypical Categories

One result of our field research was the finding that speakers rejected forms such as **ceeneeteen-ooceihi-t* 'it is a blue/green rope' or **wonoon-ooceihi-t* 'it is a new rope' with the *-oocei-* classifier included. They readily understood what the form meant, but said that such forms were not used, and that instead one would use a general AI verb form, plus the independent noun if the referent was not clear from context: *ceeneeteeneihit* (*seenook*) 'a blue/green rope' and *wonooneihit* (*seenook*) 'a new rope'. In relation to ropes, in particular, they rejected classificatory-medial verbs for 'blue/green', 'red', 'orange/yellow', 'heavy', 'old', 'new', and even 'braided' ropes. On the other hand, verb forms that did use the classificatory medial and were accepted by speakers specifically for referring to ropes included

heey-ooceihi-t	long
too'-ooceihi-t	short
3oo'-ooceihi-t	frayed, coming apart
tenei'-ooceihi-t	strong
hoow-tei'-ooceih	weak ('not strong')
cenee'-ooceihi-t	with a lump or a knot
heeces-ooceihi-t	thin
tonoukut-ooceihi-t	tangled
bee3o'-ooceihi-t	stiff
nenei'-ooceihi-t	tight (as in 'a tightly woven rope')
koox-ooceihi-t	cut in half; broken
ceneiw-oocei-o'oo-'	twisted or crooked
nenisih'-ooceihi-t	brown
woo'teen-ooceihi-t	black
nonook-ooceihi-t	white

This shows that classificatory medial verbs exist in common usage in Arapaho only for qualities that are considered common or prototypical of ropes or other string-like objects, but at the same time not so prototypical as to be scarcely worth noting ('braided'). This is a very interesting finding in that it suggests that the Arapaho classificatory medials are not "classifiers" in the classical sense of that term, in that they are not required to be used, even with the most prototypical members of the string-like category. Rather, they retain elements of typical noun-incorporation strategies. This finding is echoed by Drapeau and Lambert-Brétière (2011) for Innu as well. Cross-linguistically, noun incorporation is used to demote the status of a noun (Mithun 1984:859, 1999). Conversely, when a noun has highly marked status, it is normally expressed as an independent nominal. The Arapaho string-like classifier shows exactly the same behavior: it is used when the qualities or actions related to the string-like object are highly typical and therefore relatively unmarked. When the qualities or actions are more unusual, less prototypical of string-like objects, and thus more marked, the classifier is not used, and an independent nominal is much more likely to occur. Thus like noun incorporation, Arapaho classifiers can be understood as functioning pragmatically, not just semantically. The same appears to be true in other Algonquian languages as well: Valentine (2001) notes that classifiers are not used with all references to a noun, and are most commonly used with stative/descriptive verbs in Nishnaabemwin. He gives the example of various classifiers all used with the initial element 'long'. While he does not specifically address restrictions on classifier use, he clearly notes a tendency for the usage to occur in certain prototypical situations.

This finding about limitations on the use of the classifier also suggests that not only are there prototypes of what counts as a string-like object in Arapaho, but there are also associated prototypes of what qualities (and actions) string-like objects can be associated with. Cross-linguistically, Denny (1986) notes that classifiers are often associated with specific verbal predicates, and are used in "setting up verb predicate expectations" (1986:303). Similarly for Innu, "a classifier can be used to replace an argument if prototypicality and context converge" (Drapeau and Lambert-Brétière 2011:306). In a language such as Arapaho—and likely other Algonquian languages, based on similar overall structure and features regarding classificatory medials—one cannot understand the distribution and usage of the medials without understanding both of these sets of prototypes. In contrast, in a "classical" classifier language, it appears that one need only know which category an object falls into, not its associated prototypical actions and qualities, since the object always takes the classificatory medial.

Even more interesting is that these prototypes are not just associated with the classifier itself, but with different kinds of objects that take the classifier. For example, although *ceeneeteen-ooceihi-t* 'it is a green string-like object (VAI)' was rejected by speakers in application to a rope, it was accepted by them in application to a snake or a vine. Similarly, although *boo'-ooceihi-t* 'it is a red string-like object (VAI)' was rejected for ropes, the classifier is used with 'red' in the nominal form for red-osier dogwood (recall (8)), where it refers to a plant stem. This shows that the string-like classifier does not just have a single set of prototypical qualities and actions associated with it, but rather that there are multiple such prototypes or radial categories, depending upon the noun to which the classifier is applied. Stated another way, the pragmatic (and cognitive) status of a green rope is quite different from that of a green snake or green vine, and this determines whether the verb *ceneeteen-ooceihi-* can actually be applied and used contextually or not, though certainly in the abstract such a verb exists in Arapaho, and certainly ropes, snakes, and vines in the abstract can all be classified as 'string-like objects' in Arapaho. This suggests that not only does the nominal category of 'string-like object' contain radial categories, but the verbal qualities and actions associated with the various nominal referents that fall under the general label of 'string-like' ALSO involve radial categories, each associated with different sets of nominal referents.

In summary, the string-like classifier in Arapaho interacts not only with the nominal referent to which it refers, but with the quality or action denoted in the initial element of the verb, and both of these working jointly can function to enable or restrict the use of the classifier. Thus there is a double "lexical selection" that occurs in classifier usage. The first stage is the selection of the noun itself, as eligible for string-like status. But the semantic and pragmatic conditions under which the classifier can be applied to the given noun are also in part controlled by the exact nature of the quality or action denoted in the nonclassifier part of the verb. The Arapaho classifiers thus do not really classify nouns. Rather, when used, they classify qualities and actions in relation to various types of string-like objects as common and unremarkable (i.e. unmarked), almost like an equals sign or semantico-pragmatic "licensing marker" in the verb: classifier usage in *bo'ooceibiis* means red is licensed for stems, in *ceeneeteenooceihit* it means green is licensed for snakes; nonclassifier usage means red and green are not licensed for ropes, thus **boo'ooceihit* and **ceeneeteeneihit* are disallowed for this noun, as being too marked. As Battistella (1990:2) explains, "at the semantic level of language, markedness is probably most easily understood as a relation between a very specific linguistic sign (the marked term) and a sign that is unspecified for the grammatical or conceptual feature in question." In the example here, ropes are unspecified for the conceptual feature of 'green/blue' or 'red', and the LACK of use of the classificatory medial—along with much greater likelihood of explicit use of the nominal itself in the clause—MARKS that relationship, whereas the presence of the classifier indicates that ropes ARE specified for 'tangled' or 'frayed'. Thus classifier usage, at least in Arapaho, must be understood not in relation to noun categorization, but in relation to the classification of complex scenarios of action and description in which nominal referents take part. The focus of the usage is on cognitively highly recognizable, socioculturally common, unmarked scenarios, and can likely be understood as an efficiency strategy for referring to these scenarios.

These general findings are borne out by examination of natural discourse. In a sample of approximately 20,000 sentences of interlinearized natural discourse, there were 51 instances of the string-like classifier, amounting to roughly 0.25% of all sentences. This shows that the classifier, while not vanishingly rare, is not especially common. We estimate that true classifiers (as opposed to noun incorporation, which refers to only a single nominal referent) occur in no more than 1%–2% of Arapaho sentences (roughly similar to what Drapeau and Lambert-Brétière 2011 report for Innu). Among the natural occurrences of *-oocei-*, we found no instances of the usages rejected by speakers during elicitation. A number of the usages were lexicalized nouns, such as the word for 'wire' and the word for 'Northern Arapaho', which is 'red willow men'. For syntactic verbal usages, the most common quality initials (parallel to example (1)) were 'long' and 'strong'. A number of initials parallel to example (2) occurred, all a single time, including 'into the brush', 'out of a location', 'to there', and 'away', all referring to movement by snakes. The most common action initials (parallel to example (3)) were 'stretch' and 'jerk back and forth'. The most common instrument initials (parallel to example (5)) were 'down/lower' and 'reach/get to'. No parallels to example (4) occurred in the data sample.

Natural discourse also revealed some additional instances of metaphorical extensions that would be difficult to obtain via elicitation. An example was the verb *heeyoocei'oo-* 'stretching in a string-like fashion over a long distance', used with the noun 'breath':

(21) heeyoocei'oo' hoowu3oow, beneesoo' hiine'etiit

heeyoocei'oo-'	hoowu3oow,	beneesoo-'	hiine'etiit,
IC.stretching.long-0s	breath	IC.big-0s	life

'Breath extends long, life is large.'

This can be compared to the examples under (3b). The overall sense of the phrase is that the path of one's life should stretch a long way: one should live (and thus breathe) for a long time—and distance. Thus it is really as much the idea of the path as the breath per se that is metaphorically compared to a long string-like object. This sentence occurred in a name-changing prayer collected by Alfred Kroeber in 1899 (see Cowell, C'Hair, and Moss 2014:450–458).

In contrast, another example involves an extension of meaning related to modern concepts and technology. The following is from a translation describing how to use magnets for science lessons:

(22) bei'ci3eiiho' niini'tonouni'i heetihnoohowu'

'Iron filings can be used to see . . .

nuh'uuno heetcowoocei'isei'i tei'ehiit.

nuh'uuno	heet-cew-oocei-isei-'i	tei'ehiit
this	where-along-string.like-lie.II-PL	energy/strength

. . . the lines of force [from the magnet].'

This sentence could be compared to the examples under (3a) (as well as to the part-whole examples (21–22) cited for Innu by Drapeau and Lambert-Brétière [2011:307–308]). Here, the lines of a force field or magnetic field are the nominal referent of the string-like classifier, based on the fact that the iron filings will line up like a series of string-like forms in relation to the magnet (which together form a loose, web-like structure).

Further Comments on Markedness and Classifier Usage

The findings about the optionality of the classificatory medials discussed earlier initially seem to be the exact reverse of the findings just discussed. In the first case, the medials occur in a highly marked situation, while in the second case, they occur only in relatively unmarked situations. However, there is an important distinction to make, and it is again based on the interaction of the classifiers with the qualities and actions in the initial elements of the verb. In the examples in the section on optional extensions of classifiers, the medial is being extended to a new, unexpected category of object. The markedness focuses on shape, and the classificatory medial highlights the unexpected shape, but otherwise extends a quite common string-like quality to the new object—just as ropes are prototypically long, the dachshund is long (*heeyooceihit*). In the examples involving optional extension, it is not really the medial per se that is being extended to a new class of objects; rather the medial AND a highly prototypical quality associated with the medial are being extended, en bloque, as an entire unit, onto a new target domain, and this metaphorical extension is what is marked. This makes perfect sense when we recall the previous finding that various nouns and verbal actions and descriptions are prototypically linked with each other as sets of prototypes and radial categories. The medial itself, in association with the quality in question, is quite UNMARKED—indeed, this is perhaps the most common initial-medial association in the entire domain of string-like objects, licensed for virtually any nominal referent normally considered string-like. In fact, it appears that only such very common initial-medial associations are normally used in these kinds of joking extensions. Certainly these were the only types volunteered by our consultants. Thus lexical selection is again double in its operation: the extension of the medial to dachshunds is linked to the choice of initial that can be used with the medial. The natural discourse examples (21–22) further reinforce these findings: creative extensions of medials occur in relation to highly prototypical initials for that medial.

Summary

The principal findings of this investigation are the following:

1. Classificatory medials are associated with nominal categories that involve prototypes with radial, metaphorical, and metonymic extensions.
2. Classificatory medials seem to always be associated with prototypical qualities and actions for the medial in question, forming a large but nevertheless limited series of classificatory verbs.
3. These verbs are then further limited in actual application and usage by the particular noun with which they co-occur and its associated prototypical qualities and/or actions (i.e., vines vs. ropes). That said, if the noun in question is one of those listed in (1), (2), (3a), or (3c), and the quality/action in the verb initial is licensed for the noun, the medial classificatory verb MUST be used, at least for older Arapaho speakers.
4. If the noun is one such as is listed in (3b), the medial MAY be used.

We also know that there are similar optional cases for nouns in the first set ((1), (2), (3a), (3c)), where certain INITIALS are marginally licensed, and allow but do not require the use of the medial. In fieldwork, there was some hesitation about the suitability of some forms, with remarks such as, "I think I heard that one time." In these cases, it was not the noun (as in 3b) that was marginal to the string-like category, but the quality or action denoted in the verb initial.

5. If the noun is one such as those listed in the optional extensions, the medial may be used, but if so, it must be used with a highly prototypical initial element.
6. Classificatory medials in Arapaho function in a way very similar to noun incorporation cross-linguistically, as they are used for common, unmarked medial/initial combinations, whose unremarkableness allows them to be expressed via an incorporation strategy. More marked combinations cannot be expressed in this way.

NOTE

1. Abbreviations used in this paper: 0 = third person inanimate, 3 = third person, 4 = third person obviative, AI = intransitive verb with animate subject, AI.O = intransitive verb with animate subject and undefined object, BENEF = benefactive, CAUS = causative, DETACH = derivational suffix which detaches prefixes from verbs, GLIDE = glide consonant, HABIT = habitual, IC = initial change, II = intransitive verb with inanimate subject, INSTR = instrumental, INCHOAT = inchoative, NI = inanimate noun, PA = Proto-Algonquian, PASSIM = imperfective passive, PAST = past tense, P, PL = plural, REDUP = reduplication, S = singular, TA = transitive verb with animate object, TI = transitive verb with inanimate object. In Arapaho orthography, "3" is used for IPA θ and a straight apostrophe is used for glottal stop.

REFERENCES

Aikhenvald, Alexandra. 2000. *Classifiers.* Oxford: Oxford University Press.

Battistella, Edwin L. 1990. *Markedness: The Evaluative Superstructure of Language.* Albany: State University of New York Press.

Bloomfield, Leonard. 1946. Algonquian. *Linguistic Structures of Native America,* ed. by Cornelius Osgood, pp. 85–129. New York: Viking Fund.

Brugman, Claudia, and George Lakoff. 1988. Cognitive Typology and Lexical Networks. *Lexical Ambiguity Resolution: Perspectives from Psycholinguistics, Neuropsychology, and Artificial Intelligence,* ed. by Steven L. Small, Garrison Cottrell, and Michael Tanenhaus, pp. 477–508. San Mateo, CA: Morgan Kaufmann Publishers.

Cowell, Andrew, William C'Hair, and Alonzo Moss Sr. 2014. *Arapaho Stories, Songs and Prayers: A Bilingual Anthology.* Norman: University of Oklahoma Press.

Cowell, Andrew, and Alonzo Moss Sr. 2008. *The Arapaho Language.* Boulder: University Press of Colorado.

Denny, J. Peter. 1986. The Semantic Role of Noun Classifiers. *Noun Classes and Categorization: Proceedings of a Symposium on Categorization and Noun Classification,* ed. by Collette Craig, pp. 297–308. Philadelphia: John Benjamins.

Drapeau, Lynn. 2014. *Grammaire de la langue Innue.* Quebec: Presses de l'Université du Québec.

Drapeau, Lynn, and Renée Lambert-Brétière. 2011. Verbal Classifiers in Innu. *Anthropological Linguistics* 53(4):293–322.

Geeraerts, Dirk. 1989. Prospects and Problems of Prototype Theory. *Linguistics* 27:587–612.

Grinevald, Colette. 2000. A Morphosyntactic Typology of Classifiers. *Systems of Nominal*

Classification, ed. by Gunter Senft, pp. 50–92. Cambridge: Cambridge University Press.

Grinevald, Colette. 2002. Making Sense of Nominal Classification Systems: Noun Classifiers and the Grammaticalization Variable. *New Reflections on Grammaticalization,* ed by Ilse Wischer and Gabriele Diewald, pp. 259–276. Philadelphia: John Benjamins.

Mithun, Marianne. 1984. The Evolution of Noun Incorporation. *Language* 60(4):847–894.

Mithun, Marianne. 1999. *The Languages of Native North America.* Cambridge: Cambridge University Press.

Valentine, J. Randolph. 2001. *Nishnaabemwin Reference Grammar.* Toronto: University of Toronto Press.

Wolfart, H. C. 1996. Sketch of Cree, an Algonquian Language. *Handbook of North American Indians,* vol. 17: *Languages,* ed. by Ives Goddard, pp. 390–439. Washington, DC: Smithsonian Institution.

The Passamaquoddy-Maliseet Language Portal

Who Uses It and How?

Julia Schulz, Robert M. Leavitt, Ben Levine, and Newell Lewey

In this paper we present the Passamaquoddy-Maliseet Language Portal (PMPortal.org).[1] The portal combines an online version of the 19,000-entry Passamaquoddy-Maliseet dictionary (Francis and Leavitt 2008) with audio recordings of the words and example sentences, along with 100 subtitled video clips of natural native-language conversation and storytelling. Words in the video subtitles are linked to the appropriate dictionary entries. The portal serves teachers and learners of Passamaquoddy-Maliseet, as well as linguists and other researchers. We will include here a brief history of the PM Portal and illustrations of the major functions of this new online technology, which addresses both linguistic documentation research and community agendas. We will provide examples of how people are using the PM Portal in community, scholarly, and educational contexts, with data drawn from personal communication as well as back-end website analytics.

To put the PM Portal in context, there are today hundreds of excellent indigenous-language online resources for languages from every part of the world, including dictionaries, audio recordings, videos, transcriptions, and linguistic studies. The websites are formatted in either the language itself or in English, Spanish, or another "official" language; often the user may choose the background language. The databases are searchable, and many include internal links between dictionary entries and other content. New websites are constantly appearing. A few examples will illustrate the scope of indigenous language projects coming to the internet.

The Ojibwe People's Dictionary has thousands of entries, audio recordings, video clips, historical and cultural photographs, and excerpts from historical documents, along with language-learning and teaching resources. The features are all easily accessible throughout the site. Entries in the Myaamia dictionary feature inflected present-tense indicative verb forms. Searching on an English term brings up sets of related words, along with example sentences. The Michif online dictionary (Gabriel Dumont Institute of Native Studies and Applied Research) also has sound recordings for each entry, and a separate section of conversational statements and questions. In addition, the Louis Riel Institute video website presents a selection of videos of Michif speakers.

Looking outside North America, Swarthmore College's Enduring Voices Project online talking dictionaries, some with thousands of entries, document languages in Latin America, Asia, Papua New Guinea, and Africa. The entries in all these dictionaries have sound recordings and images. The Australian Society for Indigenous Languages has compiled Aboriginal language dictionaries in the form of word-lists for more than a dozen languages. The lexicons can be sorted by semantic category, and many of the dictionaries are available as tablet or smartphone apps.

The Passamaquoddy-Maliseet Language Portal combines features found in all of these online language resources. The 19,000 dictionary entries contain lexical and grammatical information, along with example sentences. The entries are keyed to charts of complete verb conjugations and noun declensions, and they each have audio recordings. Entries are also linked to the collection of nearly 100 subtitled video clips of natural language conversation, storytelling, and activities in Passamaquoddy-Maliseet. Reciprocally, words in the subtitles and video transcripts are linked back to the dictionary entries, so that users can find the entry headword for an inflected form. The video clips themselves, and the example sentences in the entries, document aspects of Passamaquoddy-Maliseet worldview and history, such as spiritual beliefs, family traditions, sustenance practices, and tribal land-claims.

The PM Portal is the culmination of four decades of work. The first standardized dictionary of Passamaquoddy-Maliseet was developed by Philip LeSourd in the 1970s and published in 1986. Building on this work, David A. Francis and Robert M. Leavitt authored a comprehensive dictionary, which first appeared online in 1995 and in book form in 2008. In 2006, Leavitt, heritage language consultant Julia Schulz, and documentary filmmaker Ben Levine facilitated a team of community participants to document a series of native-language conversations, eventually presented on DVDs, which came to be known as the Language Keepers project (see Levine and Leavitt 2012). Later, in 2010, the Passamaquoddy-Maliseet Language Portal was built, using open-source software, by the Scholarly and Academic Technologies team at the University of New Brunswick, to merge the Language Keepers video archive of facilitated natural group conversation and activity with the online dictionary. (For more on this speaker-driven documentation process, see Apt and Schulz 2012). More than 100 fluent first-language speakers of Passamaquoddy-Maliseet contributed to the dictionary and participated in the filming. The dictionary, DVD, and PM Portal projects were supported by grants from the National Science Foundation. The Passamaquoddy-Maliseet Language Portal went live in August 2011. At that time, a grant from the Administration for Native Americans (ANA) funded community members to create an archive of audio recordings of each dictionary entry and many example sentences. The audio-recording process paired tech-savvy young adult language learners with speaker-elders. When the recorders posted audio files on social media the language became more visible, the elders' skills increased in value and prestige, and more community members were motivated to learn to speak and read the language. The PM Portal has been a creative part of the process of Passamaquoddy and Maliseet people reclaiming their language, leading to new initiatives in preschool immersion and language reacquisition programming. In July 2017, the PM Portal was upgraded to the most current software, to improve video playback and other functions. (For more information, see Credits, at PMPortal.org). The PM Portal is currently administered by a team consisting of dictionary coauthor Robert Leavitt, community research coordinator Margaret Apt (Passamaquoddy), and Passamaquoddy tribal administrator Donald Soctomah.

The Passamaquoddy-Maliseet Language Portal now gives users access to three interoperable databases: a 19,000-entry dictionary with notes about usage and related words; a collection of videos of natural native-language conversation, storytelling, and teaching in a variety of settings with many speakers; and audio recordings of words and sample sentences. As noted above, words that occur in the video subtitles and transcriptions are linked to their respective dictionary entries; this is helpful where the form used in a particular sentence differs markedly from the entry headword.[2]

The dictionary entries and video transcriptions are fully searchable, either globally or by querying specific dictionary entry fields, such as the definition, notes, or example sentences. Both English and Passamaquoddy-Maliseet search terms

Start Time	Passamaquoddy-Maliseet	English
01:14	'Tiyali-kiluwahtuniya elihpihtit.	They (eagles) are looking for something to eat.
01:40	Nmiyawinomon your truck.	I like the looks of your truck.
01:42	U, ya?	Oh, really?
01:44	Yut ehtahc kpistehsinupon, in there.	We will go land, in there.
01:47	Yuta?	Here?
02:10	Wolikonul?	Are they good?
02:11	Yes, sir, good one...	Yes, sir, good one...
02:12	Boy.	Boy.
02:19	Suwonol.	Cranberries.
02:20	Iyap. Wolihpukotul tehna.	Yes. They are good tasting, too.
02:29	Ansa ponapskul metehtehsok.	It's like the sound of stones falling.
02:43	Tan ci wisokolamsok...	When it's very windy...
02:45	Iya	Yes.
02:46	...monolamsonul-ote mipiyil.	...the leaves blow off.

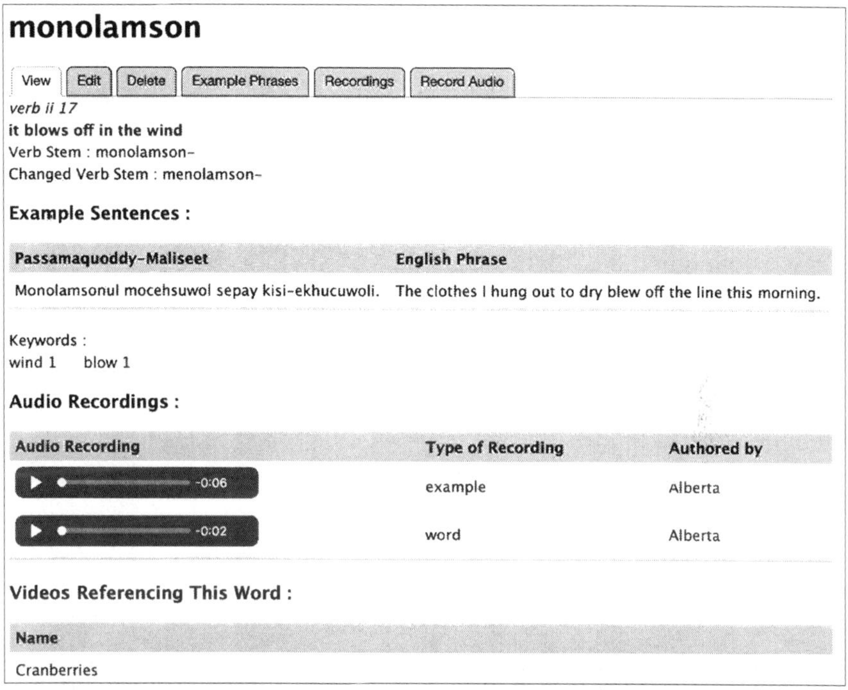

FIGURE 1 (*opposite, top*). Portal video player displaying "Cranberries" video

FIGURE 2 (*opposite, bottom*). Partial transcription/translation for "Cranberries." Highlighted words are hyperlinked to the dictionary.

FIGURE 3 (*above*). Dictionary entry page for *monolamson*

may be used, including partial strings. This feature enables users to find related words built on a specific root. Each dictionary entry page also displays one or more keywords, which, when clicked, lead to lists of related words. For example, in the entry for *ckuhqepu* 's/he sits facing this way, facing toward here', "sit" and "facing" are listed as keywords.

To understand who uses the PM Portal and how they use it, we consulted first Donald Soctomah, Passamaquoddy tribal historian and tribal administrator for the PM Portal. Soctomah reported that in the past he used to get phone calls asking for translations of specific words. Now people consult the PM Portal instead. He said the biggest users locally are tribal members, the schools, and the new immersion preschool staff and families. He related a story from within the community: a group of elders was working on baskets, talking about a word that is not in use much now. It was the word for the splitter used to make ash-splints. Soctomah went to the portal and was able to find the word *pihtuhtamut* and play the audio for it. This triggered memories. Elders said, "I heard that from my mother and grandmother all the time." A flow of recollections came back, and more basket-making terminology with them, according to Soctomah. He reports that, for speakers, "the portal brings the words back to living memory."

Soctomah sees Passamaquoddy and Maliseet language learners using the PM Portal for their posts on Facebook. They look for words on the portal and string sentences together in Passamaquoddy. For example, artist Stephanie Francis uses the portal for titles and descriptions in postings of her photos and other artwork. When the portal became available on mobile devices, Soctomah received many positive comments, especially as users consulted the audio archive to check their pronunciation on the spot. We have heard from Passamaquoddy people in the diaspora, especially younger ones, that it gives them a connection to the culture across the distance between learners and speakers.

One group of young people are the students of Lynn Mitchell, language teacher and Passamaquoddy tribal member. "Yes!" replied Mitchell, "I use the portal quite often, sometimes signing in at least four times per week. I use it for looking up words and seeing how they are used in sentences. I also use the videos. I have created comprehension questions, which students can answer only by watching the video. And as we watch and listen we also identify the words they already know. Although it is not my only resource tool, it is my biggest."

Outside the Passamaquoddy community, Maliseets in Houlton, Maine, have started using words from the PM Portal in their communication. Non-Natives, university students, teachers, and government entities often look for indigenous words or search for the history of the language. Staff at the US National Park Service Saint Croix Island International Historic Site near Calais, Maine, report they use the PM Portal to check pronunciation and sometimes to understand place-names and other words. The park site has trilingual interpretive signs and audio guides, in Passamaquoddy, English, and French, which were prepared by professional translators (see https://www.nps.gov/sacr/index.htm). It is also common for people to search the PM Portal to select a name for a pet. Yet Donald Soctomah says he is nervous that the PM Portal gives users a false sense of confidence about the language. As with any dictionary, words can be taken out of context, and users may inadvertently choose a culturally or grammatically inappropriate translation.

Among scholars and linguists who study Passamaquoddy-Maliseet and closely related Algonquian languages, Jessie Little Doe Baird, vice chairwoman of the Mashpee Wampanoag Tribe, reports: "I do use the portal quite often, probably three or four times per month. I find it extremely helpful rebuilding items and checking corresponding forms. I am actually in the portal right now. It helped me with the formula to make words for some geometric shapes this morning."

Linguist Philip LeSourd, at Indiana University Bloomington, who began fieldwork on Passamaquoddy and Maliseet in the 1970s, now sees the PM Portal as an essential tool for his research and for his work with students. He uses the PM Portal almost daily, either to see whether a word is attested in the extensive database, or to check his knowledge of meaning or pronunciation of a word. He uses the PM Portal to track down examples of sentence types that he needs to be able to cite in writing about Passamaquoddy syntax.

LeSourd has also been working with graduate students to investigate pitch accent in Passamaquoddy and to learn how the accentual properties of words interact with the intonation patterns that are assigned to phrases and sentences of various types. The sound files that accompany the entries in the PM Portal have proven invaluable for this work. The sound recordings for words are useful, and the sound files of example sentences make it possible to tell how words are pronounced in different contexts.

The PM Portal's large number of video recordings, with sound files and transcriptions for the accompanying texts, provide even more readily accessible data for linguistic work. There are extensive cross-references in the texts to entries in the dictionary, making it easy to use this material. Finally, LeSourd's anthropology students profit from the richness of the record of Passamaquoddy lifeways that the example sentences and the videos provide. LeSourd reports that "being able to refer students in a recent seminar on Passamaquoddy language and culture to the portal is really what made the course possible."

As a linguistics master's candidate as well as Peskotomuhkat/Wolastoq, Newell Lewey uses the PM Portal daily in his coursework at the Massachusetts Institute of Technology. With his professor, Norvin Richards, Lewey uses the PM Portal, for example, to find correct spellings and to see how to form plurals. They use the audio recordings of dictionary entries and example sentences to hear subtle difference in pronunciation, such as *'koselomal* 's/he loves h/' versus *koselomol* 'I love you' (entry *'koselomal*). The PM Portal is useful for viewing verb stems, along with prefixed and unprefixed verb stems. Lewey and Richards also review the verb charts included on the PM Portal, in order to see all of the various forms of a particular verb.

Linguist Conor Quinn reports using the PM Portal frequently in many ways, especially in teacher training with teachers of Maliseet language. He finds it a powerful resource for language learning: "Hands down, the best aspect of the portal for language learning is the videos." And Quinn recommends adding to the PM Portal a layperson's interlinear gloss in at least some of the transcriptions in order to show learners the literal meanings of words and phrases.

Kristine Hildebrandt, a linguist who specializes in Himalayan languages, uses the PM Portal along with other web materials in an English department undergraduate course she teaches on language endangerment at Southern Illinois University in Edwardsville, Illinois. The students are assigned to explore the Passamaquoddy-Maliseet Portal in depth early in the course "to get students warmed up to how the internet is a place for representation of research, preservation, revitalization, etc." Hildebrandt then asks students to compare the PM Portal to other endangered language sites, such as the Myaamia Dictionary, and discuss similarities and differences in goals, resources, intended audience, and structure of the sites.

Hildebrandt reports: "In this course, students examine the PM Portal closely because their semester-long, final project is to build their own 'web portal' (using Omeka.net) on an endangered/vulnerable/threatened/revitalized language of their own choosing, using materials they find via library and online research activities. So the Passamaquoddy (and other) portals serve as models of what students should think about in structure and content."

For the past five years, Arthur Haines, a botanist living in western Maine, has been using the PM Portal in multiple ways. He is learning the language, for personal reasons, by reading the entries and their example sentences, and by listening to the audio recordings and watching the videos. Haines has identified typos in dictionary entries and corrected or updated species names in a number of the plant-name entries. Also a student of Penobscot language, he has suggested cognates of botanical items not yet in the dictionary, some of which have been confirmed by Passamaquoddy-Maliseet speakers.

Haines's questions about words often lead to the creation of new entries, for example, alerting us to the absence of a TI verb's TA counterpart. Recently, Haines noticed that the dictionary listed the word *nahsehtun* for 'getting dressed' but this word only means 's/he puts on something inanimate (a hat or sock)'. The dictionary had not included *nahsehlal,* which means 'she puts on something animate (a shirt or mitten)'. In another example, the dictionary listed *saht* for 'blueberry' and our contributing botanist found the related word *sahtemus* 'blueberry bush' in Chamberlain's 1899 Maliseet vocabulary. This has now been confirmed and added to the dictionary corpus. In this way, Haines has both drawn from, and added to, the PM Portal in a truly interactive way. His more than 200 e-mails to the dictionary coauthors attest to his long-term commitment.

We used Google Analytics to get back-end data on PM Portal use. In results from a search of the past nine months, and removing the testing data from the University of New Brunswick, we found 18,400 total sessions, with 3,700 users; 7,800 (42%) of the sessions were on mobile devices.

The number one country was the United States, with 9,100 sessions. Canada was not far behind, with 7,700 sessions. Number three was India, with 250 sessions. More than 20 other countries had up to 100 sessions each. In the United States, 47% of the sessions originated in Maine, with the greatest concentration in Washington County, home of the two principal Passamaquoddy communities. Massachusetts had 850 sessions over this period, mostly in the Cambridge/Boston area. Other notable states were North Carolina, New York, Texas, and New Hampshire. There were PM Portal sessions in every state in the country during this nine-month period, and we suspect this may reflect the breadth of the Passamaquoddy diaspora.

In Canada, the greatest use was in New Brunswick, with 68% of all sessions. Ontario, Quebec, and Nova Scotia followed, in that order. During this period someone was looking at the PM Portal in every province and territory, including Nunavut.

The two videos seen most often were "Star People" and "Little People." The fact that these two titles appear at the top of the list of 93 videos probably accounts for their popularity. In the number three slot was "Sweetgrass," which appears at the bottom of the first page of the video list. All three were filmed near the shores of Passamaquoddy Bay in Sipayik, and in each case, Margaret Apt facilitated the conversations. The cultural information transmitted in these videos may be contributing to their popularity. A hallmark of the filming is the way it shows the language as it is actually lived, preserving and transmitting the associated cultural context.

We looked at landing pages to determine the most popular PM Portal pages. The top (with 300 sessions) was the Browse Dictionary page, and the top word searched was *woliwon* 'thank you', followed by searches for 'wolf'. In third place was the Video page, followed by *wolastoqewi* 'Maliseet'. About 100 sessions were searches on *koselomol* 'I love you'.

We found that use over the years has been steady from the initial climb at start-up. Use is higher during weekdays and lower on Saturdays and Sundays. Since the upgraded PM Portal went online in July 2017, half of the users have been new and half of the users have been returning. On a typical day, there are 144 PM Portal sessions, with 55 of those (38%) on mobile devices. Of the 18,400 sessions over the past nine months, the majority lasted from three to ten minutes, with over 30,000 total page views. A close second were sessions lasting one to three minutes, with 16,600 total page views. There were 806 sessions that lasted more than 30 minutes.

The integration of videos on the PM Portal has changed how dictionaries are built. Nearly 1,000 new words have been added to the Passamaquoddy-Maliseet dictionary from the videos of natural group conversation. And the PM Portal allows for continued updating, correction, and expansion of the dictionary and video archives, from a variety of administrators wherever they may be situated. The latest version of the dictionary lives online now. One limiting factor in the online PM Portal is that, like all websites, there are periodic maintenance costs. Security updates, bug fixes, and periodic upgrades may be daunting for communities to undertake on their own. These are now increasingly part of collaborating institutional research contributions.

This PM Portal has inspired a new endangered language portal for Ayöök (Mixe), the indigenous language of the community of Totontepec Villa de Morelos, Oaxaca, Mexico. The Ayöök Language Portal is an extensive video archive of Totontepecano conversations and activities linked to an 8,000-word Ayöök dictionary (in process). In this case, a trained video team of Totontepec community members produced most of the videos. This was a project led by linguist Daniel Suslak and filmmaker Ben Levine, and funded by the National Endowment for the Humanities.

Plans are in the works for multilanguage portals, which would allow for further efficiencies both for linguists monitoring several documentation projects in related languages simultaneously and for several related groups to share the cost of portal construction and maintenance. Multilanguage portals would also encourage research based on searches between archives of related languages as well as helping communities share data, media, and methods, which can motivate revitalization, for instance, building or expanding dictionaries and educational materials directly from video documentation.

Originating in dictionary development these portals (and their related documentation methods) are interoperable and interdisciplinary, integrating online technologies to better serve both linguistics research and community needs. They offer new opportunities for science and community partnerships and encourage intergenerational collaboration within the community. We hope you explore how you might use the PM Portal and stay tuned as new material and functionality are added to this PM Portal and as similarly integrated dictionary-video-audio portals come online.

NOTES

1. The authors are grateful to all those who contributed their experiences with the Passamaquoddy-Maliseet Language Portal in personal communication, as well as to Heather Souter, who provided the Michif language sources.
2. Color versions of the figures may be found under Supplementary Materials on the Algonquian Conference website at https://algonquianconference.atlas-ling.ca/eng/supplementary-materials/.

REFERENCES

Apt, Margaret, and Julia Schulz. 2012. "Language Keepers": The Role of the Facilitator in Documenting Passamaquoddy-Maliseet Group Discourse. *Papers of the Fortieth Algonquian Conference,* ed. by Karl S. Hele and J. Randolph Valentine, pp. 1–12. Albany: State University of New York Press.

Australian Society for Indigenous Languages. Aboriginal Language Dictionaries. http://ausil.org.au/.

Enduring Voices Project (Living Tongues Institute for Endangered Languages). *Talking Dictionaries.* Website hosted by Swarthmore College. http://talkingdictionary.swarthmore.edu/.

Francis, David A. and Robert M. Leavitt. 2008. *A Passamaquoddy-Maliseet Dictionary: Peskotomuhkati Wolastoqewi Latuwewakon.* Orono: University of Maine Press; Fredericton, New Brunswick: Goose Lane Editions.

Gabriel Dumont Institute of Native Studies and Applied Research. Michif Online Dictionary. http://www.metismuseum.ca.

LeSourd, Philip S. 1986. *Kolusuwakonol: Passamaquoddy-Maliseet and English Dictionary,* ed. by Robert M. Leavitt and David A. Francis. Fredericton, New Brunswick: Micmac-Maliseet

Institute, University of New Brunswick.

Levine, Ben, and Robert M. Leavitt. 2012. Language Keepers: A Documentary Film Process for Stimulating Passamaquoddy-Maliseet Language Documentation and Revival. *Papers of the Fortieth Algonquian Conference,* ed. by Karl S. Hele and J. Randolph Valentine, pp. 210–222. Albany: State University of New York Press.

Louis Riel Institute. *Michif-Cree Video Samples.* http://www.louisrielinstitute.com/.

Miami Tribe of Oklahoma. *Myaamia Dictionary.* https://myaamiadictionary.org/.

Nichols, John D. (ed.). Ojibwe People's Dictionary. Minneapolis: Department of American Indian Studies, University of Minnesota. https://ojibwe.lib.umn.edu.

Omeka (a web publishing platform). http://www.omeka.net.

Passamaquoddy-Maliseet Language Portal. https://pmportal.org/.

Saint Croix Island International Historical Site, US National Park Service. https://www.nps.gov/sacr/index.htm.

University of Indiana. *Ayöök Language Portal.* https://ayportal.indiana.edu/.

Names and Name Formulae in Literary Plains Cree

H. C. Wolfart

While the grammatical status of proper names is remarkable in a wide variety of languages, Cree names stand out further by their low frequency in every genre of discourse, from casual conversation to formal literature and ritual formulae.

In this paper we document the major productive patterns used to form personal names in Plains Cree, setting aside other proper names such as technical terms and, especially, place-names. In exploring some of the grammatical structures in which personal names appear, we also draw attention to the cultural contexts of Plains Cree name constructions.

Simple Noun Stems as Personal Names

In the least-marked type of name formation, the name (here cited as an inflected form rather than as a stem and, since the stem class is always NA, identified only as WN 'woman's name' or MN 'man's name') is identical to an ordinary noun, for example, *iskwêw* WN 'woman' (cf. *iskwêw*–NA); *nêhiyaw* WN 'Cree' (cf. *nêhiyaw*–NA).[1] Names may also be derived from inanimate stems, but the personal name is always animate, for example, *wataniy* MN 'Tailfeather' (cf. *wataniy*–NI). In the case of monosyllabic stems, which do not occur without an inflectional ending such as the proximate singular *-a,* the suffix also appears in the personal name, for example, *êsa* WN 'Shell' (cf. *êsa* 'shell', stem *ês*–NA); *maskwa* MN 'Bear' (cf. *maskwa* 'bear', stem *maskw*–NA).

Diminutive nouns are common as personal names, for example, *môniyâs* MN 'Little-Whiteman' (cf. *môniyâw*–NA); *piyêsîs* MN 'Bird' (cf. *piyêsiw*–NA). Note also *cimikwayâs* MN 'Short-Neck' (cf. root *cimi-, -kwayaw-* NDI 'neck'); *kîskanakwâs* WN 'Cut-Sleeve' (cf. root *kisk-* 'cut', *-anakway-* NDA 'sleeve').

Names Derived from Verb Stems

Names derived from verbs typically show a complex stem, for example, *wâpanohtêw* MN 'Walks-til-Dawn' (cf. [*wâpanohtê*–] VAI, with the final *-ohtê-* 'walk'); they are most often based on a stative verb, for example, *okimâwikâpaw* MN 'Stands-as-Chief'(cf. [*okimâwikâpawi*–] VAI, with the final *-kâpawi-* 'stand'). Several such names appear among the authors of the Bloomfield texts (1930, 1934), notably *nâh-namiskwêkâpaw* MN 'Stands-with-Head-Shaking' (cf. [*nâh-namiskwê*–] VAI 'shake one's head') but also *sâkêwêw* MN 'Comes-into-View' (cf. *sâkêwê*–VAI).[2] As the examples ending in *-kâpaw* illustrate, names formed from complex intransitive verbs often show the stem truncated.

Agent nouns are freely formed from transitive verb stems by the discontinuous formative *o- -w-,* for example, *onîpawihêw* MN 'Makes-Him-Stand' (cf. *nîpawih*–VTA 'make s.o. stand'). They may also be formed from intransitive stems that are themselves secondarily derived from transitives, for example, *otâcimôhiwêw* MN 'Makes-People-Tell-Stories' (cf. *âcimôhiwê*–VAI 'make people tell stories'; *âcimôh*–VTA 'make s.o. report, make s.o. tell stories'; *âcimô*–VAI 'report, tell a story'); *opitihkwahâkêw* MN 'Makes-a-Thudding-Sound-Thereby' (cf. *pitihkwahâkê*–VAI 'cause the making of a thudding sound with (it)'; *pitihkwah*–VTA 'cause s.o. to make a thudding sound'; *pitihkwê*–VAI 'make a thudding sound').

Complex Noun Stems

Nouns with two or more constituents fall into two types: UNIT WORDS and COMPOUNDS. In a unit word, neither the INITIAL nor the NONINITIAL (MEDIAL OR FINAL) constituent may be in a form that can occur in isolation, and the morphophonological rules that govern their combination are those of INTERNAL SANDHI. In compounds (orthographically identified by a hyphen), at least the final member is a freely occurring noun stem, joined to the preceding member largely by the optional rules that apply between words, those of EXTERNAL SANDHI. (For a general summary of the morphological and phonological manifestations of this distinction cf. the appendix.)

In personal names, the two patterns are found side by side. The distinction is most obvious where the noun stem, for example, *maskw*–NA 'bear', is paralleled by a noninitial of divergent shape, in this case *-askw-* (which lacks the stem-initial nasal of the independent noun). In the compound *mistahi-maskwa* MN 'Big-Bear', for instance, the common adverbial particle *mistahi* 'much, greatly' is treated as a prenoun to the stem (which retains its inflectional suffix *-a*), while the unit noun *apiscaskos* MN 'Little-Bear' shows the root *apist-* 'small' construed with the noninitial *-askw-* 'bear';[3] before the diminutive suffix *-is-* all instances of *-t-* are palatalized to *-c-*, and postconsonantal *-w-* coalesces with *-i-* to *-o-*.

Where the stem is segmentally identical to the corresponding noninitial, the distinction may manifest itself in the type of sandhi rule in force. The unit word *mistawâsis* MN 'Big-Child', for example, shows internal sandhi, with noninitial *-awâsis-* beginning in a short vowel; cf. the stem *awâsis*–NA 'child'. The compound *ôhôw-âwâsis* MN 'Owl-Child', by contrast, shows the particle-final *-i-* of *ôhôwi-*'owlish' apocopated with compensatory lengthening of the first vowel of the noninitial.

In unit words the initial is typically a root, for example, *mist-* 'big' in *mistawâsis* or *kotokw-* 'twisted' in *kotokwaskisin* MN 'Crooked-Moccasin', but full noun stems may combine with classificatory medials, as in *nôtokwêwikamik* WN 'Old-Woman's-Lodge' (cf. *nôtokwêwikamikw*–NI). Noninitials are often truncated, for example, *piyêsîwiyin* MN 'Thunderbird-Man' (cf. *iyiniw*–NA), and if *wîhkasko-kisêyin* MN 'Sweet-Grass' [lit., 'Sweet-Grass-Old-Man'] (cf. *kisêyiniw*–NA) follows the same pattern, it might be analyzed as a unit word, too. The noninitial *-sip-* (cf. *sîsîp*–NA 'duck') of *osâwisip* WN 'Yellow-Duck' is common in species terms, and *-âp-* (cf. root *wâp-* 'light, vision, eye') appears in a number of names, for example, *têyâp* WN 'Aching-Eyes' or *wâscêyâp* MN 'White-on-Eyes' (cf. *wâstêyâpi*–VAI 'have a bright spot on one's eyes, have cataracts').

In compounds the initial is normally a particle, for example, *mistahi* 'much, greatly'. Many of the particles functioning as the initial of a compound are secondarily derived from noun stems by the particle-final *-i-*, which in *masko-nôcokwêsiw*

WN 'Bear-Little-Old-Woman' coalesces to *-o-* with the postconsonantal *-w-* of the stem *maskw–*NA 'bear'. The apocope of particle-final *-i-* also defines names that consist solely of a particle, for example, *tahkohc* MN 'On-Top' (cf. *tahkohci* 'on top').

Names, whether unit words or compounds, may also give rise to further derivatives. In *kihci-wâpi-mâkwa* MN 'Great-White-Loon', for example, the prenoun *kihci* 'great' has scope over the unattested compound [*wâpi-mâkwa*] 'White-Loon'.

Of course many names defy morphological and phonological analysis. In one of Bloomfield's texts, for example, the hero's name *wacôw-awâsis* MN 'Clot-Child' is consistently written as a compound even though it shows neither particle-final *-i-* nor compensatory lengthening. In other names, while the postvocalic *-w-* of the initial may suffice to mark the transition between the morphemes, stems ending in postconsonantal *-w-* would be expected to show either the particle-final *-i-* or the extended formative *-iwi-* (cf. the final for verbs of existence), as in *kinêpiko-maskotêhk* PN 'at Snake Plain' (cf. *kinêpikw–*NA 'snake') or in *pîsimôw-âwâsis* MN 'Sun-Child' (cf. the particle *pîsimôwi-* 'sun-like' and the homonymous VAI stem 'be sun-like', both derived from *pîsimw–*NA 'sun'). Neither of these patterns is evident in the classical name *atâhk-akohp* MN 'Star-Blanket' (cf. *atâhkw–*NA 'star').

Nor is this the place to survey the types of constituents found in names, which range from monosyllabic roots like *kisk-* 'cut' to complex stems like *takwa-himinân–*NI 'chokecherry', itself secondarily derived from a verb *takwahiminê–*VAI 'crush berries' incorporating the patient nominal *-min-* 'berries'; the noninitial *-ihkomân-* corresponds to *môhkomân–*NI 'knife', while *-âhtikw-* is a classificatory medial for bushes or trees: *kiskihkomân* MN 'Cut-Knife', *takwahiminânâhtik* MN 'Chokecherry-Tree'.

No systematic attempt has been made, finally, to compare names from the early records to those of the modern texts such as *osâkikwanêwisk* WN 'Emerging-Down-Woman' and *yîkicikâwiskwêw* WN 'Slow-Woman', in which the verb-based initials [*osâkikwanêwi-*] 'show down emerging' and *yîkicikâwi–*'be a slow runner' are construed with the full and truncated noninitials *-skwêw-* and *-skw-*.

Simple *kâ*-compounds

The most distinctive and probably also productive type of personal name reflects a verb form with the relative preverb *kâ*. In verb forms, *kâ* obligatorily governs the conjunct order. The *kâ*-compounds on which personal names are modeled are always inflected for the third-person singular.[4]

Personal names based on *kâ*-verbs with the conjunct are not very common but are found with transitive and intransitive stems alike, for example, *kâ-pêtwêwêmât* MN 'Brings-Him (Thunderbird)-in-by-Singing' (cf. VTA); *kâ-wîhkaskosahk* WN 'Burns-Incense' (cf. VTI); *kâ-nîsocihcêpit* WN 'Sits-with-Two-Hands' (cf. VAI). With stems beginning in a vowel, the preverbal *-â-* may be apocopated and the opening vowel of the stem, if not already long, shows compensatory lengthening, for example, *k-âpîstawât* MN 'Sits-by-Them' (cf. *apîstaw*–VTA); *k-ây-atâhkôwit* MN 'Star-at-Times' (cf. *ây-atâhkôwi*–VAI 'be a star from time to time', with *-ây-* marking distributive reduplication).

The vast majority of *kâ*-names show a highly marked construction that is restricted to personal names: a verb form inflected in the independent order. Among the verbs on which these names are based, transitive stems are rare; hence most examples show the third-person singular ending *-w-* of the VAI paradigm, for example, *kâ-nîpitêhtêw* MN 'Walks-Abreast'; *kâ-kîsikâw-pîhtokêw* MN 'Coming-Day'; *k-ôsihkosiwayâniw* MN 'Has-an-Ermine-skin' (cf. the syntactically transitive VAI stem *osihkosiwayâni*–VAI-T 'have (it as) an ermine-skin').

Remarkably, some names are found in both forms, with the verbal constituent inflected either for the conjunct or the independent. In the case of *kâ-pimwêwêhahk* MN 'Goes-Along-Drumming', this is the form which the bearer of the name gives in his texts; in discussing his book, a fellow ritualist of another band insists on *kâ-pimwêwêham*—presumably defaulting either to an archaic or a more productive pattern. In the texts recorded by Bloomfield in 1925 the variants represent different speakers: two instances of *k-ôsôsimânisit* MN 'Little-Snowdart' (cf. *osôsimânisi*–VAI 'have a snowdart') by *mimikwâs* and 13 instances of *k-ôsôsimânisiw* (and one for *osôsimânisiw*) by *sâkêwêw.*

That *kâ*-compounds can serve as the basis for further derivation suggests a degree of internal stability. The distributive locative *-inâhk* (originally the locative of a noun stem derived by *-inâw-*) is found with animal terms, ethnonyms, and personal names, for example, *mostosonâhk* 'in the buffalo country' (cf. *mostosw*–NA), *iyinînâhk* 'in the land of mortals' (cf. *iyiniw*–NA), *kîskihkomâninâhk* 'in Cut-Knife country, among the Cut-Knife people' (cf. *kîskihkomân*–MN 'Cut-Knife'). Thus also *kâ-pitikônâhk* 'on Thunderchild Reserve, among Thunderchild's people' (cf. *kâ-pitikôw* MN 'Thunderchild [lit., 'Doubles-Himself-Up']').

Phrasal *kâ*-compounds

The most prominent type of *kâ*-compound shows the *kâ*-plus-verb complex together with an inflected noun. In these phrasal compounds, the verb shows the conjunct ending exclusively.

With intransitive verbs (VAI), the names in effect replicate relative clauses with the agent noun preceding, for example, *iyiniw-kâ-kîskwêt* MN 'Crazy-Man'; *asiniy-kâ-mihkosit* MN 'Red-Rock'; *pihêw-kâ-mihkosit* MN 'Red-Pheasant' (also reported as *kâ-mihkosit-pihêw*).

With transitive verbs (whether VTA, VTI, or VAI-T), the patient noun that precedes the *kâ* shows the appropriate inflection: the animate obviative *-a,* which is number-indifferent, in *miscanikocâsa-kâ-pimwât* MN 'Shoots-the-Gopher' (cf. *pimw–*VTA 'shoot s.o.') or *acâhkosa-k-ôtakohpit* MN 'Has-Little-Stars-on-His-Blanket' (also 'Star-Blanket'; cf. *otakohpi–*VAI-T 'have (it/him as) a blanket'); and the (homonymous) plural inanimate *-a* in *mahkwana-kâ-sakahahk* MN 'Nails-the-Heels' (cf. *sakah–*VTI 'fasten s.t.').

With transitive and intransitive stems alike, the noun included in the phrase may show the locative ending *-ihk,* for example, *kîsikohk-k-âpit* WN 'Sits-in-the-Sky' (cf. *kîsikw–*NI, *api–*VAI); *mîkwanihk-kâ-nîpawit* MN 'Stands-on-a-Feather' (cf. *nîpawi–*VAI 'stand'). In *wâwikanihk-k-ôtâmahoht* MN 'Struck-on-the-Spine' (cf. *otâmahw–*VTA 'strike s.o.'), the dependent noun stem *-âwikan-* 'spine, backbone' shows the personal prefix of the third person, *w-,* and the verb the conjunct suffix *-iht* (indefinite acting on third).

Names with Determiners and in Apposition to Kin-Terms

Names are commonly construed with determiners, even when there is no change in obviation status that would normally require a determiner, for example, *awa* 'the, this':

> *nipâw. . . . , mêkwâc ê-nipât* ***awa wîsahkêcâhk,*** *kêtahtawê sisikoc k-ôhpahoyit pihêwa.*
> 'He (3) slept. . . . , while that (3) Wisahketchahk (3) was (3) yet asleep, suddenly up flew (3′) the partridges (3′).' (ET)

They also occur freely in apposition to kin-terms, for example, *kistêsinaw* 'our (21) elder brother' or *nisîm* 'my younger sibling':

> *. . . , â, êkot[a] êkwa kâ-kî-wiyakimât* ***kistêsinaw wîsahkêcâhk****, . . .*
> '. . . , it was then that our elder brother Wisahketchahk gave him his charge, . . . ' (MT)
> ***nisîm k-ôsôsimânisiw*** *mîsihtâw.*
> 'My brother Little Snow-Dart has a store of meat.' (ET)

Often the nominal phrase includes both a determiner and a kin-term, for example, the emphatic deictic *êwakw âwa* 'that one' and *nimosôminân* 'our (1P) grandfather':

> *. . . , êwako nêhiyawasinahikan kâ-kî-osîhtât,*
> ***êwakw âwa nimosôminân "cascakiskwês"*** *kâ-kî-itiht, . . .*
> '. . . , he made it the Cree document of the treaty,
> it was our grandfather *Cascakiskwês* as he was called, . . . ' (MT)

Only simple names are found inflected for obviation, for example:

> *tâpwê tawinamawêw* ***wîsahkêcâhkwa****.*
> 'Accordingly, she opened the door for Wisahketchahk.' (ET)
> *êkota ohci wanihêw anihi,* ***êbramwa****;*
> 'from that point on he lost that one, Abram.' (MT)

For complex names this is quite rare (and no analogous construction has been found for *kâ-* names):

> *"êkosi; pasikô," itêw* ***manitôwi-kihiwah****, "tapasîtân."*
> '"So then, arise," said he to Spirit-Eagle, "let us flee."' (ET)
> *. . . , êkwa off and on kâ-kî-wîc-âyâmât ôhi* ***slim-mêrîwa****, . . .*
> '. . . , and off and on she had lived with Slim-Mary, . . . ' (MT)

Names and Their Frames: Plain Presentation

The names appearing in name formulae are by definition quoted material and as such extrasentential. Nonetheless, agreement between the name and the frame with respect to gender and number is the most common pattern when both are third-person forms, for example:

> *êwako awa, "piyêsîs" kî-isiyîhkâsow awa kâ-wî-âcimak.*
> 'He was (3) called *Piyêsîs* (3), the one of whom I am about to tell.' (MT)
> *kotak**ak** mîna onîmihitow**ak** "pihêw**ak**" isiyîhkâsow**ak**.*
> 'The dancers of another society were (3P) called *Partridges* (3P).' (ET)

In the case of non-third persons, the agreement is attenuated, for example,

> *"'yîkicikâwiskwêw' **k**-êsiyîhkâso**n** ôta ohci," ê-kî-itât anihi, . . .*
> '"*Yîkicikâwiskwêw* (3) you shall (2) be called from here on in," he said to her, . . . ' (MT)

The special extrasentential status of the quoted name is most obvious when name and frame disagree as to gender, for example,

> ***êwak ôma** pêyak kâ-wî-âtotamân, "kâ-piyêsîsiwit" kî-isiyîhkât**am**.*
> 'the one [story] I am about to tell he used to call *He-who-was-a-Bird*.' (MT)

The patient nominal is the inanimate emphatic deictic phrase *êwak ôma* 'that one', matching the VTI stem *isiyîhkât–*'name s.t. thus'. The name serving as the title of the tale is a standard *kâ*-compound with the VAI stem *piyêsîsiwi–*'be a bird' and the conjunct third-person ending *-t*.

Name and frame may also be discrepant with respect to number and obviation, for example,

> *êwakw ânim ês ê-kî-kwayâci-wîhtam**âkot** nisis aya, kayâs **anih** ôkimâhkân**a** aya, "k-ôsihkosiwayâniw" kâ-kî-isiyîhkâso**yit**.*
> 'That is reportedly what my father-in-law was told in preparation by that chief of long ago, that *K-ôsihkosiwayâniw* as he was called.' (MT)

The agent throughout is obviative, marked both in the 3′–3 ending (*-ikot,* coalesced with stem-final *-aw-*) of the main verb and the noun phrase consisting of the determiner *anihi* 'that (3′)' and the noun itself with its ending *-a;* that this is the bearer of the name is made explicit by the obviative ending of the predicate *kâ-kî-isiyîhkâso**yit*** 'as he (3′) was called'. But the name itself shows not the least sign of obviative status. Much the same situation obtains in the following example, in which an ethnonym is defined:

> ***ômis*** ***îsiyihkâsoyiwah*** *kâ-ntonawât: "kinêpikoyiniwak"* ***isiyîhkâsoyiwa.***
>
> 'This was the name of the people they were seeking out: *Snakes,* was their name.' (ET)

While the frame identifies the Cree adventurers as proximate (and, literally, singular) and the intended victims as obviative, their tribal name appears in the proximate plural, marked by the ending *-ak.*

The name is not inflected as obviative even if it is the patient of a transitive verb that otherwise would require it, for example:

> *"pîhkahtêwâhtik" isiyîhkâtêw êsah* ***ôhi*** *oskinîkiskwêwah.*
>
> '*Burnt-Stick* it seems that he called the young woman.' (ET)

The transitive stem *isiyîhkât–*VTA is inflected by *-êw* for 3–3′, and the patient noun phrase with which the name stands in apposition shows the expected obviative demonstrative *ôhi* 'this' and the obviative ending *-a.* But the name does not.

While the preceding sentence was recorded in 1925, exactly the same pattern, with the verb inflected for 3P–3′ and the patient noun phrase unambiguously obviative (*anihi êkoni, anihi*), is documented in 1988:

> *. . . , êkos êkwa, mâka mîna nêhiyawak,*
>
> *"otâcimôhiwêw" kî-isiyîhkâtêwak anihi êkoni, anihi, . . .*
>
> '. . . , and so the Crees of course used to call that one *Makes-People-Tell-Stories, . . .*' (MT)

Again, the cited name remains unaffected.

Primary Framing Verbs

The indifference that name and frame show in the matter of agreement is in part due to the particular type of verb serving as the prototypical frame. The paired stems *isiyîhkâso–*VAI 'be called thus, have such a name' and *isiyîhkât–*VTA 'call s.o. thus' (and the matching pair *isiyîhkâtê–*VII 'be called, named thus' and *isiyîhkât–*VTI 'call s.t. thus', which can largely be ignored in a study of personal names) are built on a root *it-* ~ *is-* 'thus, thither', which presupposes an antecedent; such roots form MANNER CONSTRUCTIONS, which in the simplest case have an interrogative as the antecedent, for example,

> *hâ, nisîm,* ***tânis*** *ôma êsiyîhkâsoyan?*
> 'Well, little brother, what is your name?' (ET)

The manner interrogative *tânisi* 'how' and the emphatic manner deictic *êkosi* 'thus' in the next example suggest that the conventional translations here given might more literally be paraphrased as 'how are you called' and 'only so we are called' (the variation between initial change and the preverb *ê* being optional):

> *. . . ;* ***êkosi*** *piko* ***ê-isiyîhkâsoyâhk.***
> '. . . ; that is the only name we (1P) have.' (ET)

The analytical emphasis on what has traditionally been called 'relative roots' as manner-and-place constructions is supported by the use of number adverbs rather than the ordinal *nîso* 'two' and the simple quantifier *mihcêt* 'many' in the following sentences:

> *kahkiyaw kêkway* ***nîswayak isiyîhkâtêw.***
> 'Everything has two names.' [lit., 'is doubly named'] (ET)
> *pêyak kêkway* ***mihcêtwayak isiyîhkâtêw,*** *. . .*
> 'But each thing has many names . . . ' [lit., 'is multiply named'] (ET)

Note that the root *it-* ~ *is-* also appears in a large set of other verbs, for example, *itakim*–VTA 'count s.o. thus, value s.o. thus'; *itâcimo*–VTA 'tell thus, tell such a story, give such an account'; *itâhkôm*–VTA 'be thus related to s.o.; use such a kin-term for s.o.'. Above all, it defines the classical quotative verbs *it*–VTA 'say thus to/of s.o., call s.o. thus'; *it*–VTI 'say thus to/of s.t., call s.t. thus'; *itwê*–VAI 'say thus; call (it) thus', in which the antecedent is the material being quoted.

Proclamatory Presentation

A repetition of the verb presenting the name renders the formula even more formal. This is accomplished by means of the manner deictic *ômisi* 'thus', which in other contexts is often accompanied by a gesture, as the antecedent of the first instance of the verb, effectively announcing the proclamation of the name.

Such sentences are typical of introductory passages setting the scene for a factual report (which may always contain mythical elements). In a sentence earlier examined for its grammatical properties, the announcement refers to the collective to be named in the obviative, marked by the ending *-yiwa* in both manifestations of the framing verb, and confirmed in the relative clause *kâ-ntonawât* VTA 3–3' 'him/them whom he sought'; the name itself is in the proximate plural, marked by the ending *-ak:*

> ***ômis îsiyihkâsoyiwah** kâ-ntonawât: "kinêpikoyiniw**ak**" **isiyîhkâsoyiwa**.*
>
> 'This was the name of the people they were seeking out: *Snakes,* was their name.' (ET)

In its most reduced form, such a sentence specifies the bearer of the name by the simple noun phrase *awa kisêyiniw* 'the old man' and the predicate ending in *-w:*

> ***ômis îsiyîhkâsow** awa kisêyiniw: "pitikwayasit" **isiyîhkâsow**.*
>
> 'This was the old man's name: *Club-Foot* was his name.' (ET)

Identifying the protagonist as part of the introduction of the text, this proclamation anchors a historical account. It is confirmed at the conclusion by the author having personally encountered the heroine.

The preposed part of the proclamation may occur without the repetition of the name predicate, for instance in a myth text where a series of performative names is being announced:

> *kotak nisîm **ômis îsiyîhkâsôw**: "kîsôpwêw nêm îskôh k-ôsêhcâk."*
>
> 'My other younger brother is called like this: *Hot-Weather-up-to-Yon-Hill.*' (ET)

The full formula appears at its most stately in the ritual imposition of a name, with *isiyîhkâso–*as the naming predicate inflected for the second-person singular:

*nôsisi, **ômisi** kik-êsiyîhkâson, . . . ;*
"watapîwiyin" kik-êsiyîhkâson. . . .
'My grandchild, this shall be your name, . . . ;
Pine-Root-Man will be your name. . . . ' (ET)

More prosaically, it is used with *isiyîhkâtê–*VII 'be named, called thus', the inanimate counterpart of *isiyîhkâso–*, in the definition of technical terms, for example:

***ômisi isiyîhkâtêw** ômah wâtihkân: "mênisk" **isiyîhkâtêw**.*
'Such a trench is called *earthwork.*'
(or, more literally: 'That is the name of this trench: it is called *mênisk.*') (ET)

Note that the same inanimate framing verb also appears with a technical term having the form of an animate third-person plural verb (ending *-cik* VAI 3P):

*ômis îsiyîhkâtêw **êwako:** "ê-ntawâhtâ**cik**" isiyîhkâtêw.*
'This is called as follows: *they went on a reconnaissance,* it is called.' (ET)

Bestowing Names

While the intransitive stem *isiyîhkâso–*VAI 'be called thus, have such a name' is ubiquitous as the predicate for name formulae, its function is almost universally limited to that of a statement of the name. The only exception is when it is construed with a future preverb and the second person:

"namêw" kik-êsiyîhkâson!
'*Sturgeon* will be your name!' (ET)

Much the same holds for its transitive counterpart *isiyîhkât–*VTA 'call s.o. thus', for example:

êkwah kiya, nôhtâh, "sâkwês," kik-êsiyîhkâtik ayîsiyiniw;
'And you, my father, *Mink,* mortal man will call you;' (ET)

Only under these conditions do these stems indicate that a name is being bestowed, but the textual examples all involve common names rather than personal ones.[5]

The ritual act of bestowing a personal name upon someone falls within the meaning of the transitive stem *wîh–*VTA 'name s.o., give s.o.'s name, mention s.o. by name' (cf. also *wîhowin–*NI 'name'), but textual instances are extremely rare. These are from a discussion of naming rituals:

. . . , êkos ê-kî-isi-miyikowisicik, kêhtê-ayak ôki ***t-êsi-wîhâcik****.*
'. . . , in this way the old people used to be granted the authority by the powers to bestow names upon them [children].' (MT)
. . . , namôy ânima konita mîna kâ-kî-miyihcik ***ta-wîhâcik****, . . .*
'. . . , that also was very much a matter of consequence that they used to be given the authority to bestow names upon them [children] . . . ' (MT)

In most ordinary contexts, however, the same stem simply denotes the act of using a name, for example:

êkosi nama wîhkâc ***niwîhânân****, . . .*
'And so we never call him by his name, . . . ' (ET)
mâka kahkiyaw êkwa ôk âya ayisiyiniwak ***kâ-wîhakik****, môy pimâtisiwak êkonik.*
'But the people whom I have named, they are all dead.' (MT)

It often seems to carry a connotation of revealing a name, for example:

anohc kâ-kîsikâk ***kika-wîhinâwâw****. . . .*
'On this day you shall speak my name. . . . ' (ET)
sêmâk ***wîhik****: "yahô, kotokwaskisin!"*
'At once the other called him by name: "Yoho, *Crooked-Moccasin!*" (ET)
–mâka namôy ***nika-kî-wîhâwak****.*
'–but I cannot mention them by name.' (MT)

While the semantic and cultural distinctions between *wîh–*VTA and *isiyîhkâso–*VAI are subtle, their existence seems confirmed by the interplay of the two terms, for example:

. . . , awiyak ***wâh-wîhicih,*** *"opipikwan-kâ-nayahtahk"* ***nik-êsiyîhkâson,*** *. . .*

'. . . , whenever anyone is to name me, *Flute-Bearer* I shall be called, . . . ' (ET)

mêkwâc anohc ôma ***nika-wîhâw ê-isiyîhkâsot,*** "Justine Littlechild," *êkos* ***ê-isiyîhkâsot*** *awa nicâhkos.*

'I will give her full name as she is called today, *Justine Littlechild,* that is my sister-in-law's name.' (MT)

The Performative Function of Names

Mirroring the cultural prohibitions that govern the use of names in Cree discourse, myth texts turning on the performative power of names provide some striking illustrations of the effect, perhaps best understood as magical, which is ascribed to names.

The popular texts of the *wîsahkêcâhk* cycle include several instances of the culture hero challenging figures he encounters about their multiple names. In his contest with a floating lump of fat, for example, he succeeds in provoking a sequence of four responses, and each time the referential meaning of the name is duly implemented, with *wîsahkêcâhk* biting off the number of pieces announced in the name:

hâw, nistêsê, ***"pêyakwâw-kâ-pahkwêmiht"*** *nititikawin.*	'Once-Bitten-from'
tâpwê, nistêsê, ***"nîswâw-kâ-pahkwêmiht"*** *nititikawin.*	'Twice-Bitten-from'
êhaq, nistêsê, ***"nistwâw-kâ-pahkwêmiht"*** *nititikawin.*	'Thrice-Bitten-from'
"nêwâw-kâ-pahkwêmiht" *nititikawin.*	'Four-Times-Bitten-from'

'Well, Older Brother, *Once-Bitten-from* is my name. . . . ' (ET)

The four responses, which in their literal consistency epitomize the laconic style of the text, make for a remarkable progression.

In a pair of classical myth texts told by *kâ-wîhkaskosahk* and *sâkêwêw,* the sequence of performative names is less stereotypically repetitive, but the individual instances are nothing short of spectacular. In the first, which shows little elaboration (and is only a third the length of the second), four young women are pitted against four young men. Without further introduction, the first woman's name is announced as follows:

. . . , nisîm awa kiwîh-wîhtamâtin tânisiy êsiyîhkâsot:
***"nêm îskoh k-ôsêhcâk pîwanoskwêw"** isiyîhkâsôw.*
'. . . , I shall tell you how my younger sister here is called:
Up-to-Yon-Rise-of-the-Land-Blizzard-Woman she is called.' (ET)

After a minimal transition, the denotation of the name becomes manifest:

*êkwa sipwêhtêwak. mistahi **misi-pîwaniyiw.***
'Then they were off again. There was a terrible blizzard.'

The same pattern holds for the second young woman and then for two of the young men, the performance of whose names the young women conclude by evaluations:

*î, tâpwê **miyoyîhkâsôw** kîtimosinaw!*
'Goodness me, really a beautiful name has our sweetheart!' (ET)
*tâpwê **âyimaniyiw** kîtimosinaw osîmah **êsiyîhkâsôyit!***
'Really, it is terrible, the way our sweetheart's younger brother is called!' (ET)

In the second text the male hero, instructed not to look at anyone, is surprised by one of a group of young women who address one another as *nitayîm* 'my fellow wife'. When they ask him for his name and he demurs, two young women give theirs for him to perform, for example:

*êhaq! **"nêmay isko kâ-nêyâk, êkotah iskoh kâ-sôskwâstimêwi-pimohtêw,"** ntisiyîhkâson, itik.*
êkwah tâ-sôskwâsit.
'Very well! *Up-to-Yon-Point-of-the-Land, Up-to-that-Place, Walks-Blown-on-the-Ice* is my name, she told him.
And then the wind was to carry him along on the smooth surface.' (ET)

The hero in turn announces his own names, repeating the first part with a slight variation:

> *. . . , **ninîsoyîhkâson**, itêw;*
> *"**nêma kisiwâk ôma kâ-nêyâk, êkotah iskoh, kâ-kisâkamitêwi-kimiwahk,**"*
> *nitisiyîhkâson, "**animah iskoh kâ-nêyâk.**"*
> '. . . , I have two names, he told them;
> *Yon-Close-by-Point-of-the-Land, Up-to-that-Place, Hot-Water-Rain* is my name, *Up-to-this-Point-of-the-Land.*' (ET)

After the briefest of transitions, the implementation is announced:

> *. . . , âsay **mâcih-kimiwaniyiw**. tâpiskôc êh-ohtêk nipiy, êkos îsi **kisâkamitêyiw**.*
> '. . . , at once it began to rain. Like boiling water, so hot was the liquid.' (ET)

The young women's evaluation is as follows:

> *hêy, tâpwê kîtimosinaw **âyimaniyiw owîhôwin!** . . .*
> 'Hey, truly a dangerous thing is our sweetheart's name! . . . ' (ET)

As soon as they reach their home while still performing his second name, the young women warn their mother not to speak:

> ***ka-pisci-wîhâw** kinahâhkisîm! **ôwîhôwin** ôma **kâ-tôtamâhk**, . . .*
> 'Before you know it, you will be speaking your son-in-law's name! It is his name, what we are doing . . . ' (ET)

The well-known taboos between mother-in-law and son-in-law, which in Cree prohibit all discourse between them, evidently extend to her speaking his name.

The Discourse Function of Names: Text Attribution

In the historical texts that constitute a defining part of Cree literature, personal names are quite rare, usually occurring only once in a particular text, mostly at the beginning or conclusion. For the balance of the narrative, either generic terms like *awa kisêyiniw* 'the old man' or kin-terms like *nisîm* 'my younger sibling' serve to identify the dramatis personae. For historical texts the authenticity of the document and the authority of the current performer are asserted—much in the manner of the incipit and seals that define a medieval diploma—by a formal statement of the original author's name.

The formal attribution of authorship, and the name itself, may come to stand at the very opening of the text:

> *"**mînakôs**" isiyîhkasow otâcimowin kâ-wî-âtotamân. ômis îtwêw:—*
> '*Mînakôs* is the name of him whose story I am going to tell. This is what he told:–' (ET)

In the limiting case, a text may be told as directly quoted speech, often punctuated after each clause by the quotative verb *itwêw* 'thus he said'. The following is a classical instance of such an opening:

> *kêtahtawê, "ê-nitopayihk niwîcihiwân," itwêw, "**watôwâpoy**" kî-isiyîhkâsow.*
> 'At one time, "As they went on a raid, I went along," he said, *Watôwâpoy* was his name.' (MT)

The use of the name predicate is typical when the author is identified at the beginning of the text.

In many texts, on the other hand, the protagonist is at first presented generically, and his or her name is not given until the end. In a classical instance from the historical oeuvre of *kâ-kîsikâw-pîhtokêw,* the hero is introduced only as *pêyak oskinîkiw* 'a certain youth'; the proclamatory presentation of the name marks an intermediate conclusion:

> *ômisi isiyîhkâsôw awa nêhiyaw k-âyimisit êh-nôtinikêt:*
> *"**wîhkasko-kisêyin**" isiyihkâsôw.*
> 'This was the name of the Cree who fought most redoubtably:
> *Sweet-Grass* was his name.' (ET)

Finally, at the conclusion of the entire text, the authenticity of the account is affirmed by a physical link between the hero or heroine and the current narrator:

> *awa **wîhkasko-kisêyin** oskotâkay wâpowayân nistomitanaw nîso ayiwâk tahtwayak, . . .*
> '*Sweet-Grass*'s rabbit-skin coat had 32 bullet holes [*gesture*], . . .' (ET)

In the introduction of another historical text by *kâ-kîsikâw-pîhtokêw* the hero's name does not figure but the authenticity of the report is asserted immediately, and in the strongest terms possible, by the author's direct knowledge of him:

> *pêyak nikîh-wâpamâw kisêyiniw; êyôkô ê-kîh-âcimot kisêyiniw ômis îtwêw, "nik-âcimon," itwêw.*
> 'A certain old man whom I am old enough to have known, used to tell this story; "I shall tell of what I have seen," he would say.' [lit., 'I used to see a certain old man, now dead; in telling this story that old man, now dead, used to speak thus, "I shall tell a factual story," he said.'] (ET)

The hero's name is supplied at the conclusion, the factual nature of his report confirmed by his status as an eyewitness, and the author's authority reconfirmed by a kinship link:

> ***nîsôtêw-mostos**, êwako ê-wâpahtahk ôma âcimowin;*
> *niya nisis êwako kisêyiniw.*
> '*Twin-Buffalo*, he is the one who had this experience;
> that old man was my mother's brother.' [lit., '. . . , he saw/witnessed the event being told about; that old man was my very own mother's brother.'] (ET)

In short, the personal name of the original author or the protagonist, who often are identical, is central in confirming the documentary status of a historical text.

Name Avoidance

The sparing use of personal names in every genre of discourse reflects two cultural traits which may well be linked: the pervasive use of kin terms and anaphoric constructions in lieu of proper names, and the strict prohibition against names in reference to certain kin types (e.g., a woman's son-in-law) and to the dead.

Conversely, personal names play a key role, along with a personal link between the narrator and the original reporter or a physically observable aspect of the case, in the authentication formulae that characterize orally transmitted historical documents.

Appendix

The structural distinction between unit word and compound is most transparent where the noun stem is paralleled by a noninitial variant of divergent shape; beside the stem *maskisin*–NI 'moccasin, shoe', for example, we find a noninitial *-askisin-* that lacks the stem-initial nasal of the free noun and also is indeterminate as to stem class. With the root *osk-* 'new' as the initial constituent, it forms the unit noun *oskaskisin*–NI 'new moccasin, new shoe'; with the root *post-* 'put on' and the VAI final *-ê-,* it also appears in the verb *postaskisinê*–VAI 'put on one's moccasins, shoes'. The root *pîswê-* 'loose, fluffy, swelling', by contrast, does not form a unit word with the noninitial *-askisin-;* instead, it enters into a compound with the noun stem: *pîswê-maskisin*–NI 'felt-shoe, bootliner'.

Unit words with the noninitial constituent beginning in a short vowel and the initial ending in a consonant or postconsonantal *-w-* are also unambiguous: in *waskitaskisin*–NI 'overshoe', for instance, the first vowel of *-askisin-* is not affected by the root *waskit-* 'over, on top of'. Contrast the compound *mistah-âtoskêwin*–NI 'big task', where under the rules of external sandhi the final *-i-* of the prenoun particle *mistahi* is apocopated and the first vowel of *atoskêwin*–'work' shows compensatory lengthening to *-â-*.

The status of the complex noun is less readily established when stem and noninitial are identical in shape and the latter begins in a long vowel; since long vowels do not show compensatory lengthening, in the case of *âcimowin*–NI 'report, story' there is no discernible difference between the unit word *takahkâcimowin*–and the compound *takahk-âcimowin*–NI 'fine story', in which the prenoun particle *takahki-* 'nice' shows apocope of the particle-final *-i-*.

The phonological properties of the initial also play a role. A root ending in *-t-* ~ *-s-*, for example, appears as *wawiyat-* 'funny' in the unit word *wawiyatâcimowin*–NI 'funny story' but since the particle-final *-i-* has palatalizing force, the preverb *wawiyasi-* shows *-s-* in the compound *wawiyas-âcimowin*–NI.

A single example will have to stand for the various complexities that arise when the initial ends in a sequence of vowel and semivowel. Regardless of the historical differences, stems in *-iw-* and *-iy-* appear with *-îwi-* in this context; thus, *kisêyinîw-âcimowin*–NI 'old men's story' (cf. *kisêyiniw*–NA 'old man'), *asinîwi-maskwa* MN 'Stone-Bear' (cf. *asiniy*–NA 'rock, stone').

It is fairly common for an intransitive verb stem to appear as the opening constituent in either unit words or compounds. In the former case, the transition between the two constituents is made by an epenthetic *-w-* with the first vowel of the noninitial remaining short, for example, *atoskêwaskisin–*NI 'work boot' (cf. *atoskê–*VAI 'work'). In the latter case, the initial member either shows the bare stem of the verb, for example, *mêtawê-maskwa* MN 'Play-Bear' (cf. *mêtawê–*VAI 'play'), or a particle derived from it by the suffix *-iwi-,* for example, *wiyâhkwêwi-âcimowin–*NI 'risqué story' (cf. *wiyâhkwê–*VAI 'swear, speak in obscenities').

It is striking, finally, given the sharp distinction between the stem *atimw–*NA 'dog, horse' and its noninitial counterpart *-astimw-*, that the former freely appears in unit words, for example, *takahkatimw–*NA 'nice horse' (cf. root *takahk-* 'nice'), *mihkwawêwatimw–*NA 'race horse' (cf. *mihkwawê–*VAI 'be red of coat, be a bay'). Note further the lengthened stem-vowel *-î-* in *âyimisîwatimw–*NA 'difficult, high-spirited horse' (cf. *âyimisi–*VAI 'be difficult, be wild'), optionally but commonly found in initials derived from VAI stems in *-i-* and, at the same time, the absence of compensatory lengthening in the leading vowel of the noninitial. Similarly note also the compound (explicitly marked as such by compensatory lengthening) *mîhkâwikîw-âtimw–*NA 'bay horse' (cf. *mîhkâwikî–*VAI 'race') beside the apparent unit word *mîhkâwikîwatimw–*NA.

In short, the distinction in principle between unit words and compounds is subject to many indeterminacies; more fundamentally, it is also "partly troubled in Cree" (Bloomfield 1930:5).[6]

NOTES

1. Unless otherwise indicated by square brackets, all illustrations are cited from spoken texts. Sentential examples are identified as ET for Early Texts (largely those dictated to Bloomfield in 1925; cf. Bloomfield 1930, 1934) and MT for Modern Texts (audio-recorded since the late 1960s by Wolfart and Ahenakew; cf. F. Ahenakew (ed.) 1986; Vandall and Douquette 1987; Bear et al. 1992; Whitecalf 1993; Minde 1997; kâ-pimwêwêhahk / Kâ-Nîpitêhtêw 1998; A. Ahenakew 2000; kêkêk / Masuskapoe 2010; kâ-mimikwatowêt / Greyeyes 2014). The codes WN, MN, and PN stand for woman's, man's, and place name; other abbreviations are as follow: NA = animate noun, NDA = dependent animate noun, NDI = dependent inanimate noun, NI = inanimate noun, s.o. = someone, s.t. = something, VAI = animate intransitive verb, VAI-T = syntactically transitive verb of the VAI class, VII = inanimate intransitive verb, VTA = transitive animate verb, VTI = transitive inanimate verb; person-number-obviation categories: 3, 3P, 3′, 2, 2P, 21, 1, 1P; stems are marked with a trailing en-dash, and compounds with an internal hyphen.

Thanks are due first and always to the generations of Cree speakers whose texts and comments constitute the empirical foundation of all linguistic analysis. For critical responses to earlier (and even briefer) versions of this essay I am also grateful to colleagues at the Regensburg conference "The Grammar of Personal Names" (2010), the UBC Algonquian Roundtable, Vancouver (2011), and the 49e Congrès des Algonquinistes, Montréal (2017). Lastly I salute the anonymous expert who caught the subtlest of bilingual typos.

2. Others in this set remain to be fully analyzed, for example, *kiyâkêskamikapiw* WN [Mrs. Adam Sakewew] or *âcênam* MN, which seems to reflect a VTI stem.
3. Noninitial *-askw-* 'bear' is rare, perhaps due to its homonymy with the very common non-initial *-askw-* 'grass, reed, brush', for example, *wîhkaskw*–NI 'sweetgrass'.
4. The *kâ*-compounds, by contrast, are never—to the extent that our textual corpus may be taken as representative—inflected for either plural or obviative. Instead, every syntactic device is deployed, often with considerable stylistic ingenuity, to keep them suffixless—i.e., unmarked. (With respect to the larger syntactic and semantic issues identified by Mühlbauer [e.g., 2008, 2012, 2015], the fact that *kâ*-names are restricted to the unmarked values of number and obviation provides a welcome syntactic test to complement that of possessed nouns, which are obligatorily obviative.)
5. The unique exception also appears in a myth: *"watapîwiyin" kik-êsiyîhkâson* 'Pine-Root-Man will be your name' (ET).
6. For further illustrations of this laconic conclusion, see Bloomfield's introduction to his first volume of texts (1930:5–6) and his textual notes (especially 1930:72 n. 1, 245 n. 1; 1934:208 n. 5).

REFERENCES

Ahenakew, Alice. 2000. *âh-âyitaw isi ê-kî-kiskêyihtahkik maskihkiy / They Knew Both Sides of Medicine: Cree Tales of Curing and Cursing Told by Alice Ahenakew*, ed. and trans., and with a glossary by H. C. Wolfart and Freda Ahenakew. Publications of the Algonquian Text Society. Winnipeg: University of Manitoba Press.

Ahenakew, Freda (ed.). 1986. *kiskinahamawâkan-âcimowinisa / Student Stories,* written by Cree-speaking students; ed. and trans., and with a glossary by Freda Ahenakew. Algonquian and Iroquoian Linguistics Memoir 2. Winnipeg: Algonquian and Iroquoian Linguistics.

Bear, Glecia, Irene Calliou, Janet Feitz, Minnie Fraser, Alpha Lafond, Rosa Longneck, and Mary Wells. 1992. *kôhkominawak otâcimowiniwâwa / Our Grandmothers' Lives as Told in Their*

Own Words, ed. and trans. by Freda Ahenakew and H. C. Wolfart. Saskatoon: Fifth House Publishers.

Bloomfield, Leonard. 1930. *Sacred Stories of the Sweet Grass Cree.* National Museum of Canada Bulletin 60. Ottawa: F. A. Acland.

Bloomfield, Leonard. 1934. *Plains Cree Texts.* American Ethnological Society Publication 16. New York: G. E. Stechert.

kâ-mimikwatowêt / William Greyeyes. 2014. The Travelling Companion, ed. and trans. by H. C. Wolfart and Freda Ahenakew. In H. C. Wolfart, Two Plains Cree Performances of a Pre-Victorian *Kunstmärchen, Anthropological Linguistics* 56(2):159–218, appendix, pp. 177–215.

kâ-pimwêwêhahk / Kâ-Nîpitêhtêw, Jim. 1998. *ana kâ-pimwêwêhahk okakêskihkêmowina / The Counselling Speeches of Jim Kâ-Nîpitêhtêw,* ed., trans., and with a glossary by Freda Ahenakew and H. C. Wolfart. Publications of the Algonquian Text Society. Winnipeg: University of Manitoba Press.

kêkêk / Masuskapoe, Cecilia. 2010. *piko kîkway ê-nakacihtât: kêkêk otâcimowina ê-nêhiyawastêki* [There's nothing she can't do: Kêkêk's autobiography published in Cree], ed. by H. C. Wolfart and Freda Ahenakew. Algonquian and Iroquoian Linguistics Memoir 21. Winnipeg: Algonquian and Iroquoian Linguistics.

Minde, Emma. 1997. *kwayask ê-kî-pê-kiskinowâpahtihicik / Their Example Showed Me the Way: A Cree Woman's Life Shaped by Two Cultures,* ed., trans., and with a glossary by Freda Ahenakew and H. C. Wolfart. Edmonton: University of Alberta Press.

Mühlbauer, Jeffrey. 2008. *kâ-yôskâtahk ôma nêhiyawêwin:* The Representation of Intentionality in Plains Cree. PhD thesis, University of British Columbia.

Mühlbauer, Jeffrey. 2012. The Relation of Switch-Reference, Animacy, and Obviation in Plains Cree. *International Journal of American Linguistics* 78:203–238.

Mühlbauer, Jeffrey. 2015. A "Presence" Paradigm in Plains Cree: Context, Form, and Content. *Anthropological Linguistics* 57(3):275–313.

Mühlbauer, Jeffrey, and H. C. Wolfart. 2010. Proper Names and Obviation in Plains Cree. Paper read at the conference "The Grammar of Proper Names," Universität Regensburg.

Vandall, Peter, and Joe Douquette. 1987. *wâskahikaniwiyiniw-âcimowina / Stories of the House People,* ed., trans., and with a glossary by Freda Ahenakew. Publications of the Algonquian Text Society. Winnipeg: University of Manitoba Press.

Whitecalf, Sarah. 1993. *kinêhiyâwiwininaw nêhiyawêwin / The Cree Language Is Our Identity: The La Ronge Lectures of Sarah Whitecalf,* ed., trans., and with a glossary by H. C. Wolfart and Freda Ahenakew. Publications of the Algonquian Text Society. Winnipeg: University of Manitoba Press.

CONTRIBUTORS

Antti Arppe is associate professor of quantitative linguistics at the University of Alberta, having been a faculty member since 2012, and the founding director of Alberta Language Technology Laboratory (ALTLab) since 2013. He received his PhD in general linguistics from the University of Helsinki in 2009. His research interests include lexical semantics, corpus linguistics, statistical and computational methods, as well as exploiting multiple methods and sources of evidence. More recently he has started work in language documentation and developing language technological tools and applications for Indigenous languages to support their revitalization, in particular for Cree but also other Canadian Indigenous languages.

Peter Bakker is associate professor at Aarhus University, Denmark. He did fieldwork on Algonquian languages in Canada and the United States, primarily on Michif. He is interested in new languages and language contact, including pidgins, creoles, and mixed languages, and works on the crossroads of typology, history, and anthropology. He has also published on deep connections between Salish and Algonquian.

Vincent Collette is sessional in linguistics at First Nations University of Canada. He holds a degree in anthropology and a PhD in linguistics. He works on the morphology and semantics of East Cree (Algonquian) and Nakota (Siouan), as well as on a grammar of Southern Auvernhat (Romance). He is also interested in historical semantics and the ethnohistory of the Indigenous populations of Canada. Recently, he started documenting and helping revitalize Nakota, a seriously endangered language of the Northern Plains.

David J. Costa is the program director for the Language Research Office at the Myaamia Center at Miami University of Ohio. He grew up in Northern California and completed his PhD in linguistics at the University of California, Berkeley in 1994. He has been studying the Miami-Illinois language since 1988.

Andrew Cowell is professor of linguistics at the University of Colorado, where he specializes in linguistic anthropology. His work focuses primarily on Algonquian languages, especially Arapaho. He recently completed an ethnography of language shift and efforts at language maintenance among the Northern Arapaho (*Naming the World,* University of Arizona Press, 2018), as well as an anthology of Gros Ventre/Aaniiih narratives with Terry Brockie (University of Regina Press, 2017). He is continuing work on an online Lexical Database of Arapaho.

Amy Dahlstrom is associate professor of linguistics at the University of Chicago. Her research deals with issues of morphology, syntax, and information structure in Meskwaki and Plains Cree.

Ives Goddard is senior linguist, emeritus, in the Department of Anthropology in the National Museum of Natural History, Smithsonian Institution. He conducted extensive fieldwork on Munsee, Unami, and Meskwaki and has written extensively on Native North American languages, cultures, and ethnohistory, particularly of the speakers of Algonquian languages.

Atticus G. Harrigan is a graduate student in the Department of Linguistics at the University of Alberta studying corpus and computational linguistics of North American Indigenous languages. His research focuses on morphosyntax, phonetics, and semantics, as well as endangered language sustainability.

Robert M. Leavitt is professor emeritus of education and former director of the Mi'kmaq-Maliseet Institute at the University of New Brunswick, Fredericton. He is coauthor of the *Passamaquoddy-Maliseet Dictionary* (University of Maine Press, 2008, pmportal.org) and most recently linguist-educator for the Passamaquoddy immersion preschools in Maine funded by the Administration for Native Americans.

Ben Levine is a documentary filmmaker with a background in clinical psychology who turned to documenting endangered languages. These documentation projects use participatory video techniques that have become a basis for language revival projects. He and his partner, Julia Schulz, are directors of Speaking Place, which has ongoing projects in nine communities in the United States and Mexico.

Newell Lewey, Passamaquoddy, received his MS in linguistics from the Massachusetts Institute of Technology in 2018 and is currently teaching Passamaquoddy language at the two Passamaquoddy reservations in Maine. Future work in this area includes teaching an introduction to Passamaquoddy language and culture at the University of Maine in Machias.

Cherry Meyer is a doctoral candidate in linguistics at the University of Chicago with a focus on Anishinaabemowin. She has worked on topics such as discontinuous constituents, word order, information structure, and, most recently, gender and classifiers.

Taylor L. Miller is visiting assistant professor of linguistics at the State University of New York at Oswego. She oversees the Endangered Languages Lab at SUNY Oswego, leading a team of research assistants in community-based fieldwork and linguistic analysis. Miller's work primarily focuses on phonological theory and documentation of Kiowa and Saulteaux Ojibwe. She received her PhD in linguistics from the University of Delaware in 2018.

Mizuki Miyashita is professor of linguistics at the University of Montana. Her current research focus is Blackfoot prosody. She is also interested in documentary linguistics and has recorded Blackfoot lullabies, narratives, and conversations.

Toby Morantz is an ethnohistorian who has been researching the Native-newcomer relations in Eastern James Bay and arctic Quebec since the 1970s. Her recent books are *The White Man's Gonna Getcha: The Colonial Challenge to the Crees in Quebec; Relations on Southeastern Hudson Bay: An Illustrated History of Inuit, Cree* *and Eurocanadian Interaction;* and *Relations on Ungava Bay: An Illustrated History of Inuit, Naskapi and Eurocandian Interaction.* She is a retired member of the Department of Anthropology, McGill University.

Margaret Noodin is director of the Electa Quinney Institute for American Indian Education and professor of English at the University of Wisconsin–Milwaukee. She is the author of *Bawaajimo: A Dialect of Dreams in Anishinaabe Language and Literature* and *Weweni,* a collection of bilingual poems in Ojibwe and English. She also serves as editor of www.ojibwe.net.

Will Oxford is associate professor of linguistics at the University of Manitoba. His research focuses on the morphosyntax of the Algonquian languages from comparative and theoretical perspectives.

Robert A. Papen is a retired professor at the Department of Linguistics, University of Quebec at Montreal. He has published extensively on the languages of the Canadian and North Dakotan Metis (Michif French and Michif), French in the Canadian Prairie provinces, the Metis of Ontario, and is currently working on French and English language contact in North America as well as on the influence of French in the history of the development of western North America.

Allison Sanders is director of Impact & Development at Impact46, a social impact accelerator that works with donors, philanthropists, nonprofits, and social enterprises throughout the world. Prior to Impact46, she was director of Strategy & Partnerships at Baan Dek Foundation in Thailand, which provides access to education, health, and safety services for vulnerable children. Before working in international aid and development, she studied field linguistics and endangered languages, and she holds master's degrees in linguistics from the University of Colorado–Boulder and Université Grenoble–Alpes.

Katherine Schmirler received her MA in linguistics from the University of Toronto and is currently pursuing a PhD in linguistics at the University of Alberta. She is involved with the Alberta Language Technology Lab's Plains Cree dictionary collaboration with Miyo Wahkohtowin Education, located in Maskwacîs, Alberta.

Julia Schulz (MA anthropology, McGill University) is codirector of Speaking Place.

A language education and resource consultant, she currently focuses on endangered language documentation and revival. Her collaborations with researchers and community language advocates include New England French, Passamaquoddy-Maliseet, and numerous Indigenous languages of Oaxaca, Mexico.

Natalie Weber is assistant professor in the Department of Linguistics at Yale University. Her main interests lie in phonology and the interfaces between phonology and other components of grammar. Her dissertation explores the relationship between word-internal prosodic and syntactic structure of polysynthetic languages. Since 2011, her empirical focus has been Blackfoot, an Algonquian language spoken in Alberta and northern Montana.

H. C. Wolfart is professor emeritus of linguistics at the University of Manitoba. He has long concentrated on the analysis of spoken texts. For Plains Cree, the results of this work include a variety of grammatical, lexical, historical, and literary studies and, most importantly, a series of text editions prepared jointly with Freda Ahenakew.

Arok Wolvengrey is professor of linguistics for the Indigenous Languages and Linguistics programs at First Nations University of Canada and the University of Regina. He specializes in Cree language studies, particularly syntax, and Algonquian linguistics in general. He has been active in Cree revitalization efforts in addition to his descriptive and theoretical linguistics research, and he serves as the series editor for the University of Regina Press's First Nations Language Reader series.